THE COMPUTER AND THE CHILD

A Montessori Approach

D1066582

THE COMPUTER AND THE CHILD

A Montessori Approach

Peter G. Gebhardt-Seele

COMPUTER SCIENCE PRESS

Computer Science Press, Inc.
1803 Research Boulevard
Rockville, Maryland 20850

1 2 3 4 5 6   Printing   Year   89 88 87 86 85

Library of Congress Cataloging in Publication Data

Gebhardt-Seele, Peter G., 1931-
    The computer and the child.

    Bibliography: p.
    1. Montessori method of education—Data processing.
2. Computer literacy.   3. Computer graphics.
4. Computer-assisted instruction.   5. Education—Data processing.   I. Title.
LB775.M8G39   1985   371.3′92′02854   84-19921
ISBN 0-88175-013-1

CONTENTS

PREFACE

Our children are growing up in a society and environment of fast change. Which is the best way to help them now and prepare them for their future?

Shall we confront them with the latest trends of our technological environment, which may well be obsolete by the time today's children are adults, or should we rather focus on "unchangeable," "basic" facts of nature and mind?

The computer in education is part of this discussion. Shall we jump on the bandwagon and put computers in our educational environment, or rather be reluctant in exposing children to new technologies? And if we decide to implement computer studies in education, how should we go about this?

In pondering these questions, the crucial test should always be: Which environment will be most helpful for any real need of the developing child? That of course brings us back to the fundamental problem: What are the needs of the developing child and how can the adult arrange his or her help to be most effective?

Maria Montessori's life was devoted to these problems. She observed children building their minds and adapting to their culture; she found rules and conditions of the growing mind and developed criteria on how to help. She came up with answers that have since then been confirmed and underlined by many other pedagogues and psychologists.

So when this book applies those models and criteria to the problem of computers in education, it pursues not only the goal of providing orientation to Montessori schools, but, in a wider sense, wants to contribute to the discussion on education in our society. May it therefore find the interest of many advocates of the child.

ACKNOWLEDGMENTS

We would like to gratefully acknowledge the publishers for granting us permission to reprint material from the following sources:

Abelson, Harold. "A Beginner's Guide to Logo, Logo is not just for Kids." *BYTE, The Small Systems Journal,* Petersborough, NH, August 1982, pp. 88–115.

Dillon, J.T. "Do Your Questions Promote or Prevent Thinking?" Reprinted by special permission of *LEARNING, The Magazine of Creative Thinking,* October 1982. © 1982 by Pitman Learning, Inc. 19 Davis Drive, Belmont, CA 94002.

Fiske, Edward P. "Computers After life of Pupils and Teachers." *New York Times,* April 4, 1982. Copyright © 1982 by the New York Times Company. Reprinted with permission.

Goldenberg, E. Paul. "Logo—A Cultural Glossary." *BYTE, The Small Systems Journal,* Petersborough, NH, August 1982, pp. 210–229.

Grady, David. "What Every Teacher Should Know About Computer Simulations." Reprinted by special permission of *LEARNING, The Magazine for Creative Thinking,* March 1983. © 1983 by Pitman Learning, Inc., 19 Davis Drive, Belmont, CA 94002.

Harwey Brian. "Why Logo? Logo is Designed to Encourage Development of Problem-Solving Skills." *BYTE, The Small Systems Journal,* Petersborough, NH, August 1982, pp. 163–193.

Lawler, R.W. "Designing Computer Based Microworlds." *BYTE, The Small Systems Journal,* Petersborough, NH, August 1982, pp. 138–162.

Lewis, Lawrence P. "Individual Instruction, Is It Montessori?" *Montessori Elementary Newsletter III/3,* Cleveland Heights, OH, 15 January 1984, pp. 1–4.

Miller, Jean K. "Piaget and Montessori—Theory and Practice and the Development of Classification Skills." *Montessori Elementary Newsletter III/3,* Cleveland Heights, OH, 1974, p. a.

Montessori, Maria. "The Absorbent Mind." All rights reserved. Reprinted by permission of Holt, Rinehart and Winston, Publishers.

Montessori, Maria. *The Advanced Montessori Method.* 2 vols., 1913. Reprint. Madras, India: Kalakshetra Publications, Inc., 1965. Vol. 1, pp. 55, 57, 64, 70, 177, 179.

Montessori, Maria. *The Discovery of the Child.* 1909; Rev. Engl. Ed. Madras, India: Kalakshetra Publications, Inc., 1966; pp. 141, 269, 374.

Montessori, Maria. To Educate the Human Potential. 1948. 5th ed. Madras, India: Kalakshetra Publications, Inc., 1973, p. 4.

Montessori, Maria. "The Four Planes of Education." (Lecture given at the Seventh International Montessori Congress, Edinburgh, 1938, combined with another lecture, London 1939), Mario Montessori, ed., published in *AMI Communications 4,* 1961.

Montessori, Mario. *The Human Tendencies and Montessori Education.* 2nd rev. ed. Amsterdam, The Netherlands: Association Montessori Internationale, 1956, p. 27, 2 lines, p. 22.

Papert, Seymour. "Mindstorms: Children, Computers, and Powerful Ideas." © 1980 by Basic Books, Inc., Publishers. Reprinted by permission of the publisher.

Standing, E. Mortimer. *Maria Montessori: Her Life and Work.* 1957, New ed., New York: New American Library, 1962, p. 238.

Watt, Daniel. "Logo in the Schools." *BYTE, The Small Systems Journal,* Petersborough, NH, August 1982, pp. 116–137.

Chapter A

GENERAL DISCUSSION

I. WHY A COMPUTER IN THE EDUCATIONAL ENVIRONMENT?

a. The Computer Is Part of the Child's Environment

There can no longer be any doubt about the computer's ever-increasing significance as part of our environment. For years now every citizen has been confronted by computers in all areas of business and administration. However, not until the development of the microcomputer did they move into the home and become part of the personal environment of the child. This development was made possible through technical advances that led to a decrease in production costs of microcomputers, making it possible today to buy one for the price—or even less—of a television set. This new size of computer, for good reasons called the personal computer, appears more and more in the immediate family environment of the child. Several sources indicate that this trend will continue:

> The home computer probably will be as basic to American living as the television. A retail market study predicts that sales of home computers and accessories will reach $5.3 billion in 1985 with unit sales of 7.9 million.[1]
>
> The astonishing conclusion of several high professional projections is that by 1995 the personal computing industry will be bigger than the automobile industry.[2]

If you think of an automobile using up a multiple of the costs and production volume needed to produce a personal computer and if, further, you think of the automobile industry providing each family with several automobiles, then

---

[1] Carol Rasmussen, "Computers in the Kitchen," *The Washington Post,* 19 September 1982, p. H4.

[2] David Bunnell, "From The Publishing Jungle," *PC Magazine,* August 1982, p. 17.

1

the latter quotation would translate into the fact that there should be several computers per family in the near future.

These and many other well-founded projections lead to the conclusion that the computer will soon be an integral part of our family environment, comparable to the car, the telephone, or the refrigerator. But do we include the study of cars, telephones, or refrigerators in the primary or elementary class?

Maria Montessori describes elementary school children as interested explorers of their environment and she advises us to aid this exploration. She describes the age between six and twelve years as

> a period for the acquisition of culture, just as the former was for the absorption of environment. We are confronted with a considerable development of consciousness that has already taken place, but now that consciousness is thrown outwards with a special direction, intelligence being extroverted, and there is an unusual demand on the part of the child to know the reasons of things. Knowledge can be best given where there is eagerness to learn, so this is the period when the seed of everything can be sown, the child's mind being like a fertile field, ready to receive what will germinate into culture. But if neglected during this period or frustrated in its vital needs, the mind of the child becomes artificially dulled, henceforth to resist imparted knowledge. Interest will no longer be there if the seed is sown too late, but at six years of age all items of culture are received enthusiastically, and later these seeds will expand and grow. If asked how many seeds may be sown, my answer is: 'As many as possible!' Looking around us at the cultural development of our epoch of evolution, we see no limit to what must be offered to the child, for his will be an immense field of chosen activity, and he should not be hampered by ignorance.[3]

One may wonder whether this "acquisition of the culture" may include the computer.

b. Computer Knowledge Is Considered Part of Literacy

Not only the computer in the home affects the child's life. The concern of parents about the future job situation is of high influence on schools. The forecaster Marvin Cetron, talking of the job market in the year 2000, mentioned among other things:

> Service sector jobs will increase from 68% to 86% with at least 44% related to information processing. . . . Computers will continue to permeate almost every field and by doing so will provide a multitude of new job opportunities. . . . You have to be computer literate or you

---

[3] Maria Montessori, *To Educate the Human Potential,* 1948. 5th ed. (Madras, India: Kalakshetra Publications, Inc., 1973), p. 4.

will just have a non-challenging job. Computer literacy will be almost like driving a car—no longer a luxury, a necessity.[4]

Another fact that puts pressure even on elementary schools is the growing tendency of colleges and universities to require that students "must have their own personal computers. . . . No matter what field they go into, they are going to have to use a computer. . . . It's a trend that's likely to increase."[5]

If our thinking is focused on the need of the child, this need of the future adult and of society as a whole may not necessarily be relevant. Indeed, the future adult and society may be better served when the children of today have a chance to develop their potential as fully as possible by satisfying their present needs as fully as possible. However, one of the children's needs is the acquisition of their culture and this includes becoming literate. Whatever computer literacy is going to mean in this society, the children will want to acquire it, just as they want to learn to write, read, and count.

c. To Get the Child Acquainted with the New Tool

For an adult, it is quite natural to realize negative feelings in encountering something unfamiliar. Our body has the peculiarity, acquired during the millions of years of evolution in the Stone Age, that unfamiliar situations release stress hormones.[6] Such a reaction was quite appropriate in a time when human activities were widely controlled by feelings, and when it was wise to back out of a situation for which appropriate behavior had not yet been developed. Our body chemistry, therefore, is perfectly attuned to the conditions of the Stone Age, when the last steps of human evolution took place.

For children, however, things are different: to them everything is unfamiliar in the beginning and their peculiarity is to absorb it all without prejudice and make it their culture. "The environment was (and is) built into the brain of the child with the cortex cells achieving completion."[7]

The understanding of this difference in adult and child behavior is important in designing an educational environment. Not only are we doing the children a service, in making them familiar with something they will have to cope with as an adult, but also will they meet these new things with joyful interest, which for adults may have a threatening aspect. There is no proof from any experience that the "poor children" may suffer at their tender young age on

---

[4] Diane Stoy "Trends: The Job Market by the Year 2000," *The Washington Post,* 2 January 1984, p. c5.

[5] Carol Clurman, *Pack Your Own Computer for College* (A report on this requirement at SIT, Hoboken, N.J., Drexel University, Philadelphia, Clarkson College, Potsdam, N.Y., and Dallas Baptist College). *USA TODAY,* 17 August 1983, p. 1.

[6] Frederic Vester, *Denken, Lernen, Vergessen* (Stuttgart: Deutsche Verlagsanstalt, 1975), p. 99.

[7] Mario Montessori, *The Human Tendencies and Montessori Education* 2nd rev. ed. (Amsterdam, The Netherlands: Association Montessori Internationale, 1956), p. 27.

being confronted by a computer. If, however, children of today have no chance to develop this feeling of familiarity with this part of their environment, once grown up they may have the same difficulties as adults have today.

d. Other Schools Have Computers

There can be no doubt that schools will react to the situation discussed above and are already doing so.

> Computers have not only arrived in the nation's classrooms, but will, in fact, be as familiar as chalk and erasers in more than half the country's sixteen thousand school districts in this academic year. The US Department of Education says about one out of every four public schools— about twenty-two thousand—currently has at least one microcomputer or computer terminal for instructional use by students.[8]

So it is no wonder that Montessori schools, faced with this development, also should take steps to adapt to this new situation. Within the last few years, many Montessori schools have acquired computers, even though some do not yet know how to implement them in the classroom. There is enormous interest in the question of how the computer is compatible with the Montessori educational philosophy.

II. WHY NOT?

a. "High Tech" and the Child

1. Hidden Sophisticated Processes

Montessori material in general avoids hidden machinery. It emphasizes clear and simple structures that can be picked up by the mind.

The concern of 'un-understood' sophisticated structures behind the surface is mentioned by Seymour Papert, although not discussed in detail, when he considers children programming "turtle geometry" (see Chapter B, section XI.b) on a computer:

> A child (and, indeed, perhaps most adults) lives in a world in which everything is only partially understood: well enough perhaps, but never complete. For many, understanding the turtle's action so completely that there is nothing more to say about it is a rare, possibly unique experience. For some it is an exhilarating one: we can see this by the children's eagerness to explain what they have understood. For all it is

---

[8] Patricia McCormack, "Political Action" (Washington, D.C.: National Education Association Press Report, 1983), p. 3.

a better model of the crispness of analytic knowledge than most people ever encounter.

The reader might object that far from understanding the turtle "fully," a child programmer hardly understands at all the complex mechanisms at work behind the scenes whenever a turtle carries out a LOGO command. Are we in fact in danger of mystifying children by placing them in an environment of sophisticated technology whose complexities are only partially understood by advanced computer scientists?[9]

These doubts are not really answered when he continues:

> These questions are very general and touch on fundamental issues of scientific method. Newton "understood" the universe by reducing whole planets to points that move according to a fixed set of laws of motion. Is this grasping the essence of the real world or hiding its complexities?[10]

The answer deals with the simplification of a scientific object but does not touch on the problem of the complexity of the instrument.

Another consideration may help here: children approach the miracle computer with the same unprejudiced sense of wonder as a germinating pea. An experiment with germinating peas[11] is based on hidden processes of enzymes working within the cells, causing the splitting and multiplication of the cells including reproduction of the total building design of the future pea plant. These hidden processes are probably more complicated than the processes within a computer that cause a turtle to move on the screen. Since the early dawn of human intellect, man has learned to cope with such unintelligible facts and to integrate them in his everyday life. Children have the special gift of being able to open the textbook of life at the back and read the user's instructions long before they understand the theoretical reasons for it.

2. Natural Versus Manmade

The criticism mentioned above is probably directed less at the complexity of the processes in germinating peas or in computers but rather at the fact that the one is part of our natural environment while the other is not.

The computer certainly is a manmade part of our environment. But with due consideration, it is clear that the larger part of our environment is manmade. Since his early days on earth, man has been working on and changing his environment. A simple piece of woven cloth is manmade in the same way as a computer.

What then is the difference between the germinating pea, the woven cloth, and the computer?

[9] Seymour Papert, *Mindstorms: Children, Computers, and Powerful Ideas* (New York: Basic Books Inc., 1980), p. 117.

[10] Ibid., p. 117.

[11] As part of the study of a plant's needs in Montessori classes for 6–12 year olds.

3. "High Tech"

The difference might be described by the terms "high tech" and "high touch" as they are introduced by John Naisbitt to discuss the balance between technology and human response: "What happens is that whenever new technology is introduced into society, there must be a counterbalancing human response—that is, high touch—or the technology is rejected." [12] In reading several examples, it becomes revealing when this pair of terms is applied to the issue of the metric system: People felt stressed with this HIGH TECH metric issue until they were allowed to go back to, and become comfortable with, the more human-related HIGH TOUCH of the American system. This sounds strange to a reader brought up in Europe, who feels threatened by the complicated relationships of inches, ounces, and gallons of which he finds nothing engrained in his emotional web, but of course feels at home with metrics. It seems that the stress of HIGH TECH has to do with something being new, not integrated during the sensitive periods of early age.

4. The Unfamiliar Causes Stress

It has already been discussed that encountering something unfamiliar in our environment causes stress reaction in our bodies. However differently we may deal with this reaction, the fact itself is caused by hormones and not controlled by our willful mind. So the metric system caused these reactions to Americans, who were unfamiliar with it, but did not cause any such reaction to a European, who had a chance to absorb this system as a child. The same is true with computers: some adults feel uneasy about them and tend to project this feeling to children. The children themselves do not experience uneasiness, as long as computers are not controlling them or are in other ways a part of a system stressful for other reasons. This latter remark relates to Chapter B, in particular to sections III, IV and VI, and of course to any educational situation detrimental to the child, whether using computers or not.

5. The Alteration of Our World Gets Out of Control

A deeper motive of criticism could be the uncomfortable feeling justified by the fact that the alteration of the world by human technology is getting more and more out of control. But even in the face of this, the uncomfortable truth remains, that we have no alternative. We cannot dismantle this technology. All we can do is decide how to deal with it.

To control the problems of worldwide technology, very opposite strategies have been suggested, ranging from total denial to uncontrolled application of modern technology.

It should become obvious through the course of this book that uncontrolled usage of modern technology does not find an advocate in the author. Rea-

---

[12] John Naisbitt, *Megatrends* (New York: Warner Books, 1982), p. 39.

sonable application, controlled by an understanding of possibilities, limits, and dangers, may serve us best. That includes being acquainted with the technology one wants to control and practicing its control.

We as educators do not have the choice of whether or not to establish the computer as part of the child's environment. All we can do is decide on the consequences that the fact of computers, as part of the child's environment, will have in our prepared environment in the school and the home.

b. Is It a Key Material?

The intention of Montessori at all age levels is to enable the child to become independent and have a meaningful interaction with the real environment. The prepared environment in the classroom is merely an instrument to reach that goal.

One principle in this education is to provide the child with the "keys" only and then let him explore on his own. "The idea is to open the door only a little, rather than to give a guided tour into the interior of all the world's knowledge." [13]

Thus, it is not the intention of the school to give all knowledge and experiences, but rather only those insights and skills (called "keys") that are necessary to explore and understand the real world. Any material that is not necessary in that sense hampers the children and is an obstacle in their way to free themselves from the material and turn toward the real world.

> An error may be committed by an excessive quantity of the educative material: this may dissipate the attention, render the exercises with the objects mechanical, and cause the child to pass by his psychological moment of ascent without perceiving it and seizing it. Moreover, such objects are then futile, and, by their futility, "the child may lose his soul." [14]

It is then assumed that the Montessori environment, as designed until now, includes all the keys necessary for the child to explore the real world and society. All essential materials are present and there is no need to develop additional ones. [15]

This understanding of the classroom obviously has prevented most Montessori schools from including all that has been developed in our modern world, such as television, gasoline motors, refrigerators, and other technological achievements in their classrooms. Is the same attitude appropriate towards the computer? Computers have become so important in controlling our environment that it may well be necessary to encourage exploring them

---

[13] Margaret Elizabeth Stephenson, Unpublished lectures, Washington Montessori Institute, Washington, D.C., 1982-83.

[14] Maria Montessori, *The Advanced Montessori Method*, 1913. Reprint (Madras, India: Kalakshetra Publications, Inc., 1965) Vol. 1, p. 64.

[15] Margaret Elizabeth Stephenson, Unpublished Lectures.

and providing certain key concepts for this task (see Chapters B, section IX and C, sections II and IV).

But there is even another aspect to be considered: the computer is not only an interesting machine, but also a tool for mental activity. We may compare it with the letters of the alphabet: these letters have been part of human environments for several thousands of years, so, of course, we are interested in them as a cultural and historical phenomenon. But once we have learned to understand the letters and to read and write them, they open a whole field of new activities for us.

> Mr. [Seymour] Papert says the effect of computers on learning and thinking is comparable to that of the invention of writing. "Socrates argued that writing would undermine the oral tradition and destroy memory," he said.[16]

Socrates was certainly right with his view on the negative impact of writing, but did not foresee the positive consequences of this new tool. In the same way that writing is a key tool today for exploring the spiritual territory of human cultures, the computer may be considered one of the helpful tools for exploring thinking (see Chapter B, sections X and XI).

c. Scientific Development of Montessori Materials

If the computer is brought into the class as a new part of the educational environment, the principles on developing this environment should be applied. They evolve from the role this environment plays in the development of the child:

> Psychical development is organized by the aid of external stimuli, which may be determined experimentally. . . . In order to expand, the child, left at liberty to exercise his activities, ought to find in his surroundings, something organized in direct relation to his internal organization which is developed itself by natural laws just as the free insect finds in the form and qualities of flowers a direct correspondence between form and sustenance. . . . It is therefore necessary that the environment should contain the means of auto-education. This means cannot be "taken at random"; they represent the result of an experimental study which cannot be undertaken by all because a scientific preparation is necessary for such delicate work; besides, like all experimental study it is laborious, prolonged and exact. Many years of research are required before the means really necessary for psychical development can be set forth. Those educationalists who leave the great question of the liberty of the pupil to the good sense or to the preparation of the master are very far from solving the problem of liberty. The greatest scientist or the person most

---

[16] Edward P. Fiske, "Computers Alter Life of Pupils and Teachers," *New York Times,* 4 April 1982, p. 42.

fitted by nature to teach could never of himself discover such because to preparation and natural gifts, the further factor of time must be added—the long period of preparatory experiment. Therefore a science which already provided the means for self education must exist beforehand. Today, he who speaks of liberty in the schools ought at the same time to exhibit objects—approximating to a scientific apparatus—which will make such liberty possible.[17]

In accordance with these principles, Montessori materials have been approved only after trial usages in a few schools under careful scrutiny.

The long trial period called for by Montessori in the above quote, unfortunately, contradicts the rapidity with which the computer is entering the classroom.

So, if any educator decides to implement computer studies, it should be kept in mind that this is, then, part of an experimental developmental process, which needs careful observation and intensive communication with other educators throughout an adaptation period. The materials, presentations, and exercises published in Chapter C are understood as part of this process. They are developed on the basis of classroom experience. Children have been observed working with them, and the design of the materials has been rearranged repeatedly, but the high standards of scientific material development as quoted above are not as yet met.

While acknowledging the necessity of this scientific development process, this book intends to accomplish a first step, by contemplating the theoretical arguments and proposing certain classroom implementations for use in this experimental process.

III. AGE LEVEL

a. Specific Developmental Tasks at Each Age

Montessori repeatedly pointed to the importance of age level in considering certain aspects of development. The child is not seen as just a miniature version of the adult species, but it is recognized that each step of development has its particular age and each age has its particular characteristics and developmental tasks. A rough classification of age levels is given as infancy (roughly age zero–six years), childhood (roughly age six–twelve years), adolescence (roughly age twelve–eighteen years), and maturity.

The characteristics of each (age level) are so different that the passages from one phase to the other has been described by certain psychologists as "rebirths." It is something similar to passing from the larva to the nymph stage in insects. The two stages are completely different. Each

---

[17] Maria Montessori, *The Advanced Montessori Method,* Vol. 1, pp. 57-60.

lasts a period of time, each has its own needs and mode of behavior. With regard to the child education should correspond to them. . . .[18]

Some narrower time periods are especially sensitive to the buildup of mental features such as language, order, fine motor movements, or hand-eye coordination.

When we come to decide on a new piece of equipment in the child's environment, such as a computer, and whether or not it serves any real need of the child, it is important to remember that these needs are different in each age level.

The argumentation in this book, except where stated otherwise, considers the six- to twelve-year-old child.

b. Age Three to Six Years

Without going into all the details of the characteristics at this age, some particularities relevant to our question may be mentioned. "Children at this age are spontaneously active. It is curious to notice that while active in a practical way not only their movements but also their intelligence develops greatly." [19] Movement in this respect includes acting out operations that we as adults do abstractly in our minds, such as lining up objects (that we call counting) or grouping objects that at the abstract level leads to the multiplication facts. Computers can be of little help in this stage, since any work on the computer is on a highly abstract level, meaning that the material object—in this case the keyboard—is totally detached from the mental object that may be represented by a picture on the screen.

Children under six are interested in their environment in a factual way, absorbing facts and their representation in language; they are interested in learning words and making statements, as opposed to the elementary child, [20] who is interested in the reasons behind things and in abstract thinking. One small scene in a Montessori school may illuminate this:

> There was an aquarium that was accessible to children from 3 to 9 years. One morning the fishes were all dead. The little ones, struck by this fact, ran to every newcomer to announce that "the fishes are dead," then ran back to their former occupation. The older children stood quietly around the aquarium saying: "Why are the fishes dead?" "Why?" "Why do things happen, how do they come about?" . . . We might

---

[18] Maria Montessori, "The Four Planes of Education" (Lecture given at the Seventh International Montessori Congress, Edinburgh, 1938, combined with another lecture, London 1939), Mario Montessori ed., published in *AMI Communications*, 4, 1971, p. 5.

[19] Maria Montessori, "The Four Planes of Education."

[20] The term "elementary" is not consistently applied throughout the educational establishment. This book follows those who use "elementary" for the age group of six to twelve years.

say that the younger children take in things sensorially. The child of 7 enters the abstract field, he wishes to know the reasons.[21]

Considering these characteristics, exploration of the computer at ages below six years may include only the names of the machine and its parts; a machine in the environment is not necessary.

Ages three to six are especially rich in sensitive periods, as mentioned in the previous chapter, where crucial achievements in the buildup of the mind are made. "These periods correspond to special sensibilities to be found in creatures in process of development; they are transitory, and confined to the acquisition of a determined characteristic. Once this characteristic has evolved the corresponding sensibility disappears."[22]

This transitory character of the sensitive periods calls in the responsibility of the educator in a special way: if the environment of the child is not suited to satisfy these sensibilities, the periods may go by without being used in full. That deficiency will never be made up in later life. Since a computer has little value in aiding the needs during these sensitive periods, it may just take away time and attention from more important activities.

At this point of the discussion, there is little purpose to be seen for a computer to be included in a class for children of age three to six years. But there are important considerations not to include it.

---

[21] Maria Montessori, "The Four Planes of Education."

[22] Maria Montessori, *The Secret of Childhood* 1936. Rev. Ed. (New York: Fides/Ballantine Books, Inc., 1966), p. 61.

Chapter B

FIFTEEN SPECIFIC APPLICATIONS AND THEIR EVALUATION

The discussion as outlined in Chapter A will not provide us with a satisfactory answer to whether or not we should have computers in the educational environment. This is due chiefly to the fact that the computer is not only an object in our environment, but a tool that can be used in many different ways. Thus far, it is comparable to a pencil: the question is not whether or not you provide children with pencils, but rather what to draw or write with them. To discuss the educational value of computers in more detail, it is necessary to focus on the different ways of using them.

This Chapter B will discuss fifteen applications of computers.

I. AN ORGANIZING TOOL

a. School Office and Library

In all areas of business and administration, computer applications for work organization already cover a wide area. This is also true in schools: computers are used in managing the finances and the school office, report writing, planning, and scheduling. In Montessori schools these applications have no importance up to date. The reason may be that Montessori schools in most cases are small, that reports are replaced by parent conferences or verbal letters, and that schedules and other organizational problems are avoided or reduced to a minimum.

Some schools discuss the application of a computer to manage the library, which, compared with the size of the school, is usually of considerable size. At present, however, for this application, the advantages of saving on work time are still balanced out by the amount of labor necessary to introduce the technology.

It should be mentioned, though, that programs available for microcomputers could be used to cover most of the office work even in small Montessori schools: data base management programs to manage student files and the library: spreadsheet programs to manage budgeting and bookkeeping: word processing (see section VIII) to manage outgoing mail such as parent letters, fund-raising efforts, newsletters.

b. Teachers' Records

One interesting organizational application is the record keeping of the teacher and the students on the student's work and its comparison with the desired curriculum. Unlike regular schools, the mixture of age groups and the individualized way of work in a Montessori school make it more necessary and also more difficult to keep such records for each student. These records have to be organized in such a way as to allow the teacher to discuss them with the students from time to time and to guide the students' work within the framework of their liberty.

A special feature of the computer is its ability to store considerable amounts of data, and to allow access to single parts of it according to different characteristics. If the lessons given to students and the work done or started by them are fed into a computer on a regular basis, the teacher or the student could ask different questions that might be meaningful in the process of work and counseling within the class, as follows:

Which parts of the curriculum did the student focus on and which did this student leave out?

Which students worked on particular material and which steps have they already completed?

When was certain material used more frequently and by which students and which materials were left alone in the recent past?

If certain sequences and priorities in curricula were programmed into the computer by the teacher, one could even envisage a student asking the computer for suggestions, the computer checking the student's past work, comparing it with a stored priority list, and printing out certain proposals from which the student then may choose. One may also imagine a teacher asking for the areas of most concern that might have been overlooked.

With all these examples, it can be seen that a computer might be helpful, but by no means can it ever replace the creative responsibility and awareness of the teacher.

At the moment this record-keeping application of the computer is not the object of discussion. Again, it would swallow up more time for the teacher to establish and adapt such a system than would be given back. However, as computers penetrate schools for other reasons and teachers become more familiar with them, this application will become of interest.

II. GAMES

a. Entertainment

The most familiar use of computers to children is for games. Since they have ample opportunity to encounter computer games in the home and other areas of society, there seems to be no need for the school to provide additional opportunities of that type.

In Montessori schools, games in general are not considered as helpful elements in the prepared environment, for reasons that are rooted in yearlong observations of children. "Indeed, every intellectual conquest is a well spring of joy to our free children. This is the 'pleasure' to which they are now most susceptible, and which makes them scorn lower pleasures; it is after having tasted of this that our little ones despise sweetmeats, toys and vanities."[1]

If one has experienced school only as a burden, it might be difficult to expect children to have fun with intellectual achievements rather than toys. A reminder is needed, that exploring, learning, and understanding in a Montessori school are allowed to develop in a spontaneous way and therefore have the joyful aspect that creative work usually has. Considering this, it may not be forgotten, however, that such satisfaction needs to be experienced and that prior to such an experience, it might be helpful for the children if their environment were rid of those temptations providing activities that never lead to the experience of the satisfaction mentioned above.

Nevertheless, the use of games as teaching material does find advocates:

> Educators who oppose this excellent form of learning, should try their hand at it and see what is involved in obtaining a high score! The benefits of hand-eye coordination, shape discrimination, cause-effect relationships, improved reaction time, following directions, increased attention span, improved spatial relations and organizing a game-winning strategy are all present. So are the rewards associated with competition and victory.[2]

Many of these practicing effects are taken care of by other activities with the Montessori materials.

The main point may be that Montessori education focuses not so much on the isolated development of skills (which is expected to come about without too much intention), but on the growth of the personality through understanding and exploring the real world. In selecting the materials for the prepared environment of a classroom, priority is given to the growth of the mind. Games in that process may be compared to candy: high in calories but detrimental to the naturally tuned system. A healthy body does not long

---

[1] Maria Montessori, *The Advanced Montessori Method,* Vol. 1, p. 179.

[2] Material description of "Creative Programming" Inc., Charleston, Ill., 1982.

for them. But to become healthy, it may well be reasonable to stay away from them.

If, with a computer in the class, game programs are not available, children even in recess times will use the computer for rather more interesting explorations, as I was able to observe in my class.

b. Educational Games

The term "games" as discussed so far is not clearly defined. An increasing number of educational games in particular may need different considerations. The following two examples can shed light on what the term "educational game" may cover:

"Story machine"[3] lets the child create short sentences by choosing from word lists containing nouns, verbs, and prepositions: such as, "The cat walks to the house." The computer then makes up a picture on the screen according to the sentence chosen by the child; in this case, a walking cat approaching a house.

Another rather different example is the "function game." This program is made for high school students to help them recognize functions of a single variable. The program draws a graph on the screen for the student to examine. "The student must then guess the name of the function and determine the value of its unknown constants. Now the student's estimate is drawn, overlaying it on the actual function."[4]

These two examples show the wide scope of programs that can be included under "educational games" and point out that this variety is not clearly set apart from computer-assisted instruction, simulation, or even programming ("Karel the Robot" is a game to teach the language Pascal[5]).

The term "game" is well known in Montessori education for a didactically controlled joyful activity, such as the "snake game" or "dot game," which are both activities to practice addition and subtraction of numbers at the age of four to six years.[6]

So the question with a particular educational game will be, "What goal does it have?"

Is it to train a narrow-minded skill, the training of which in a Montessori school should be done preferably in a context of a more open-ended study?

---

[3] Priscilla Waynant, "Creative Ways of Introducing Language Arts Instruction." Paper read at: Marilyn Church and June Wright, "Using the Microcomputer Creatively with Young Children," in *Proceedings of National Educational Computing Conference 1983, Baltimore, MD.* (Silver Spring, MD: IEEE Computer Society Press, 1983.) p. 272; "Story Machine" is produced by Spinnaker Software.

[4] Ed Zeidman, *The Function Game* (Baltimore, MD: Muse Software Inc., 1982), p. 2.

[5] John J. Hirschfelder, "Karel the Robot," *Creative Computing,* April 1983, pp. 154-156.

[6] Montessori Special Education Course, *Unpublished Lectures on Montessori Primary Materials* (Munich: Aktion Sonnenschein e.V., 1976-77).

Is the particular goal covered in a better way by already existing Montessori materials? This should be considered with the game "Story machine," which should not replace the activities with the movable alphabet.

Another consideration concerns the gamelike features in graphics and sounds that provide rewards for the involved child. Are these features related to the subject with which the game is dealing; or are they wild fantasies, which on the other hand distract from that subject? The distinction between intrinsic and extrinsic rewards is important here. "Research by Mark Lepper, David Greene, and others indicates that extrinsic rewards may actually decrease students' intrinsic motivation."[7]

Other aspects with games are the amount of violence included and the bad or good taste in graphics applied. In most games, the objective is to shoot, kill, hit, or trap any human or animal or their vehicles, or otherwise be shot or hit. The intended educational goal may often be surpassed by the unintended achievement of training the child in violence and bad taste, and by overstimulating unreal fantasies.

So before putting any such program into the classroom, there should be a careful check as to whether the subject taught is really intended and not done in a better way by the existing material, whether the programmer is being trapped by the temptation of using the full scale of the graphics and sound capabilities, flooding the child with fantasies and impressions far from the original educational goal, and whether violence or bad taste is predominant.

III. COMPUTER-ASSISTED INSTRUCTION

a. What It Is

The term "Computer-Assisted Instruction" (CAI) is used in different ways, some authors[8] including several activities, which are dealt with in other sections in this Chapter. I will use the term in a more narrow sense for an instructional process, which was derived from programmed instruction.

CAI in this sense can be seen as a particular form of programmed instruction: the computer offers printed, drawn, or spoken information, and puts questions in front of the student that are to be answered at the keyboard. The computer then evaluates the answers and picks the appropriate part of the program according to these answers.

So far, CAI is comparable to programmed instructions provided by books or filmstrips, with the additional advantage that the flexibility of a computer

---

[7] Tom Malone, "On Intrinsically Motivating Games," *Classroom Computer News*, April 1983, pp. 17-23.

[8] Digital Equipment Corporation. *Introduction to Computer Based Education.* Marlborough, MA, 1983, p. 23, provides an overview, using the term CAI for all kinds of learning such as drill and practice, dialogues, testing, problem solving, games, simulation, discovery learning.

makes it possible to adapt the program to the student in a way not possible with less sophisticated media.

A recent development brings another advantage of the computer into this field: the combination of the computer with the newly developed video disk allows random access in a very short time period to a large amount of audio-visual materials on the disk, and thus provides a combination of high flexibility of branching programs with rich audio-visual information.[9]

The answer solicited from the student, however, is still the multiple choice answer, selecting the appropriate answer from a set of three to five answers provided by the program.

It should be mentioned that in few examples available, a less restricted way of student answers to the computer's questions is provided. Methods of artificial intelligence are applied to work on a student's free-formulated answer. Of course, the reaction of the computer can never be very specific, since the level of understanding is low.[10] Other programs encourage free formulated answers but do not evaluate them. They rather provoke the answers as a step toward developing the student's own thinking.[11]

Since these options are still exceptions in the software available today, the following considerations will deal with computer-assisted instruction, which uses multiple choice answers or comparable techniques.

Many schools and educators have given their special attention to this application of computers, and for schools as well as for learning at home, program-producing companies have worked out a considerable amount of material that allows the use of computers as teachers.

> According to a recent survey by Market Data Retrieval Incorporated at least fifteen thousand of the nation's one hundred thousand elementary and secondary schools are using microcomputers as teaching tools. In most cases the machines are used to teach ideas and skills that have previously been presented in books or on blackboards.[12]

Is this enthusiasm for CAI justified, if we look at education as a help for children to unfold their potential?

---

[9] David H. Ahl, "The State of the Art in Educational Software." Paper read at National Educational Computing Conference, 6 June 1983, at Baltimore, MD.

[10] Ibid.

[11] Helen Schwartz, "Aids to Organization." In Mary Dee Harris, Fosberg and Donald Ross: "Word Processor in the Composition Classroom." In *Proceedings of National Educational Computing Conference 1983, Baltimore, MD.* (Silver Spring, MD: IEEE Computer Society Press, 1983.) p. 368.

[12] Edward P. Fiske, "Computers Alter Life of Pupils and Teachers," *New York Times,* 4 April 1982, p. 42.

b. Different Views on the Learning Child

Computer-assisted instruction is based on scientific research of the learning process. The speed of the computer's response to the student's answers is highly effective in retaining the given information in the student's mind. The flexibility of the computer to choose program branches according to the answer pattern of the student makes it possible to individualize the learning process. The combination with graphic and sound includes all the benefits of audio-visual teaching materials. For all these reasons the computer is a marvelous tool, when a certain piece of information is to be learned.

The question is: Is that the goal in education?

Maria Montessori sees the task of the child not so much in filling the mind with information as one would fill an empty sack, but rather constructing that mind by working as its builder.

> There is undoubtedly a fundamental difference between understanding and learning the reasoning of others, and being able "to reason". . . .
> In the mind of one who "learns the things of others" we may find, as in a sack of old clothes hanging over the shoulders of a hawker, solutions of the problems of Euclid, together with the images of Raphael's works, ideas of history and geography, and rules of styles, huddled together with alike indifference and alike sensations of "weight." While, on the other hand, he who uses all these things for his own life, is like the person who is assisted in attaining his own welfare, his own relief, his own comfort by those same objects which are merely burdens when in the sack of the hawker. Such objects are, however, no longer huddled together without order and without purpose in a closed bag, but set out in the spacious rooms of a well ordered house. The mind which constructs may contain a great deal more than the mind in which pieces of knowledge are heaped up as in the bag; and in that mind, as in the house, the objects are clearly divided one from another, harmoniously arranged, and distinctive in their uses.[13]

The building of this mind where "objects are harmoniously arranged" is not done by mere instruction, but by the activity of this mind according to its inner drive and own schedule and executed in liberty.

Jean Piaget, whose view on the learning child is very similar to that of Montessori, uses the term "operational processes" to describe the growth of intelligence through the operating mind as opposed to "figurative processes" obtained by mere instruction. This becomes particularly clear in his criticism of audio-visual and programmed methods of teaching:

> Thus the use of audio-visual material such as films and television is seen as producing "figurative processes" rather than true operational processes. By this Piaget means that they produce perceptions or mental

---

[13] Maria Montessori, *The Advanced Montessori Method*, Vol. 1, p. 177.

images which are merely precise copy of what has been seen rather than really flexible reversible stable understanding. This is the same kind of rote learning approach that Piaget criticizes in programmed learning machines. Skinner's "Teaching Machines," he says, are a great success, if by success is meant merely the verbal reproduction of the desired answer.[14]

The sentimental and the natural worriers have been saddened by the fact that schoolmasters can be replaced by machines. In my view . . . these machines have performed at least one great service for us, which is to demonstrate beyond all possible doubt the mechanical character of the schoolmasters' function as it is conceived by traditional teaching methods: if the idea of that method is merely to elicit correct repetition of what has been correctly transmitted, then it goes without saying that the machine can fulfill those conditions correctly.[15]

c. CAI and the Properties of Montessori Materials

1. The Function as "Means of Development"

Montessori sees the material in the prepared environment of a class not merely as a didactic help as used in other teaching. She relates to this material as

> . . . those means of development, those external impressions, necessary to unfold the inner life, and an exact correspondence to the psychical needs of formation is essential in their construction.
>
> Up to a certain point, they might correspond with the so called didactic or objective material of the old methods. Their significance, however, is profoundly different. The objective material of the old schools was an aid to the teacher in making his explanations comprehensible to a collective class listening passively to him. . . .
>
> Here, on the other hand, the means of development are experimentally determined with reference to the psychical evolution of the child; and their aim is not to give mere instructions; they represent the means which induce a spontaneous interpretation of the internal energies.[16]

Can computer-assisted instruction function that way? It has certain features in common with the Montessori materials. Can it therefore occupy the same place?

> Surely Montessori material has obvious control of error. It is coded or ordered for easy use by the child; it is inviting in design; it progresses in difficulties; it has sensory appeal; it isolates concepts. Individualized

---

[14] Marianne Spencer Pulaski, *Understanding Piaget* (New York: Harper & Row, 1971), p. 202.

[15] Jean Piaget, *Science of Education and the Psychology of the Child.* 1969 Engl. Ed. (New York: Orion Press, 1970), p. 27.

[16] Maria Montessori, *The Advanced Montessori Method,* Vol. 1, p. 70.

instruction material participates in these qualities of Montessori material. But Montessori material has an open-ended quality and many layers of significance that other materials do not. . . .

The Montessori material gives keys to categorization that reveals the world about him. The material opens the mind, senses, personality to perceive even more of reality. . . . The materials can lead the child on to greater insights, self-realization. Without such material the teacher must put his understanding of a point directly into the mind of the child through book, tape, film or word—hardly a system that respects the individual child's perception of the same phenomena.

Truly Montessori material has latent within it several truths, aspects of reality, be they relationship between shape and number, numerical facts, sensorial gradations, or historical perspectives. The material is not simply good for just one thing. . . .

The teacher involves the child with the initial activity and lets the child discover the reality himself. The Montessori directress does not use the material to prove a point, to "teach" the child a fact or a concept. . . . Montessori materials have latent within them aspects of reality, basic relationships, truths that the child can discover and gradually make his own: and most of all in this process of concentration and repetition he makes himself. He builds as befits his personality, personal order and perceptiveness.[17]

From this it might be more understandable why few Montessori teachers include computer-assisted instruction in their classrooms, even if it otherwise is used so intensively.

With respect to the importance of this issue, further analysis may be suitable on how computer assisted instruction would satisfy the properties of Montessori materials.

2. Activity and Manipulation

"A . . . character of the material of development is that it must lend itself to the activity of the child. The possibility of rousing the interest and attention of the child does not depend so much on the quality of things as on the opportunities which they offer for doing something with them."[18]

The exploration of a theoretic fact is connected with activity of the hands, eyes or even more, the whole body. So, for example, with the grammar boxes, the parts of speech are studied by manipulating the colored cards containing the words of the sentence studied. Hands and eyes in cooperation find the

[17] Lawrence P. Lewis, "Individualized Instruction, Is It Montessori?," *Montessori Elementary Newsletter*, 15 January 1984, pp. 1-4.

[18] Maria Montessori, *The Discovery of the Child* (Madras, India: Kalakshetra Publications, 1966), p. 141.

respective card within the compartments of the box according to the judgment of the mind about the particular part of speech.[19]

In principle, the manipulative ability follows the pattern of the theoretical facts and therefore is by far preferable to the manipulative activity of punching the keys of a computer. The term "manipulate" is derived from the Latin "manus," which means hand. Montessori emphasizes that "the skill of man's hand is bound up with the development of his mind. . . . We may put it like this: the child's intelligence can develop to a certain level without the help of his hand. But if it develops with his hand then the level it reaches is higher and the child's character is stronger."[20] These insights have strong support from recent research with handicapped children, who cannot work with their hands in a normal way, and therefore are deprived in developing abstractions such as the concept of numbers, derived from touching a number of things, or the concept of prepositions abstracted from being "under" or "over" the table. Even the language preserves this insight when mental processes are expressed in terms of body movements such as, "I grasp this," to say, "I understand it." Applied to our topic of the computer as a teaching tool, it is clear that children need hand activities that are closer related to the abstractions they want to derive from them as can be expected from pushing buttons.

3. Tactile Stimuli

Tactile stimuli improving fine motor control and using tactile memory: This principle, which is obvious, for example, with the bead materials in many areas of arithmetic,[21] serves independently from the particular problem, using the tactile memory as well as improving the fine motor skills. These functions again are not taken care of in the work with a computer.

4. Aesthetics

"Another character of the objects is that they are attractive. Color, brightness and harmony of form are sought after in everything which surrounds the child. Not only the sensorial material, but also the environment is so prepared that it will attract him, as in nature brilliant petals attract insects to drink the nectar which they conceal."[22]

In working with a computer, aesthetics may have a certain importance in the way the screen picture is designed. Unfortunately, in the available programs, this point does not take high priority and has not always been guided

---

[19] Maria Montessori, *The Advanced Montessori Method,* Vol. 2, p. 47.

[20] Maria Montessori, *The Absorbent Mind* (Translated from the Italian by Claude A Claremont) (New York: Holt Rinehart and Winston, 1967), pp. 150-2.

[21] Maria Montessori, *The Discovery of the Child,* p. 324; idem, *The Advanced Montessori Method,* Vol. 2, p. 188.

[22] Maria Montessori, *The Discovery of the Child,* p. 141.

by good taste. And, of course, the aesthetic aspect of material such as beautiful wood is not covered at all. The skillful craftwork of wood or glass beads in the hands of children is of another power than mere optical presentations on a screen.

5. Physical Structure Conveys Abstract Concepts

In many cases, the arrangement in space given to the material is an important means to clarify and memorize abstract concepts. So, for example, the squares on the checkerboard[23] where the bead bars are to be placed are arranged in a way that immediately leads to the arrangement of numbers in the abstract process of multiplication.

These messages built into the material are more than just verbal information. They are described by E. M. Standing as "ideas":

> These objects are not chosen at random, or because they happen to arouse the passing interest. Each possesses as it were within it an idea to be realized—not an idea to be announced by the teacher and handed over directly from her to the child. Rather the idea is implicit in, or latent in the material itself. As the material is used, this idea becomes presented—if one might say so—materially and spread out in space. And in time, too, for it is only as the child works with the materials, lives with it . . . hours at a time and day after day—always active with hand as well as brain—that the idea inherent in the material comes off from it into the child's mind (as a transfer that has been soaking a long time in water comes off on a piece of paper). Or, to vary the metaphor, the idea seems to detach itself from the material, quietly, gently, unobtrusively, as an exhalation or perfume—or even a spiritual emanation—thus entering the child's mind to become part of his very self.[24]

6. No Questions

One aspect of computer-assisted instruction to be considered is how it depends heavily on questions. Montessori teachers rarely ask questions, preferring them to be aroused in the child's mind.[25] The ineffectiveness of questions to stimulate thinking is also a criticism of other educators.

> Teachers often ask questions, hoping to stimulate students' thinking, to open up a dialogue, to draw out responses and to keep a discussion

---

[23] Nienhaus-Montessori: Catalogue of Montessori Apparatus. Zelhem, Holland and unpublished lectures at Washington Montessori Institute, Washington, D.C., U.S.A. 1982.

[24] E. M. Standing, *Maria Montessori, Her Life and Work* (New York: New American Library Inc., 1962), p. 238.

[25] Montessori Elementary Training Course, *Unpublished Lectures,* Washington Montessori Institute, Washington D.C., 1982.

flowing. But what the teacher actually does is initiate, indeed institute, a question and answer exchange that has little chance of evolving into true classroom discussion. Far from promoting expressiveness, active participation and independent thinking, the teacher has established a process that encourages student reactivity, passivity and dependence.[26]

7. Conclusions

All these arguments concerning teaching technologies, although not intensively discussed in the Montessori community, are obviously well understood by all the teachers, who shape their classroom environments. They may have led to the fact that little material of either programmed or audio-visual instruction can be found in Montessori classes.

This widely practiced rejection of all educational technology in Montessori schools is in contrast to the readiness with which computers are being brought into Montessori classes. Pondering on this fact, two assumptions come to mind: Montessori teachers are well aware of the superiority of Montessori materials for the child's learning process over modern educational technologies. One may therefore assume that computers are not intended to be used for computer-assisted instruction. The computers taken into the classrooms obviously are not meant as another type of educational technology, as a teaching instrument. Maybe they are seen rather as a part of the environment that was not there before, but is now, and therefore should be reflected in the environment of the class.

Whatever the reasons in those schools out there in the country, it is important to differentiate between the uses of the computer—the use for instructing the child is not compatible with the educational model of Montessori.

IV. DRILL AND PRACTICE

Drill and practice, in order to develop certain skills and memorize certain information, do not play a central role in Montessori education. (See section III this chapter.) There are, however, areas where the necessity is seen, such as memorizing the arithmetic facts. To a high degree this memorization is integrated in different areas of study. But particular materials are provided for memorizing facts only; for example, the finger charts.[27]

Therefore, there is no need to replace these materials with computer drills, and a computer should not be bought just for this reason. But once it is

---

[26] E. T. Dillon, "Do Your Questions Promote Thinking?," *Learning, The Magazine for Creative Teaching* October 1982, pp. 51-57.

[27] Montessori Special Education Course, *Unpublished Lectures on Montessori Primary Materials* (Munich: Aktion Sonnenschein e.V., 1976-77).

there, this application might be considered as a chance for "repetition through variety" (another principle of Montessori education). In my own class, programs for practicing arithmetic facts were created by the eight-year-old students, not for the purpose of practicing, but for the purpose of learning programming. Once the programs were there, they were also used by the six-year-olds. They liked them and it provided an additional incentive through variety for practicing facts.

With computers for drill and practice, the same cautioning remark is necessary as in section IIb. Drill programs will include rewards for correct answers. For the reinforcing impact of these rewards, the mere statement that the answer is correct is sufficient. The children want to master the times tables that they are practicing and therefore the message that an answer is correct is the best reward they can get. There is no need to wrap the whole activity into a fantasy world of dragons and supermen, and all kinds of graphic and sound effects. Extrinsic rewards of this kind, which have no relationship to the matter at hand, are detrimental. The equipment for this use of computers can be quite simple—almost any computer will do. If, however, programs are bought, they may come on disks necessitating a disk drive.

The age group depends on what is to be practiced: for arithmetic facts, the age six to seven years may be considered. Mere drills should not take place before the child has had enough chance to build up an understanding of the concept concerned, such as multiplication or addition.

V. TOUCH TYPING

One skill the computer can teach especially well is typing. Since the computer includes a keyboard similar to that of a typewriter and can monitor and react to it immediately, it provides the perfect way of learning to type.

Typing is not included in most elementary school curricula, therefore, there is no need to use a computer for this reason. However, wherever teaching of this skill is demanded, for example, because it is a necessary skill in our working society, a computer program for touch typing is an appropriate teaching method.

One special reason for teaching touch typing would be if a computer was used for word processing (see section VIII). To prevent children from developing bad typing habits, it is appropriate to let them work through a touch typing program before going on to word processing activities. Children usually enjoy this and their typing skills develop fast.

The configuration of a computer for this purpose can be rather simple: any computer that is equipped with a full typewriter keyboard will do.

VI. TESTS

a. The Computer as a Powerful Tool

Computers are used for tests in two ways. Evaluation of written tests can be done with a computer, if a scanner device for reading marked papers is available. The computer then reads the test forms marked by students and evaluates the test for the single student as well as calculates certain average data for the whole group. Another way to give the test is on the computer itself. This process is similar to the computer-assisted instruction, except that the focus is on the questions rather than giving instructions. The questions put in front of the child on the screen are answered on the keyboard and the answers are evaluated immediately or in a final score.

b. Educational Aspects of Testing

In applying computers for testing, the educational question is not so much on whether to apply computers, but whether to apply tests. Despite the fact that tests seem to be an integral part of most school systems, we should realize that they are detrimental to the work habits and the psychic development of the child.

Testing, as a measure for assessing a child's achievements, inhibits rather than promotes the child's growth. The mental growth of a child may be compared to that of a flower: the flower cannot grow if you keep opening the bud in order to check how far the work is completed.[28]

The benefits or dangers of tests depend for a good part on what is done with the results: they can provoke feedback, which spoils the free working attitude of the children and endangers the spontaneous interest by an element of fear and pressure. This may occur when the test results are taken by parents or teachers as a source of criticism, maybe even combined with punishment. Whenever tests are given, it is therefore important to deal with the results in a casual and reasonable way.

While the test results should be discussed with the child, one has to be careful that this is done in a positive and helpful way, and if the results are passed on to parents or other teachers, the same caution is exercised.

But even if tests never result in criticism or punishment, they create an atmosphere of competition, which may be detrimental to the natural interest in the subject matter. In this context, it is important to see that stress and challenge may be helpful for healthy personalities, but may slow down the psychological growth of children who still have to struggle for their security. These considerations of Montessori are confirmed from a different point of

---

[28] Margaret Elizabeth Stephenson, *Unpublished Lectures,* Washington Montessori Institute, Washington D.C. 1982-83.

view in the psychology of Abraham Maslow.[29] He makes clear that the growth of the personality depends on the satisfaction of the psychological needs rather than training to cope with stress and competition.

All this applied to tests in schools would rather call for no tests at all.

Some schools, however, feel that taking tests needs skills that should be developed in order to give the child a chance in his future scholastic life. With that goal in mind, tests are given for practicing purposes rather than assessing achievements.

VII. SIMULATION

a. Simulation in the Montessori Class

The term "simulation" is applied to a learning process, where a certain aspect of reality, which cannot be explored live, is simulated and therefore made accessible for the child's exploration.

In the prepared environment of the classroom, we always prefer to give the child a chance to explore real nature. There are, however, certain subjects that cannot be explored in reality, but are still interesting for the children and necessary as a key to understand their environment and function in society. For example, the relationship between sun and earth and the resulting changes in day and night, seasons and temperatures are difficult to observe in nature: only a careful observation over a certain period of time will show that the points of sunrise and sunset move north through the first half of the year and south through the second half of the year. Nevertheless, it took us millions of years to come to the understanding of the sun and earth as we know it today. For this reason, we provide the children with a model simulating these relationships: a ball represents the earth and a lamp the sun. With this simulation, the children can explore and understand the reasons behind their observations of day and night, and changes in seasons and temperatures.

In order to decide how simulation models in general fit into our Montessori view, there is little help from the literature. The term "simulation" was just not considered; maybe because without computers, there was little chance to simulate realities that could not be directly explored.

But even if the term "simulation" is not yet used, the concept is used in simple applications, as with the globe and the lamp. Another example would be the use of magnets to give a sensorial impression of gravity. Since gravity is hard to experience with small objects that would fit into a classroom, the impression of traction is given with magnets, even if the force of a magnet is very different from that of gravity. For some story problems in math, the reality is simulated graphically in order to give an impression of the rela-

---

[29] Frank Goble, *The Third Force, A.H. Maslow's Contribution for a Psychology of Psychic Health* (New York: Grossman Publishers, 1970).

tionship of the factors involved, and to help the child derive the calculation. The protractor chart in the geography study is a simulation model for the changes of seasons according to the changing position of the sun.[30]

These examples and others include the concept of replacing reality with a model in order to study it more easily and they allow for the conclusion that simulation is considered a help for the child's exploration, where reality itself is not accessible.

b. Examples of Computer Simulation

The computer is an extraordinary tool to provide simulation on a high level. As an example, a study of economics is developed in detail in Chapter C, section V.

Two well-known examples for simulation problems are "Oregon Trail" or "The Search Series:"

> "Oregon Trail" simulates a trip over the Oregon Trail from Independence, Missouri, to Oregon City, Oregon, in 1847. Your family will cover the 2,040-mile Oregon Trail in five to six months, if you make it alive . . . Students are asked to make a series of decisions, initial ones about how they wish to allocate $700 for food, oxen, clothing, bullets, miscellaneous supplies and cash reserve; then later ones about whether to stop and hunt or visit a fort for more supplies, about how well to eat . . . and about how to react to any riders who appear on the trail . . . Although the game messages allow ample opportunity to fantasize about dangers and calamities, there is no hint in them about reality of bonegrinding weariness and the value of stamina or about the spiritual life that comes from encountering magnificent vistas and the exuberance of success.[31]

Within "The Search Series," the "geology search provides a simulation with all clues you need to discover oil without going broke. The map of an island is given and a choice of certain scientific tests reveals information about the geological strata underground. On the basis of this information the student has to decide where to drill and what other measures to spend money on."[32]

A more sophisticated example of the application of a computer for simulation is mentioned in section XI, b.3 with the "Dyna Turtle," a help to explore sensorially Newton's laws of mechanics.

---

[30] All examples are taken from Montessori Elementary Training Course, *Unpublished Lectures,* Washington Montessori Institute, Washington D.C., 1982.

[31] David Grady, "What Every Teacher Should Know about Computer Simulations," *Learning, The Magazine for Creative Teaching,* March 1983, pp. 34-46.

[32] T.S. Snyder, *The Search Series, Five Simulations in Social Studies and Science,* (New York: McGraw Hill, 1982).

c. Critical Notes

By considering these examples, it should be clear that through simulation the child has a chance to explore and understand reality. However, one has to keep in mind, that the child does not study reality itself, but what the programmer considers reality and has put so far into the program. So, in acquiring a simulation program, the same care should be taken as with a book: the teacher has to make an assessment, whether the student should be exposed to the particular view of reality that is acquired with the program.

VIII. WORD PROCESSING

a. A Tool for Writing

Word processing uses the ability of the computer to store and rearrange alphanumerical information. After a certain text is typed into the computer and stored in its memory, the text can be recalled on the screen and changes can be made easily. If, for example, a word should be added, the whole text is moved to make space for the new word. If the order of a sentence should be changed, that can be done on the screen by pushing a few keys. If a whole paragraph has to go in another place, even that can be done without scissors and glue by moving it within the computer memory. After all these changes, the new text can be printed on a printer attached to the computer and will always look perfect.

For the writing adult, the computer as a word processing instrument is invaluable. Any changes of the text become so simple that the attention of the writer can be applied fully to the content, and is not distracted by cutting, gluing, erasing, or writing manipulations. The proposal to provide this advantage also for students in order to give them a new incentive for intensive changing work with their own writing, is discussed by Seymour Papert:

> For me, writing means making a rough draft and refining it over a considerable period of time. . . . but I would not be able to afford this image if I were a third grader. The physical act of writing would be slow and laborious, I would have no secretary. For most children rewriting a text is so laborious that the first draft is the final copy, and the skill of rereading with a critical eye is never acquired. This changes dramatically when children have access to computers capable of manipulating texts. The first draft is composed at the keyboard. Corrections are made easily. The current copy is always neat and tidy. I have seen a child move from total rejection of writing to an intense involvement (accompanied by rapid improvement of quality) within a few weeks of beginning to write with a computer. Even more dramatic changes are seen when the child has physical handicaps that make writing by hand more than usually difficult or even impossible. This use of computers

is rapidly becoming adopted wherever adults write for a living. . . . The image of children using the computer as a writing instrument is a particularly good example of my general thesis that what is good for professionals is good for children.[33]

The application of word processing computers for handicapped children as mentioned here has certain advantages as opposed to the adaptation and use of typewriters as presently done: the arrangement and manipulation of the text, as well as any changes, also are done on the keyboard. After all the changes have been made, the tidy printout can be released through keyboard operations.

b. A Help in Improving Style

Word processing in a wider sense may also include certain checking operations by the computer on the essay typed in. The simplest action could be checking on spelling mistakes by comparing all words with a dictionary contained in the computer's memory. Of course, this check cannot discriminate as to whether an existing word is used in the wrong place. However, a good portion of spelling mistakes can be detected and brought to the writer's attention.

How far the possibilities in checking and aiding the student in his or her style can go may be seen in a program for college students called "Writer's Workbench,"[34] developed by Bell Laboratories and running on computers larger than microcomputers. Some features performed by the program are as follows:

1. It counts all words in each paragraph and thus checks for suspicion of insufficient development;
2. It checks the frequency of words and thus makes one aware of overused words;
3. It checks for throwaway words;
4. It checks on vague words, comparing them with a built-in dictionary of 120 words such as 'bad', 'most', 'all', 'very', and so on;
5. It checks on the length of sentences and its variety being arranged around an average of fifteen words;
6. It checks on the beginnings of sentences that should not constantly begin with a noun;
7. It checks on nominalization of verbs, being changed to nouns;
8. It checks on punctuation and possible grammar errors, which are brought to the attention of the student.

---

[33] Seymour Papert, *Mindstorms: Children, Computers, and Powerful Ideas,* p. 30.

[34] Kathleen Kieffer and Charles Smith, "Writer's Workbench: Teaching Aid and Learning Aid." In Mary Dee Harris, Fosberg and Donald Ross: "Word Processor in the Composition Classroom." In *Proceedings of National Educational Computing Conference* 1983, Baltimore, MD. (Silver Spring, MD: IEEE Computer Society Press, 1983), p. 368.

This level of sophistication may not be applicable in a Montessori elementary class and is not available on microcomputers. However, simplified versions are available and useful. The important feature with this help of the computer in evaluating style is that it is not a personal criticism, like coming from the teacher or parents, but it is given in a neutral way by a machine. The next advantage is that this help based on a detailed check of the student's written work can be given much more frequently than the teacher's capacity would allow.

Of course, the teacher would still be needed to give the necessary help to the student to draw conclusions from the computer's comments and to organize future work accordingly.

c. The Role of Handwriting

How far the positive argumentation for the application of word processing in normal schools has to be modified if applied to Montessori schools is now to be considered. The Montessori child has a far more positive relationship to handwriting.

"In general, children from four years of age onwards are keenly interested in writing. . . . Writing constitutes one of the easiest and enjoyable achievements gained by our children." [35]

It is also important to see that writing here is not only seen as an instrument to create a text, but is considered in its complex wholeness as a fine motor activity, calling for a combination of eye and hand, together with an intellectual process:

> Writing begins with the more complicated group of touch exercises in which the light hand is trained to move in specific directions, the eye is taught to analyze outlines and abstract forms, the hearing to perceive the sound of the voice which speaks framing the words according to their component sounds. . . . Such conquests are powerful manifestations of internal energy, and occur like sudden eruptions; the outbreak of higher activities is accompanied by the enthusiasm and joy of the child. [36]

In fact, one may observe in the elementary school that children like writing as much for its beauty as for the satisfaction derived from filling several pages with a story or a report.

In some cases, however, the willingness to work on the created text, to change and improve it, is tempered by the need to rewrite it. In those cases, one could try to see what results that work with a word processing computer can achieve on intensive exercises that improve and refine a certain text.

---

[35] Maria Montessori, *The Discovery of the Child,* p. 269.

[36] Ibid, p. 374.

The total replacement of handwriting by a computer is not desirable and cannot be achieved anyway because it would necessitate the availability of a whole series of word processors. For all the reasons given, a Montessori school would not want that in any case. But the availability of such a tool for special exercises may be welcome.

d. Equipment

A powerful word processor as desired by a professional writer or for use in the office would need a personal computer in the upper price range. To store a long text, one needs enough internal memory space. To put the text on the screen in the same way as it would appear on a letter-size page, one needs a high resolution screen with eighty columns of letters, and in order to make the printout, a printer is necessary.

In particular, the printer needs careful consideration: if the final document is supposed to look typewritten, a more expensive printer (a daisy wheel printer) may be considered. If a high printing speed is desired, a dot matrix printer is recommended.

However, for classroom use, much simpler equipment may do, if only short pieces of texts are handled and if the arrangement on the screen does not need to reflect that on a letter-size page. Since in the classroom the shape and beauty of characters is not first priority, one of the less expensive printers may be chosen.

IX. STUDY OF THE COMPUTER ITSELF

a. The Child's Drive to Explore the Environment

In Chapter A, section I, we found a serious reason for putting a computer in the class in the interest of the children to explore their environment. For the child of below six years, this means merely absorbing facts and their names, but for the child aged six to twelve years, the questions how? and why? are exciting. It should be clear by now that none of the applications of computers discussed so far would satisfy these questions. To explore the computer itself needs certain arrangements that are different from just using the computer in any of the usual ways.

Exploring the computer as a powerful tool in the technological revolution also includes an important educational task: there are not many man-made things in our immediate environment that are so complex and therefore so easily misunderstood as a mysterious means of infinite possibilities as the computer. In order to understand its limits and be able to put it to work reasonably, it is necessary to know its functions and to know how to handle it.

b. Different Levels of Exploring

Such "getting acquainted" can as always be dealt with on different levels: If the questioning person, for example, meets a computer programmed for a game, the questions may proceed as shown in Figure B.1.

This chart with the progressing questions reminds us that "explaining" never means a complete understanding, but rather only reduces one part of a questionable aspect to another that sounds more familiar. Children in the elementary school may not always penetrate through the bottom of this chart.

A first interest may concern the programs which one can run on a computer. Satisfying this interest is an important part of providing computer literacy. In particular, the general programs used in business applications, such as data base management, spread-sheets, word processing, and bookkeeping ledgers, may be explained to the children, but without sophisticated applications. It might be part of the practical life in the classroom to use a data base management program to organize the class student list or the class library.

Question	Items to invesitgate
1. What do I see, etc.?	Sensorial impressions, Screen picture, buttons, etc.
2. How does the game work?	Rules of the game
3. What does the program do?	Structural diagram of the program.[a,b]
4. What does the program look like?	Program list, Functions of single commands [a,b]
5. What does the computer perform obeying a given command?	Interpreter subroutines, translating from programming language to machine language [b]
6. What happens within the computer at a given machine language command?	Parts of the Computer (different memories, calculator, central processing unit, screen, keyboard, peripheral units, etc.) and their functions [b]
7. How are numbers and letters represented and processed as electric currents?	Logical circuits, Boolean algebra, dual numbers [c]
8. How are logical circuits represented by real electrical switches?	Model circuits consisting of real transistors, diodes, resistors, etc.
9. How does an electric switch work?	Model of a transistor
10. Why do electrons work that way?	Physics of particles, charges, and fields
11. Of what kind is that "law" in nature?	Philosophy of the bases of physics
12. Why is there such "law" in nature?	Theology

[a] Covered by learning programming, sections X and XI, this chapter.
[b] Partially covered by PACS, the material described in Chapter C, section IV.
[c] Covered by the Electronic Circuits Material, Chapter C, section II.

Figure B.1 Questions in front of a computer.

A very vital interest of the child certainly reaches down to question 4 on our chart, which includes programming, because that concerns one's own activity, one's own power to control the computer. The answer to this question will be dealt with in section X, this chapter. Continuing down the chart, with questions 7 and 8, the investigation of the hardware will become interesting. Material for this exploration is described in Chapter C, section II: "Electronic circuits doing math." At the end of that chapter, some ideas are developed of how the exploration may proceed further.

As the questioning mind continues on to questions 9 or 10, then general physics are concerned and it has to be decided which key concepts out of that area are to be given on a level appropriate to an elementary child.

At questions 11 and 12, we reach the general area covered by the great story of "God without hands." This story shows in a most beautiful way how all particles follow certain laws, implanted into them by the creator, giving these facts in a way that stirs the imagination and starts off the interest of the child. This great story is one example of how Maria Montessori wanted the teacher to be a "storyteller of the truth."[37]

In order to give a complete picture, it must be mentioned that exploring the computer includes learning about the social issues connected with it: the history of computers, the new ethical problems connected with the new possibilities, the social impact on our society, and vocational choices connected with computers.[38] These topics of course can be dealt with as parts of history and social studies, and do not in themselves necessitate having a computer in the class.

X. PROGRAMMING

a. Benefits and Warnings

It was mentioned that a core part of exploring the computer as part of our environment is introducing the child to programming. Also in order to help children experience the limits of a computer and enable them to put it to work reasonably, it seems necessary to understand the process of programming.

During my own trial introduction of seven-to-nine-year-old students in a Montessori elementary class to programming, I observed remarkable interest and the high readiness for hard work usually connected with it. I also realized that introducing the child to programming simultaneously involves practicing other skills, and introduces new math concepts without the difficulties one comes to expect with that. The skills practiced were writing, comprehensive

---

[37] Montessori Elementary Training Course, *Unpublished Lectures.*

[38] Rachelle S. Heller and C. Dianne Martin, *Bits'n Bytes about Computing, A Computer Literacy Primer* (Rockville, MD: Computer Science Press Inc.), 1982.

reading, following directions, and arithmetic; the math concepts introduced were variables, x and y coordinates, priorities of operations in larger arithmetic terms.

The most important observation seemed to me the child's realization that this machine does not think, but merely gives back what was thought of by the human user beforehand. So, for example, the math-fact-practicing programs produced by Bobby included answers like, "Right, smarty pants," or, "Wrong, dummy," but it was obvious that these were not spontaneous reactions of a sort of smart computer, but the language of a class comrade Bobby, and were understood as such.

The possibility of teaching programming to children is described by Papert as

> learning paths that have led hundreds of children to becoming quite sophisticated programmers. Once programming is seen in the proper perspective, there is nothing very surprising about the fact that this should happen. Programming a computer means nothing more or less than communicating to it in a language that it and the human user can both 'understand.' And learning languages is one of the things children do best. Every normal child learns to talk. Why then should a child not learn to 'talk' to a computer?[39]

A further motive to introduce children to programming a computer is this: programming calls for and practices, more than any other activity, that double focus on the subject as well as the thinking process, which is so essential for all scientific work. Programming is an exercise in thinking. "In teaching the computer how to think, children embark on an exploration about how they themselves think."[40]

Not all authors, however, share this positive attitude:

> Some educators fear that there is a possibility of negative consequences from the widespread use of computers in schools, such as an overemphasis on problems and ideas that lend themselves to quantification.[41]

> The danger is that we will end up thinking like a computer and that the only things we will recognize as legitimate problems are those where quantification and calculation play a big role.[42]
> Debate over such issues is only beginning in academic circles, and some educators say it is too early to come to any profound conclusion about the effects of computers on learning and thinking.[43]

---

[39] Seymour Papert, *Mindstorms,* p. 5.

[40] Ibid, p. 19.

[41] Edward P. Fiske, "Computers Alter Life of Pupils and Teachers," *New York Times,* 4 April 1982, p. 42.

[42] Professor Joseph Weizenbaum, M.I.T. Quoted after *New York Times,* 4 April 1982, p. 42.

[43] Edward P. Fiske, "Computers Alter Life of Pupils and Teachers," p. 42.

It should be clear at this point that our question is not whether to replace the present material in the classroom by computers, but merely to consider the arguments on whether to accept a computer as another part in that environment. Therefore, any concern on overemphasis should be held against the limited way that this part of the environment is allowed to emphasize at all. If a Montessori school is considering installing a computer, it should be clear that there has to be a healthy balance, in the same way as there must always be a balance between the considerable amount of math work and other activities such as story writing or art.

It should also be mentioned, that for many programming tasks, the emphasis is on logic rather than quantification or calculation.

b. Educational Approaches

If for any reason the school decides to include programming in its curriculum, then the more difficult question arises as to which materials and methods to use. Programs offered by the computer itself to introduce programming are offered by many computer manufacturers. They are, however, geared mostly to older students or even adults.

Recently, more materials have been offered, which provide the student with the opportunity to be active at the real computer, starting with simple tasks and thus building up skills.

Some approaches start with and stress graphics and sounds.[44] Others use the PRINT command to organize little designs on the screen.[45] The material described in Chapter C, section IV, the "Paper Computer Simulator," is not a hands-on approach in the beginning, but provides the children with material whereby they assume the role of the computer, in order to experience step by step the functioning of a machine.

For several computer languages, there now exist educational ideas to introduce the language by a little creature on the screen that takes commands to perform movements and graphics. The most widely known example of this approach is the turtle in Logo (see this chapter, section XI), which has also been applied to other languages such as PILOT and BASIC. Another approach of that kind is "Karel the Robot,"[46] a symbolized robot drawn on the screen that walks through a street maze and picks up beepers. Another such approach may be mentioned with "Antfarm."[47] This puts several ants on the screen, which move and eat according to commands.

---

[44] Atari Inc., Sun Valley, CA. Unpublished Instructions for a Computer Camp, 1982.

[45] "Creative Programming" Inc., Charleston, IL, 1982.

[46] John J. Hirschfelder, "Karel The Robot," *Creative Computing,* April 1983, pp. 154-156.

[47] Jacques Lafrance, "Crisis in Programming, or History Does Repeat Itself," In *Proceedings of National Educational Computing Conference 1983, Baltimore, MD.* (Silver Spring, MD: IEEE Computer Society Press, 1983.)

c. Which Computer Language to Teach?

As should be clear by now, some teaching approaches come with different programming languages. It should then be considered which programming language to choose when teaching programming. This question is discussed widely and, without going into more detail, a few results of this discussion may be stated here:

For the high school and university level, Pascal was chosen as the language required for the College Board Advanced Placement Exam in computer science.

> Pascal is a recent programming language, developed by Niklaus Wirth at The Swiss Institute of Technology in Zurich. . . . Pascal was designed . . . to be adaptable to more modern structured programming techniques. . . . It is not designed for trial-and-error . . . methods.[48]

Pascal encourages problem-solving strategies but lends itself rather to a hand-off approach, meaning a teaching approach that uses paper and pencil rather than the computer. Since for high school and university classes, the necessary computer time for a hands-on approach would not be available anyway, Pascal seemed to be the reasonable choice. Pascal also requires a certain math background from the student and a high level of logical organization; therefore, it is not recommended for children under twelve years.

Until recently, BASIC was considered a good choice for beginners. It should be mentioned, however, that BASIC is difficult for the novice, because a good deal of understanding is required before being able to do reasonable programs. BASIC may be easy for the adult, but it is not for the beginning child.

For smaller children, Logo is the better choice, having been designed with that purpose in mind. Details will be discussed in this chapter section XI.

Many authors also consider BASIC as outdated and therefore not the best choice for teaching programming. Since it was developed at a time when modern programming techniques such as "structured programming" had not been developed, scholars are afraid that studying BASIC may develop programming habits that perpetuate outdated methods.

> The increasing cost, unreliability, complexity and unmaintainability of programming efforts of the 1960's gave rise to the discipline of structured programming. We face a similar crisis in microcomputer software today because of a new generation unfamiliar with the past. New approaches to introducing programming are needed to solve the problem.[49]

---

[48] I.R. Wilson and A.M. Addyman, *A Practical Introduction to Pascal.* (New York/Heidelberg: Springer Verlag, 1978).

[49] Jacques Lafrance, "Crisis in Programming, or History Does Repeat Itself." p. 126.

However, at the moment, most microcomputers provide BASIC as their language and therefore it makes sense to introduce the students to it, preferably as a second language. And, besides, with a computer that doesn't speak Logo, BASIC is still the easiest way to introduce programming. BASIC has enough capability for problem-solving strategies and provides an easier way to understand the function of a computer, since a computer handling Logo has to perform far more sophisticated processes.

It should also be mentioned that as one reaches higher levels of sophistication in programming, Logo becomes very powerful, but more difficult.

> While Logo is superior to BASIC as an introductory language, it has some important limitations which we feel are not well known. We believe that the best computer literacy curriculum right now involves teaching Logo to beginning students, quickly switching to some intermediate language and finally moving on to Pascal for students who need a powerful application language.[50]

In any case, it is a good idea, after a thorough introduction to the first language, to teach another language in order to let the child discover the different characteristics of computer languages.

d. At What Age Can We Teach Programming?

Programming can be taught to children of age six to twelve years. Simplified versions of Logo are developed for children four to six or even pre-reading children. These versions use a few single keys, which can be marked by stickers on the keyboard to direct the turtle and even name a procedure and call it back.[51]

Another approach for preliterate children is given in "KIDBITS", which is "a programming system in which icons (pictures that represent actions, or objects upon which actions occur) are assembled into sequences to achieve some desired effects."[52]

Since the period of three to six years has so many and important developmental tasks (see Chapter A, section III), it may be questioned whether computers should be brought in at that age. The children enjoy these activities. In only a few cases, however, can they be arranged in such a way that the child can work without the immediate help of an adult to bridge organizational manipulation of the computer and debug programs. We should wait for more

---

[50] Robert Tinker, "Logo's Limits Or Which Language Should We Teach?," *Hands On! Microcomputers in Education—Innovations and Issues,* pp. 1-5.

[51] Examples are Spinnaker Software. *"Delta Drawing."* Cambridge, MA: 1982 and Terrapin Inc. *"Instant Logo."* Cambridge, MA: 1982.

[52] Charles E. Hughes and J. Michael Moshell, "A Programming Environment for Preliterate Children." In *Proceedings of National Educational Computing Conference 1983, Baltimore, MD.* Silver Spring, MD: IEEE Computer Society Press, 1983.

research to be done on the question of whether any of these activities satisfies a need, which has a sensitive period in the age of three to six.

XI. LOGO AND TURTLE

Logo is the name of a newly developed computer language. In a wider sense, this name also describes a whole package of educational ideas, including a new geometry, all based on a particular view of the child's learning process.

a. Piagetian Learning

The computer language Logo and the educational model and materials described by that name were developed at the Massachusetts Institute of Technology (MIT). Its fathers were "over the past twelve years, the Logo group at MIT under the direction of Seymour Papert, along with colleagues at a few universities and research centres around the world."[53]

The Logo project was primarily geared to educational goals, wherein the role of the educator, (based on Piaget), was seen to provide an environment fostering spontaneous learning activities of the child. Motives of catering to the needs of a computer-oriented society and teaching the art of programming were marginal. Papert's position is rather critical toward existing society and in that it is comparable to that of Maria Montessori, especially when he criticizes the traditional school for being more interested in providing information than catering to the needs of growth in the children:

> In most contemporary educational situations where children come into contact with computers, the computer is used to put children through their paces, to provide exercises of an appropriate level of difficulty, to provide feedback, and to dispense information. The computer is programming the child. In the Logo environment the relationship is reversed: the child, even at pre-school ages, is in control, the child programs the computer.[54]

The view of the learning child underlying the further-developed model is claimed to be taken from Piaget. Says Papert,

> The powerful image of the child as epistemologist caught my imagination while I was working with Piaget. In 1964, after five years at Piaget's Centre of Genetic Epistemology in Geneva, I came away impressed by his way of looking at children as the active builders of their own intellectual structures. But to say that intellectual structures are built by the learner rather than taught by a teacher does not mean that they

---

[53] Harold Abelson, "A Beginner's Guide to Logo, Logo is not just for Kids," *BYTE, The Small Systems Journal,* August 1982, p. 88.

[54] Seymour Papert, *Mindstorms,* p. 19.

are built from nothing. On the contrary: like other builders, children appropriate to their own use materials they find about them, most saliently the models and metaphors suggested by the surrounding culture.[55]

Children seem to be innately gifted learners, acquiring long before they go to school a vast quantity of knowledge by a process I call 'Piagetian learning' or learning without being taught. For example children learn to speak, learn the intuitive geometry needed to get around in space, and learn enough of logic and rhetoric to get around parents— all this without being "taught." We must ask why some learning takes place so early and spontaneously while some is delayed many years or does not happen at all without deliberately imposed formal instruction.

If we really look at the "child as builder" we are on our way to an answer. All builders need materials to build with.[56]

I see Piaget as the theorist of learning without curriculum and the theorist of the kind of learning that happens without deliberate teaching. . . . But "teaching without curriculum" does not mean spontaneous, free from classrooms or simply "leaving the child alone." It means supporting children as they build their own intellectual structures with materials drawn from the surrounding culture. In this model educational intervention means changing the culture, planting new constructive elements and eliminating noxious ones.[57]

With the example of children building up the mathematical concept of numbers, Papert explains the learning model of Piaget and continues:

And all this is done through what I have called Piagetian learning, a learning process that has many features the schools should envy: it is effective (all the children get there), it is inexpensive (it seems to require neither teacher nor curriculum development), and it is humane (the children seem to do it in a carefree spirit without explicit external rewards and punishments).[58]

The most obvious example for this way of learning is the language which each child builds up without pain, school organization and didactic. Papert calls on this picture:

Two fundamental ideas run through this book. The first is that it is possible to design computers so that learning to communicate with them can be a natural process, more like learning French by living in France than like trying to learn it through the unnatural process of American foreign language instruction in classroom. Second, learning to com-

---

[55] Ibid, p. 19.

[56] Ibid, p. 7.

[57] Ibid, p. 32.

[58] Ibid, p. 42.

municate with a computer may change the way other learning takes place. The computer can be a mathematics speaking and alphabetics speaking entity. We are learning how to make computers with which children love to communicate. When this communication occurs, children learn mathematics as a living language. Moreover, mathematical communication and alphabeitc communication are thereby both transformed from the alien and therefore difficult things they are for most children into natural and therefore easy ones.[59]

b. What is Logo?

"Logo is the name of a philosophy of education in a growing family of computer languages that goes with it."[60]

1. Turtle Geometry

Part of this educational method is a new geometry, and since it seems to be easier to explain Logo with examples taken from that geometry, it may be explained right here.

An important didactic vehicle for teaching geometry is the turtle, which gives us the name: "turtle geometry."

> Turtle geometry is a different style of doing geometry, just as Euclid's axiomatic style and Descartes' analytical style are different from one another. . . . Euclid built his geometry from a set of fundamental concepts, one of which is the point. . . . Turtle geometry, too, has a fundamental entity similar to Euclid's point. But this entity which I call a 'turtle,' can be related to things people know because unlike Euclid's point, it is not stripped so totally of all properties, and instead of being static it is dynamic. . . . A turtle is at some place—it, too, has a position—but it also faces some direction—it's heading. In this, the turtle is like a person—I am here and I am facing north—or an animal or both. And from these similarities comes the turtle's special ability to serve as a first representative of formal mathematics for a child. Children can identify with the turtle and are thus able to bring their knowledge about their bodies and how they move into the work of learning formal geometry.
>
> To see how this happens we need to know one more thing about turtles: they are able to accept commands expressed in a language called TURTLE TALK. The command 'FORWARD' causes the turtle to move in a straight line in the direction it is facing. . . . To tell it how far to go, FORWARD must be followed by a number: FORWARD 1 will cause a very small movement, FORWARD 100 a large one. In

---

[59] Ibid, p. 6.

[60] Ibid, p. 217.

Logo environments many children have been started on the road to turtle geometry by introducing them to a mechanical turtle, a cybernetic robot, that will carry out these commands when they are typed on a typewriter keyboard. This "floor turtle" has wheels, a dome shape, and a pen so that it can draw a line as it moves. But its essential properties— position, heading and the ability to obey TURTLE TALK commands— are the ones that matter for doing geometry. The child may later meet the same three properties in another embodiment of the turtle: a "light turtle." This is a triangular shaped object on a television screen. . . .

Two other commands change the heading without affecting the position: RIGHT and LEFT cause a turtle to "pivot." Like FORWARD, a turning command also needs to be given a number—input message— to say how much the turtle needs to turn. An adult will quickly recognize these numbers as the measure of the turning angle in degrees. For most children the numbers have to be explored, and doing so is an exciting and playful process.

A square can be produced by the commands

```
FORWARD      100
RIGHT         90
FORWARD      100
RIGHT         90
FORWARD      100
RIGHT         90
FORWARD      100
RIGHT         90      .   .   .   .
```

Since learning to control the turtle is like learning to speak a language it mobilizes the child's expertise and pleasure in speaking. Since it is like being in command, it mobilizes the child's expertise and pleasure in commanding. To make the turtle trace a square you walk in a square yourself and describe what you are doing in TURTLE TALK. And so, working with the turtle mobilizes the child's expertise and pleasure in motion. It draws on the child's well-established knowledge of "body geometry" as a starting-point for the development of bridges into formal geometry.[61]

One may easily visualize how this instrument is applicable to drawing all standard geometric figures, but also to drawing objects like houses, flowers, birds, including making discoveries about geometrical relationships, angles, symmetries, and so forth, and such theorems as the sum of angles in a triangle.

---

[61] Ibid, pp. 55-58.

2. Properties of the Logo Programming Language

The short example of a Logo program as given above shows the properties of the Logo language: [62]

Logo is interactive, meaning that typed-in commands may be executed immediately. This facilitates a trial-and-error approach to programming.

In this respect, Logo may be compared to the cylinder blocks in a Montessori class: The material provides immediate feedback on the child's attempts to solve a problem, and thereby stimulates and satisfies further trials. With the cylinder blocks, the problem is to fit the wooden cylinders into the right holes and thereby develop the necessary fine motor skills and hand-eye coordination. If the cylinder does not fit the hole, the child feels it immediately. The same is true on a higher level with Logo: If the turtle does not perform what the child wanted to program, it will be felt immediately, not by the criticism of an adult, but by the feedback of the material itself.

Logo is user friendly. One example is its simple and clear program structure: simple mnemonic commands; no line numeration; changes in the program done right on the screen; and easy access to program parts, since these parts have names.

Logo is tuned for interesting applications. This means that there is more opportunity for the learning programmer to use his or her skills on objects that make sense in themselves, instead of meaningless tasks given only to teach programming.

Mentioned above is the application with turtle geometry. Another example is its ready application for language problems, since letters, words, and sentences can be dealt with in their natural hierarchy while most other programming languages consider sentences merely as sequences of letters and spaces, which makes programming of language problems more difficult.

Logo is easy for the young learner. Its introduction with turtle geometry gives the child opportunity to work and explore independently after picking up only two commands. Even sophisticated program structures such as procedures or recursion can be introduced quickly.

Logo is extensible, which means that new procedures defined by the user look like normal commands. In this way, Logo allows one to be creative and to create new commands. From the point of view of the program, this is done by subroutines that have a name that allows them to be called without any further complications. An example follows:

```
TO SQUARE
  REPEAT 4 [FORWARD 100 RIGHT 90]
END
```

---

[62] Brian Harwey: "Why Logo? Logo is designed to encourage development of problem-solving skills," *BYTE, The Small Systems Journal,* August 1982, pp. 163-193.

After this little program is created, it can be called on in all future occasions merely by entering the command, "SQUARE."

Another example follows:

```
TO TRIANGLE
  REPEAT 3 [FORWARD 100 RIGHT 120]
END
```

The two new commands could be used to draw a house, which in itself could become a new command:

```
TO HOUSE
  SQUARE
  TRIANGLE
END
```

> The technique of regarding a procedure (even a complex procedure) as a black box whose details you needn't worry about at the moment is a crucial idea in programming or, indeed, in any kind of design enterprise. Each time you define a new procedure, you can use it as a building block in more complex procedures, and in this way you can build up very complex processes in what Papert refers to as mindsize bites.'[63]

Friendly attitude to bugs. The example above is used by Papert to introduce a further element of the method above that is also found in Montessori: Errors and mistakes are not forbidden, but are taken as an interesting occasion to understand the problem even better. The program just mentioned, which was supposed to create a house, instead will produce the following:

> The triangle came out inside the square instead of on top of it! Typically in math class, the child's reaction to a wrong answer is to try to forget it as fast as possible. But in the Logo environment, the child is not criticized for an error in drawing. The process of debugging is a normal part of the process of understanding a program. The programmer is encouraged to study the bug rather than forget the error.[64]

The creation of new commands includes two further particularities of Logo:

---

[63] Harold Abelson, *Apple Logo* (New York: McGraw Hill Byte Books, 1982), p. 28.

[64] Seymour Papert, *Mindstorms,* p. 61.

Logo is procedural, meaning that a program and procedures may be built up from smaller building blocks and therefore are easier to develop and understand.

Logo is recursive, meaning that the name of a particular procedure can be used within the same procedure. As an example, we may look at the program that creates a spiral:[65]

```
TO SPIRAL :DISTANCE
   FORWARD :DISTANCE
   RIGHT 90
   SPIRAL :DISTANCE + 5
END.
```

> It's hard to explain in a simple way why recursion is important. The idea behind recursion, though, has profound mathematical importance. By allowing a complicated problem to be described in terms of simpler versions of itself, recursion allows very large problems to be stated in a very compact form.[66]

The example simultaneously showed the application of variables in Logo: The word "DISTANCE" is the name of a variable that may take on different values. Names of variables in Logo need no specification whether they are meant for numbers or letters, and these names can be words of considerable size, which facilitates dealing with them. A similar advantage lies in the use of lists, which may consist of numbers, letters, lists, or lists of lists.

All these properties make Logo a language that, for the computer, is very demanding. Handling Logo on a computer calls for a memory capacity of at least 64K bytes, meaning a memory with 64,000 letters or numbers capacity. Some applications also call for rather fast computers.[67]

However, the same properties make Logo a very flexible and easy instrument for the user and enable programmers to keep their attention fully on the problem without being confused by programming difficulties.

3. Applications

Applications of this programming language reach from geometric explorations for primary children through sophisticated problems on the theory of relativity for university students.[68]

Turtle geometry therefore is not limited to simple tasks as described above. As soon as the child tries to make the turtle draw a circle, this "places the

---

[65] Ibid, p. 71.

[66] Brian Harwey, *Why Logo?* p. 166.

[67] Ibid, p. 193.

[68] Ibid, p. 186.

child in contact with a cluster of ideas that lie at the heart of the calculus, . . .
not learning about the formalism of calculus, . . . but about its use and its
meaning. In fact the turtle circle program . . . is a powerful carrier of ideas
behind the differential." [69]

As an example of how far Logo can be taken, the introduction to Newton's
laws of mechanics may be mentioned. This program includes an extension
of the turtle vocabulary:

> These new turtles, which we call "dynaturtles," are more dynamic in
> the sense that their state is taken to include two velocity components
> in addition to the two geometric components, position and heading, of
> the previously discussed geometry turtles. [70]
>
> The physics microworld we shall develop, the physics analogue of
> our computer-based Mathland, offers a Piagetian learning path into
> Newtonian laws of motion, a topic usually considered paradigmatic of
> the kind of knowledge that can only be reached by a long, formalized
> learning path. [71]

This example indicates the possible extensions within the educational model
of Logo. However, next to the possibilities to include all kinds of subjects,
the formal learning processes are also of particular importance.

> To give ourselves a more systematic overview of what children learn
> from working with the turtle we begin by distinguishing between two
> kinds of knowledge. One kind is mathematical: the turtles are only a
> small corner of a large mathematical subject, turtle geometry, a kind
> of geometry that is easily learnable and an effective carrier of very
> general mathematical ideas. The other kind of knowledge is mathetic:
> knowledge about learning. . . . [72]

This idea is very important in Logo, namely, seeing ideas from computer science not only as instruments of explanation of how learning

---

[69] Seymour Papert, *Mindstorms*, p. 66. Further application containing an introduction to calculus,
see Harold Abelson and Andrea diEssa, *Turtle Geometry: The Computer as a Medium for
Exploring Mathematics* (Cambridge, MA: MIT Press, 1981). An application for primary children,
see R. W. Lawler:

R. W. Lawler, Designing Computer Based Microworlds, *BYTE, The Small Systems Journal,*
August 1982, p. 144: "The beach microworld . . . this microworld helped my three year old
daughter learn to read with minimal direct instruction."

"A microworld is a well-defined, but limited, learning environment in which interesting things
happen and in which there are important ideas to be learned," E. Paul Goldenberg, Logo—A
Cultural Glossary, *BYTE, The Small Systems Journal,* August 1982, p. 218.

[70] Seymour Papert, *Mindstorms,* p. 122.

[71] Ibid, p. 123.

[72] Ibid, p. 63. ". . . the stem 'math' in Greek means 'learning' in a general sense." (p. 39).
"Mathetics is the set of guiding principles that govern learning." (p. 52).

and thinking in fact do work, but also as instruments of change that might alter, and possibly improve, the way people learn and think.[73]

As an example of such heuristic strategy processes, the work with the touch turtle is mentioned: The turtle, which is sensitive to touch, is to be programmed in a way that lets it surround objects.

It is a very instructive project for a group of students to develop this (or an equivalent) program from first principles by acting out how they think they would use touch to get around an object and by translating their strategies into turtle commands.[74]

We also find applications mentioned that are totally different:

The students wrote programs that could translate English to "pig Latin," programs that could play games of strategy, and programs to generate concrete poetry.[75]

4. Educational Results

With the poetry program, an encouraging example is mentioned of a seventh grader who, after yearlong drills in grammar, still did not understand the difference between nouns and verbs and adverbs.

One day Jenny came in very excited. She had made a discovery. "Now I know why we have nouns and verbs" she said . . . In order to "teach" her computer to make strings of words that would look like English, she had to "teach" it to choose words of an appropriate class. What she learned about grammar from this experience with a machine was anything but mechanical or routine. Her learning was deep and meaningful. . . . She not only "understood" grammar, she changed her relationship to it. It was "hers," and during her year with the computer, incidents like this helped Jenny change her image of herself. Her performance changed too; her previously low to average grades became "straight A's" for her remaining years of school.[76]

Besides this story of Jenny, a few other encouraging experiences are mentioned.[77]

One may be quoted:

Kim was a fifth grade girl who invariably came out on the bottom on all school arithmetic tests. She hated math. In a Logo environment she became engrossed in programming. . . . One day a visiting educator

---

[73] Ibid, p. 208.

[74] Ibid, p. 219.

[75] Ibid, p. 218.

[76] Ibid, p. 49.

[77] Ibid, p. 65, 104, 151.

remarked to her that "computers made math fun." Kim looked up from her work and said very angrily: "There ain't nothin' fun in math." The instructor in her class had not thought it advisable to discuss with her whether what she was doing with the computer was "math." Clearly, anything that was good was definitionally not math. But by the end of the year Kim made the connection herself and decided that mathematics was neither unpleasant nor difficult.[78]

Although there are not yet scientifically secured reports on the usage of Logo in school, "during the past year, the use of Logo in schools has jumped from less than a dozen sites to hundreds. By the end of the coming year, it may involve thousands of classrooms with tens of thousands of students."[79]

The article quoted here tells about four projects and their evaluation. A cautious summing up states:

> Logo can be effective for all students in a school setting. In fact a regular theme for all the projects cited is the success of students who previously had been unsuccessful in school . . .
>
> In no case has the "full potential of what might be possible" with Logo been realized. It will probably take a lot of time and many diverse efforts, before the learning potential of Logo can be fully understood and utilized.[80]

One particular use of Logo is obviously the help for handicapped children. It has already been mentioned that children with gross or fine motor problems can be greatly helped by a word processing computer. The advantages for these children in a Logo environment go far beyond that.

> The Cotting School for the physically handicapped in Boston has been the site of a series of projects conducted by Dr. Sylvia Weir of MIT. In these projects, Logo has enabled students with cerebral palsy, previously unable to communicate effectively, to begin to realize their intellectual potential. Of all the Logo projects, this has been the most dramatic in demonstrating Logo's effectiveness for students who previously had not been successful in academic settings.[81]

All these reports provide a very positive picture; however, they do not give a scientifically controlled verification on the advantages of Logo applications in schools. Where Logo is based on the pedagogy of Piaget, his careful and long-ranging studies may be taken into consideration. At points, however, where Piaget is interpreted or where the limits set by him are exceeded, a careful and scientific evaluation would be desirable. This is not the place to

---

[78] Ibid, p. 151.

[79] Daniel Watt, "Logo in the Schools," *BYTE, The Small Systems Journal,* August 1982, p. 134.

[80] Ibid, p. 133.

[81] Ibid, p. 132.

do so. But it is obvious that even without that evaluation, the new concept of Logo is making big strides to enter the reality of education. It therefore may be necessary and worthwhile to consider its compatibility with Montessori principles.

c. Logo and Montessori

The previous pages could not give more than a short outline of the educational philosophy behind Logo, just as much as was necessary to discuss them in our context. Unfortunately, it also was not possible to convey the exciting atmosphere of original thinking. In spite of this necessary briefness, one striking aspect should be clear—the remarkable relationship of the philosophy behind Logo with Montessori education.

1. Children as Builders of Their Own Minds

The relationship of the philosophies underlying Logo and Montessori can be seen most clearly in the way that children are considered the builders of their own potential and in how learning is seen as a function of that building process. Besides that most fundamental aspect, a few more parallels between the two educational systems also will be outlined here, each of which individually may not be that important, but as a whole underline the stated relationship.

It should not be surprising that the Logo system based on Piaget has points in common with the philosophy of Montessori:

> During this century the paths of Montessori and Piaget crossed a number of times. Piaget attended many of the international congresses of the Association Montessori Internationale which were held in Europe between 1929 and the outbreak of the Second World War, and he served as president of the Swiss Montessori Society. To those who know both Piagetian theory and Montessori theory and practice, the similarities are very striking.[82]

Among the many parallels between both theories, the one that is important here is the view on the learning child and the resulting necessity of a prepared environment:

Piaget—"The goal in education is not to increase the amount of knowledge, but to create the possibilities for a child to invent and discover. When we teach too fast, we keep a child from inventing and discovering for himself . . . Teaching means creating situations where structures can be discovered; it does not mean transmitting structures which may be assimilated at none other than a verbal level."[83]

---

[82] Jean K. Miller, "Piaget and Montessori—Theory and Practice and the Development of Classification Skills," *Montessori Elementary Newsletter*, p. a.

[83] Piaget cited according to J. Miller, ibid., p. p.

Montessori—"Education is not something which the teacher does, but it is a natural process which develops spontaneously in the human being. It is not acquired by listening to words, but in virtue of the experiences in which the child acts on his environment. The teacher's task is not to talk, but to prepare and arrange a series of motives for cultural activity in a special environment made for the child."[84]

Even the choice of words expresses this common basis of the two theories: Both describe the child as "builder of his own potential"; they both talk about the "material" and the "environment" prepared for the child and about the importance of "independence of the child." The quote given in section XIa, this chapter, about "learning without curriculum" would fit perfectly into a book of Montessori.

Other parallels may be of minor importance, but underline the common basis of both educational philosophies:

2. Isolation of Difficulties

The principle of "isolation of difficulties" is expressed differently for the materials of Montessori and for the microworlds of Logo; however, it is the same principle.

> It is in fact easy for children to understand how the turtle defines a self-contained world in which certain questions are relevant and others are not. . . . This idea can be developed by constructing many such "microworlds," each with its own set of assumptions and constraints. Children get to know what it is like to explore the properties of a chosen microworld undisturbed by extraneous questions.[85]

With Montessori, the isolating of difficulties means to analyze certain aspects and offer one aspect at a time in order that the child is not confronted with different difficulties at the same time. This principle is particularly obvious with the sensorial materials.[86] It is, however, applied throughout the materials of the elementary school as well. The basic idea common to both educational theories is to provide children with a material allowing them to focus on certain aspects of reality without being distracted by other difficulties.

3. Positive Attitude Towards Mistakes

The attitude towards mistakes in the child's work has already been mentioned.

> Errors benefit us because they lead us to study what happened, to understand what went wrong, and, through understanding, to fix it.

---

[84] Maria Montessori quoted according to J. Miller, ibid, p. p.

[85] Seymour Papert, *Mindstorms,* p. 117.

[86] Compare Maria Montessori, *The Discovery of the Child,* p. 138.

> Experience with computer programming leads children more effectively
> than any other activity to "believe in" debugging.[87]

This quote sums up an interest of Papert, which is far more important to
him than can be shown in our short introduction. The positive attitude towards
the error as a source of learning stimulations can be found as well in Montessori.

"Supposing we study the phenomenon of error in itself; it becomes apparent
that everyone makes mistakes. This is one of life's realities, and to admit it
is already to have taken a great step forward. . . . So it is well to cultivate
a friendly feeling towards error, to treat it as a companion inseparable from
our lives, as something having a purpose, which it truly has.

. . .

It will be remembered that one of the first exercises done by our children
is that with a set of cylinders of equal height but varying in diameter, which
fit into corresponding sockets in a block of wood. The first thing is to realize
that all are different; the second is to hold them by the knob at the top of
each, using the thumb and first two fingers. The child begins fitting them
one at a time into their sockets, but finds when he comes to the end that he
has made a mistake. One cylinder is left which is too large for the only
remaining hole, while some of the others fit too loosely. The child looks again
and studies them all more closely. He is now faced by a problem. There is
that cylinder left over, which shows that he has made a mistake. Well, it is
just this that adds interest to the game and makes him repeat it time after
time.

. . .

If in the daily routine of school we always arrange for errors to become
perceptible, this is to place us on a path to perfection, the child's interest in
doing better, and his own constant checking and testing, are so important to
him that his progress is assured.

. . .

Errors divide man, but their correction is a means of union. It becomes a
matter of general interest to correct errors wherever they may be found. The
error itself becomes interesting."[88]

4. Normalizing Effect of Focused Work

The normalizing effect of focused work and of satisfying the need of free
learning may not be expressively mentioned by Papert, but it is clear that he
thought of it as important. The following description of a situation by Papert

---

[87] Seymour Papert, *Mindstorms,* p. 114.

[88] Maria Montessori, *The Absorbent Mind* (Madras, India: Kalakshetra Publications, 1967), pp.
246, 249, 250.

recalls immediately the famous quote of Montessori which tells about the repetitious work of a child with the cylinder blocks.[89]

Here is Montessori's story:

> At San Lorenzo ... I happened to notice a little girl of about three years old deeply absorbed in a set of solid insets, removing the wooden cylinders from their respective holes and replacing them. The expression on the child's face was one of such concentrated attention that it seemed to me an extraordinary manifestation; up to this time none of the children had ever shown such fixity of interest in an object; and my belief in the characteristic instability of attention in young children who flit incessantly from one thing to another, made me peculiarly alive to the phenomenon.
>
> I watched the child intensely without disturbing her at first, and began to count how many times she repeated the exercise: then, seeing she was continuing for a long time, I picked up the little armchair in which she was seated, and placed chair and child upon the table; the little creature hastily caught up her case of insets, laid it across the arms of the chair and gathering the cylinders into her lap set to work again. Then I called upon all the children to sing; they sang, but the little girl continued undisturbed, repeating her exercise even after the short song had come to an end. I counted forty-four repetitions; when at last she ceased, it was quite independently of any surrounding stimuli which might have distracted her, and she looked round with a satisfied air, almost as if awaking from a refreshing nap. ... And each time that such a polarisation of attention took place, the child began to be completely transformed, to become calmer, more intelligent and more expansive.

And here is Papert's story:

> Deborah, a sixth grader with problems with school learning was introduced to the work of screen turtles. ... Deborah found it frightening, the reaction she had to most of what she did at school. In her first few hours with turtle work she developed a disturbing degree of dependence on the instruction, constantly asking for reassurance before taking the smallest exploratory step. A turning point came when Deborah decided to restrict her turtle commands, creating a microworld within the microworld of turtle commands. She allowed herself only one turning command: RIGHT 30. To turn the turtle through 90°, she would repeat RIGHT 30 three times and would obtain the effect of LEFT 30 by repeating it eleven times. To an onlooker it might seem tedious to obtain simple effects in such complicated ways. But for Deborah it was exciting to be able to construct her own microworld and to discover how much she could do within its rigid constraints. She no longer asked permission

---

[89] Maria Montessori, *The Advanced Montessori Method,* Vol. 1, p. 55.

to explore. And one day, when the teacher offered to show her a "simpler way," to achieve an effect, she listened patiently and said, "I don't think I'll do it that way." She emerged when she was ready, several weeks later, with a new sense of confidence that showed itself not only in more ambitious turtle projects but in her relationship to everything else she did at school.[90]

Although both quotes describe different situations, the parallels lie in these aspects: the simplicity of the activity, making no sense to an unprepared adult; the stunning multitude of repetitions; the abstinence of the adult from insisting upon a faster and more rational process; and, finally, the normalizing effect, which involves the whole personality and goes far beyond the situation at the moment.

5. Meaningful Learning

Turtle geometry was specifically designed to be something children could make sense of, to be something that would resonate with their sense of what is important. And it was designed to help children develop the mathetics strategy: in order to learn something, first make sense of it.[91]

When Montessori confronts the three-year-old child with the "exercises of practical life," one of the goals is to let the child participate in what is important in family life. In the elementary school, this principle works by offering learning materials according to the interest of the six-to-twelve-year-old child, "in acquisition of culture . . . and to know the reasons of things."[92] Accordingly, children are helped to explore how the constellation of sun and earth causes the world's climatic regions, or how photo-synthesis within the leaf builds up plant food, all of this, of course in a method adapted to the age.[93]

In another way, the same principle appears for the twelve-to-fifteen-year-old, when Montessori sees life and work in nature and involvement in economic and social processes of society as the constituents of her Erdkinder model.[94]

Therefore work on the land is an introduction both to nature and to civilization and gives a limitless field for scientific and historic studies.

---

[90] Seymour Papert, *Mindstorms,* pp. 118–119.

[91] Ibid, p. 63. The author uses the term "mathetic" as "having to do with learning," see page 39.

[92] Maria Montessori, "To Educate the Human Potential," p. 4.

[93] Montessori Elementary Training Course, *Unpublished Lectures.* Washington Montessori Institute, Washington, D.C., 1982.

[94] Maria Montessori, *From Childhood to Adolescence.* 1948, New Engl. Ed. (New York: Schocken Books, 1973). p. 105.

If the produce can be used commercially this brings in the fundamental mechanism of society, that of production and exchange, on which economic life is based. This means that there is an opportunity to learn both academically and through actual experience what are the elements of social life.[95]

The remarkable difference, of course, is that Montessori seeks meaningful learning, not primarily in an aesthetic playful aspect, but in the function of the acquired skills and knowledge within human society. In common with Logo is the fact that the child is not asked to acknowledge such meaningfulness, nor is there any inscription on top of the school door, "We learn for life"; but the meaning is found as a powerful agent within the child. It might be necessary to add that Logo also does not stop with aesthetic playful meaningfulness, but the spontaneous fascination of deeper mathematical and language structure is seen and intended. "A child who draws a turtle circle wants to draw the circle; doing it produces pride and excitement."[96]

6. Importance of Language

Papert spends a whole chapter making clear that the learning and the application of a computer language introduce and practice new concepts that enable us to express and conceptualize new thoughts and structures in an adequate way. "In a computer-rich world, computer languages that simultaneously provide a means of control over the computer and offer new and powerful descriptive languages for thinking will undoubtedly be carried into the general culture. They will have a particular effect on our language for describing ourselves and our learning."[97]

Papert then describes the anecdote of Descartes watching a fly on the ceiling, which triggered in his mind the famous coordinate system, which in turn brought about the language that is so necessary for science and economy today.

The relationship with Montessori lies in the importance seen in language as an instrument for thinking and spiritual order. "The child with three years of age has already acquired the language of the environment and in our Montessori environment we help him to make conscious what he already possesses in order to use it for his further development. . . . We provide him with the trust, to express himself and his thoughts with a clear and precise vocabulary."[98]

---

[95] Ibid, p. 107.

[96] Seymour Papert, *Mindstorms,* p. 63.

[97] Ibid, p. 98.

[98] Hildegard Solzbacher, "Schreiben und Lesen" in *Die Montessori-Paedagogik und das behinderte Kind,* ed. Theodor Hellbruegge and Mario Montessori; trans. Peter Gebhardt-Seele (Munich: Kindler Verlag, 1978), p. 81.

This principle of creating an instrument of thinking through a refined language is observed through all the school years, especially through the focus on those materials that clarify the logical structure of the language to the child at a relatively early age: the parts of speech, sentence analysis, and other parts of grammar and syntax.

7. Importance of Mathematics

The importance of mathematics as a principle is obvious in Logo. But also in the Montessori method, it is well understood that mathematics is not only one among other school subjects, but an important aspect of human thinking and the development of the human mind.

> Of its nature, the mind not only has the power to imagine (i.e., to think of things not immediately present) but it can also assemble and rearrange its mental content, extract—let us say—an "alphabet of qualities" from all those numberless things that we meet in the outside world. This it does by the power it possesses of abstract thought.
>
> . . .
>
> In our work, therefore, we have given a name to this part of the mind which is built up with exactitude, and we call it "the mathematical mind." I take the term from Pascal, the French philosopher, physicist and mathematician, who said man's mind was mathematical by nature, and that knowledge and progress came from accurate observation.[99]
>
> Man not only has been endowed with a mathematical mind, but also with the urge to use it . . . If mathematics have come to be applied, it means that in the nature of man the tendency towards mathematical conception exists! . . . If mathematics are introduced in the life of the child in the way Dr. Montessori taught, children delight in them.[100]

This understanding characterizes the place that mathematics holds in Montessori education through all age levels.

8. Serving Function of the Material

Papert makes it clear that "although technology will play an essential role in the realization of my vision of the future of education, my central focus is not on the machine but on the mind, and particularly on the way in which intellectual movements and cultures define themselves and grow. Indeed, the role I give to the computer is that of a carrier of cultural 'germs' or 'seeds' whose intellectual products will not need technological support once they

---

[99] Maria Montessori, *The Absorbent Mind*, p. 183.

[100] Mario Montessori, *The Human Tendencies and Montessori Education* 2nd rev. ed. (Amsterdam, The Netherlands: Association Montessori Internationale, 1956), p. 22.

take root in an actively growing mind." [101] The picture of "seeds" can be found with the same term and the same meaning in the words of Montessori. [102]

The serving and transitional function of the materials and their help to develop mind structures that then will function in themselves is an important principle in the Montessori method. So, for example, the steps introducing material are organized in such a way that at the end, they lead to an abstract definition of the process, which then can be handled without the material. Thus, in the introduction of square roots, the geometrical structures on the pegboard provide an opportunity to experience the mathematical structures in a visual, tactile, and motor way, with the final goal being, however, to go beyond the material and solve the math problem without it. [103]

d. Logo In The Class

The parallels in the pedagogies of Montessori and Logo show in their sum that the two are closely related. This may well be an indication that it is reasonable to use Logo in a Montessori class. So it is understandable that Montessori schools in increasing numbers are looking for more information on Logo.

Of course, there are concerns and arguments against this application. One has already been mentioned in Chapter A, Section IIb: the principle of Montessori that limits the materials to only those that are "keys" in order not to clutter the class with unnecessary items, the key materials already being developed in full.

Within this concern one would have to consider how far Logo provides "keys." It certainly is true for the areas of geometry, language, and Newton's mechanics. However, the areas of geometry and language are covered well by the classic Montessori materials. It might not be desirable to replace proven materials by computer exercises.

Another principle in Montessori is "repetition through variation," which replaces the repetitious exercises of ages three to six in the elementary class. [104]

In realizing this principle, it might be desirable to provide variation in geometry through another type of exercise. More detailed studies may answer the question of whether the geometry exercises in Logo and in Montessori really cover the same geometrical problems. If they do not, both exercises could be valuable to supplement each other.

Certainly a key is to be seen in the insights, which are provoked by Logo, about what Papert describes by the term "mathetic." [105] These insights into

---

[101] Seymour Papert, *Mindstorms*, p. 9.

[102] Maria Montessori, *To Educate the Human Potential*, p. 4, quoted in Chapter A, Section Ia.

[103] Montessori Elementary Training Course, *Unpublished Lectures*.

[104] Montessori Elementary Training Course, *Unpublished Lectures*.

[105] Seymour Papert, *Mindstorms*, p. 52.

one's own thinking and one's own learning process are especially important in our times, where learning continues for a lifetime.

Besides the subjects that may be learned by dealing with Logo in the classroom, Logo could also be chosen simply as a computer language in order to teach programming (see section X). After our brief introduction to the properties of this language, it may now be clearer why Logo, as a computer language, is more appropriate for younger children than any other.

The configuration of a computer needed to teach Logo is more expensive than for simpler languages. Although the advantage of Logo is its simplicity for the programmer, it is not all that simple for the computer. It needs a memory capacity of at least 64K, which the cheaper computers on the market are not always able to handle. Although the major manufacturers of the microcomputer do provide Logo in their products, that is not true for everyone.

Some computers have versions of Logo that include only the turtle graphics, not the whole scope of the Logo language. Some have adapted turtle graphics to other computer languages, which, of course, provide interesting work for the child, but not the full scope of the educational purpose of Logo.

XII. PROBLEM SOLVING

The technique of using a computer for problem solving is employed in high school for more sophisticated math problems, with the intention that while the students program the computer to solve the problem, they must analyze the problem themselves and develop solving strategies. These features are also applicable to simpler problems.

Important arguments in connection with this method are discussed in the previous chapter. The possibilities of problem-solving methods, however, go beyond those mentioned there. For example, if a student were to program a computer to solve a square root, the student's knowledge of the abstract rule has to be actualized in a very intensive way. This rule, developed with the pegboard and applied to the abstract process on paper, has to be transferred now to a higher level of understanding by isolating each step into a sequence of program commands and then putting together all the steps into a whole program.

Another application of problem-solving strategies would be to use the particular ability of the computer for iterative processes. That means not to take a formula, for example, to draw the square root, but to take the very basic understanding of the concept of roots that the square of the root would end up as the number. So, a computer programmed to take all numbers from one on, square them, and compare the result with the number where the square root is to be drawn from, still would be fast enough in finding the correct answer.

The program a student may come up with could look like this (in Logo):

```
TO ROOT  :NUMBER  :A
  IF (:A * :A > :NUMBER) PRINT :A−1 STOP
  ROOT :NUMBER :A+1
END
```

To produce such a program would be another exercise at the point when the concept of square roots is consolidated by drawing roots from two digit numbers with beads, probably at age seven to eight years.

A similar program could be done to dwell on multiplication being a series of additions. By deliberately not using the computer's ability to multiply, the task for the student would be: "program the computer to multiply 2 numbers by using the addition capacity only." The program may turn out like this:

```
TO MULTIPLY :MULTIPLICAND :MULTIPLIER
  MAKE "ANSWER 0
  REPEAT :MULTIPLIER [ MAKE "ANSWER :ANSWER
+
   :MULTIPLICAND ]
  (PRINT :MULTIPLICAND "* :MULTIPLIER" =
   :ANSWER)
END
```

Division may be programmed similar to the root program as a series of trial multiplications until arriving at the dividend: "Make a program for division of 2 numbers by using the multiplication capacity only." The student would have to consider division as a conversion of multiplication. Or: "Program division of 2 numbers by using the subtraction capacity only." This means dealing with division as a series of subtractions and would result in a program similar to the MULTIPLY program.

Even the idea underlying addition can be explored: "Program addition of 2 numbers by using addition commands with 1 only." The result may be as follows:

```
TO ADD :A1 :A2
  REPEAT :A2 [ MAKE "A1 :A1+1 ]
  (PRINT [ THE ANSWER IS ] :A1 )
END
```

These exercises, mentioned only as examples to illustrate problem-solving strategies by computer programming, provide opportunities to apply and sharpen mathematical thinking, which is the main purpose of any mathematical studies.

Of course, this application of a computer is only reasonable after a certain level of programming skills has been achieved.

XIII. CREATIVE USES

a. Art

With the ability to fill the screen with colored lines and areas comes the possibility of doing art in this way. Most computers on the market provide this graphics capability, and most languages provide a set of commands to light up or erase certain points, lines, or areas in certain colors. There are even programs for very young children to draw on the screen with the help of a joystick, which moves an invisible pen on the screen.[106]

The reasons given for these activities with young children are to develop hand-eye coordination, to develop creative abilities, and, more especially, to introduce children to the idea that the computer is an instrument that they can command.

More research must be done to determine whether hand-eye coordination between looking at the screen and moving the joystick should come only after a thorough development of the immediate coordination between the drawing hand in contact with the real drawing. According to Montessori and other investigators, the sensitive periods for developing the sensorial abilities, especially the eye and touch organs and their coordination, are at the age of zero to six years. It therefore seems appropriate to let this natural process come to a certain level of completion before bringing in the more sophisticated relationship between seeing a movement on the screen and manipulating the joystick.

Of the art aspect, one may ask whether the immediate contact of hand and product would be a better choice for the creative process.

Finally, the aspect of teaching children that they may be in command of the computer should also be considered in the context of whether it satisfies any need during the period of three to six years. This can be experienced later as well. There are already many things to be experienced and built up at this young age, such as being in command of one's own muscles and movements and of the immediate natural environment.

All these questions must be considered carefully before installing a computer for three-to-six-year olds as a tool to work creatively in graphics.

Of course, this does not at all question the capability of the computer as a tool in the hands of an artist. Exciting artworks such as those by Melin Prueitt are certainly proof of this capability.[107] It should be understood, however, that in dealing with education, the simple tools must be mastered prior to introducing sophisticated ones.

---

[106] Mina Bell, "Joystick/Keyboard Applications in Preschool Computer Program." Paper read at: Marilyn Church and June Wright, "Using the Microcomputer Creatively with Young Children," in *Proceedings of National Educational Computing Conference 1983, Baltimore, MD.* (Silver Spring, MD: IEEE Computer Society Press, 1983), p. 272.

[107] Melin L. Prueitt, "Cray on Art," *Discover,* November 1983, p. 69.

b. Music

Most computers today are equipped with a sound-producing circuitry that can be controlled by certain commands, included in the computer's language repertoire. To improve the sound quality, it is possible in certain cases to attach a hi-fi speaker. Even then, however, the sound quality is limited by the fact that the sound is produced in an electronic circuit and not by a naturally moving string or membrane. Some manufacturers also allow for the application of piano-type keyboards replacing the typewriter keyboard. The important difference then from a computer equipped in this way versus an electronic organ is the fact that the computer can store certain tunes or pitches played on the keyboard in its memory, combine it with program rhythms, and play it back in a variety of ways. This indeed opens up certain opportunities for exploration in music that were not previously available.

For the basic exploration of pitch, simple tunes, and simple harmonies, the Montessori class has the set of bells and tone bars, which give immediate access to the phenomenon of sounds and their arrangement in musical patterns. The work with this material allows musical phenomena connected to the arrangement in space and combined with a concrete movement of hands and objects. These materials in their simplicity and beauty are designed specially for the young child. It would make little sense to replace them with a machine.

However, at the more advanced level of musical studies, the point may be reached where the manual skills of the children set limits that cannot be exceeded. Since music happens at a certain speed and rhythm, the manual performance cannot be slowed down deliberately. At this point, the computer may provide some help: While the students can input the different elements of music in a slow and isolated way such as tunes, rhythms, harmonies, they can then program the computer to play it back at the right speed and in the right combination, and do that repetitiously. The age for such studies will probably not be earlier than ten years.

Although most computers come equipped with these sound capabilities, for serious studies, care should be taken for good sound quality and a piano-type keyboard would be desirable.

XIV. SCIENCE EXPERIMENTS

In high schools, computers are used increasingly to control, survey, and evaluate physics experiments.

Montessori elementary schools provide simple equipment to do experiments. These, however, focus on giving sensorial impressions rather than scientific evaluations.

Since an important characteristic of children aged six to twelve is seen in their powers of imagination, impressions through pictures and experiments are used as a help to understand natural phenomena, for example, those connected with the history of our earth.[108] The level of scientific exactness and sophistication in experiments, which would call for a computer as a reasonable tool, is not reached until high school. Therefore, the use of computers in Montessori elementary schools for this purpose is not a matter of discussion.

XV. COMPUTERS FOR HANDICAPPED STUDENTS

This chapter concerns all the uses so far discussed, and for each kind of handicap, different opportunities and problems are to be considered. It is, therefore, not possible within the limits of this book to do more than direct attention at the new possibilities and illustrate that with some examples.

The Montessori school, with its special features of individualized work and its focus on the child's sensorial and rational development, has special capabilities to mainstream handicapped children of different kinds of handicaps,[109] and may then be interested in the special help, which computers can provide. But of course, the applications of computers for handicapped students mentioned here are not exclusive to the Montessori class, but are developed and used in all kinds of schools.

a. Examples with Physically Disabled

One special feature of the computer is to provide help for the moving impaired. The computer allows one to control processes on the screen and with the printer through a limited number of body movements, which also can be defined in very different ways. One such way is to control programs by single switch control on the keyboard. For example, the program could provide menus from which the students may choose by pushing single keys on the keyboard.

For heavily impaired students, these single keys can be replaced by single body switches that may be attached to that part of the body which functions best, such as the feet, head, or for gross movements of the hands. Even switches to be acted on by blowing or sucking have been developed, as have speech discriminators, where the switch is controlled by sounds given by the student.

One example for such an application could be the work with Logo. The turtle graphics are controlled by the same commands as mentioned in this chapter, Section XI, except that these commands are not typed into the keyboard but are given as a menu on the screen. The program provides a

---

[108] Montessori Elementary Training Course, *Unpublished Lectures.*

[109] For details on this wide topic, see Theodor Hellbrügge and Mario Montessori, eds. *Die Montessori-Pädagogik und das behinderte Kind* (Munich: Kindler Verlag, 1978).

cursor moving at a slow pace through the menu and the student, by acting on the single switch, gives an impulse at the moment when the cursor stands next to the command the student wants to choose.[110]

In general, these techniques can be applied to any kind of teaching equipment, including audio-visual presentations, computer-assisted instruction, drills, and so on.

"With these interfaces a handicapped student can have access to the tremendously wide range of software currently available for microcomputers. This could aid in education as well as in communication and daily routines for individuals with a broad range of handicaps."[111]

There are also programs for special handicaps such as the visually impaired: these programs use access technology, which "means the voice output or braille output device they are using as an alternative to the screen."[112] Another example is the communication device for students with cerebral palsy, providing the opportunity to communicate with computer-produced sounds and written messages that the students control to what they can do with any part of the body.[113]

b. With Mentally Disabled Reconsider Previous Chapters

With learning disabled children, the considerations on computer-assisted instructions, drills, and practices may be revised in as far as these children are not able to build up their natural thinking processes through exploration and interest as do healthy children. This question, however, still needs more research and the answers will probably depend very much on the individual case.

More examples of the special usefulness of computers with handicapped children are given in Sections VIII (Word Processing) and XI (Logo).

It should be understood from these short remarks that the computer can be of special help for handicapped students in almost all aspects of class life.

---

[110] Warren R. Brown, "Project CAISH Second Year Update." In Rita Horan; Warren R. Brown; Mary Russo; Dr. Nancy Jones; Sharon Smaldino; and Patrick Schloss: "Computing for the Learning Disabled or Handicapped." In *Proceedings of National Educational Computing Conference 1983, Baltimore, MD*. (Silver Spring, MD: IEEE Computer Society Press, 1983.)

[111] Robert Tinker, "Special Interfaces for Special Students," *Hands On! Microcomputers in Education*, Vol. 6, No. 2, 1983, pp. 5-8.

[112] David Holladay, "Programs for the Visually Impaired," *Computers Closing the Gap for Handicapped*, June 1983, p. 6.

[113] John Bennin, "The Talking Wheelchair," *Computers Closing the Gap for Handicapped*, June 1983, p. 7.

XVI. SUMMARY

In this Chapter, the argumentation on application of computers in the classroom was deferred for a detailed consideration of different applications. So far, fifteen types of application have been mentioned:

- The computer as an organizational help poses no real educational problem. Its use in the office and for report writing might never hold great importance for Montessori schools except perhaps for the organization of the library. One interesting use may be seen in organizing the teacher's record keeping, especially once the teacher and the students have become acquainted with the computer for other reasons.
- The general principles on games in the Montessori education are applicable for computer games. Even the many skills that some educators claim to be acquired from computer games are not of great interest here since the priority of Montessori is not on isolated teaching of skills, although that is accomplished in connection with other educational activities. With computer games in particular, a warning is necessary: Many overemphasize aggressiveness and killing and overstimulate an unreal fantasy.

  A somewhat different conclusion may be reached with certain educational games. That, however, depends on the individual program and its educational implications.

- Computer-assisted instruction can be seen as an advanced method of programmed instruction, which, for good reasons, has not yet been applied in Montessori schools. The Montessori material with its properties of providing activity, tactile stimuli, practice for fine motor coordination, its aesthetics and its built-in didactic structure shows it to be superior to the keyboard of a computer. What is even more important is the educational intention: Montessori sees the work of the educator as providing opportunity to children to build up their minds rather than instruct them. The open-endedness of the Montessori materials and their limitation to being a stimulus for the child's own working mind are not provided by computer-assisted instruction.
- The application of computers for drill and practice, to teach touch typing, or to take tests is of advantage if these activities are desirable in the classroom. The argumentation here does not concern the computer but the activities themselves.
- The use of a computer for simulation models may be of help in cases where the model has become rather complicated. The Montessori materials include simulation models on the level of simple mechanical experiments. However, more sophisticated aspects of reality, such as Newton's mechanic or the economic laws can only be molded into a simulation model by computers.
- Word processing on a computer may provide a chance to get certain children interested in refining their written work. This computer appli-

cation, however, should not replace handwriting, although there is little chance for this to happen, since with one computer in a classroom, access to it would be so limited and other applications would take up enough time that word processing could happen only in narrow limitations.

• The study of the computer itself would become important, if one were to come to the conclusion that the computer is an important part of the child's environment and an important instrument in his or her future life. It also seems part of our educational responsibility to show the children the limitations and capacities of this man-made instrument, which in science fiction stories is brought near to them as an omnipotent being in its own right.

As a help for studying the computer hardware, one could think of manipulative materials oriented on the four basic ideas of a computer. One such is described in Chapter C, Section II. Going even deeper into the question of electronic networks could lead to an exploration into electronics and physics.

To make the child acquainted with general business software and to include the social aspects of the computer such as its history, impact on society, and jobs related to it is part of the teacher's responsibility for computer literacy.

• Exploring the computer's capacity in learning how to program is even more important if one wants to understand the power and limitations of a computer. Programming therefore serves four purposes: It is part of the study of the computer; it means gaining power over the computer as an instrument; it provides the skills necessary to do problem solving on the computer; and it is an exploration of one's own thinking. In deciding which computer language to use, Logo is the first choice for children four to twelve. Pascal is important at the high school level, particularly since it is now part of the College Board Advanced Placement Exam. BASIC, as a second language to be taught in the elementary school, makes sense, since it is still the language that most microcomputers speak as they come from the manufacturer. Logo comes with a whole educational system that combines teaching of programming with exploration in geometry and other areas.

• Besides being a computer language, Logo provides an opportunity to explore one's own thinking and learning process while dealing with geometry, basic mathematical concepts, and other subjects. It is based on a philosophy that sees the child in a very similar way to that of Montessori. In particular, it focuses on the idea of providing the children with an environment that enables them to explore independently and thus undergo a learning process that is internally controlled rather than directed by the teacher. Application of Logo in a Montessori class depends on whether one considers the concepts acquired to be key concepts important to be given to the child.

In as far as the subjects taught run parallel with those dealt with in

Montessori materials, such as parts of geometry, the question arises as to whether Logo is welcome as a method of "repetition through variety."

- Problem solving gives an opportunity to explore certain mathematical and physical problems by programming them on a computer. Both the traditional way of solution and iterative solutions in particular for the work of a computer may be explored. The techniques of problem solving provide opportunities for independent work and study, after the key concepts are understood with a different process, which in Montessori classes, of course, would be the work with the Montessori materials.
- Creative uses are possible with computers in art and music. Little reason can be seen in replacing original creative activities with computer graphics. The same is true for replacing the work with the bells and tone bars in the Montessori class by a sound program on computers. However, for advanced studies in music, the computer may come in handy to compose music that the children with their limited manual capabilities cannot yet play on the piano.
- Science experiments can be controlled and evaluated by computers. This application, however, is more geared to high school, whereas the experiments in Montessori elementary schools are still simple enough and focus on giving impressions.
- For handicapped students, the computer can be an important help in all areas of school life. Equipped with single key controls, the handicapped student can be enabled to work through educational programs or use the computer to control other processes during class life.

We have seen several uses that are not compatible with the Montessori education. Others were seen as growing out of a philosophy very similar to that of Montessori and therefore deserve serious consideration.

As always, the deciding factor should be not a desire to be modern or conservative, nor the fun or rejection of new technology by the teacher, but solely the child and his or her healthy development.

Chapter C

IMPLEMENTATION IN CLASS: MATERIALS, PRESENTATIONS, EXERCISES

I. SOME GENERAL GUIDELINES

a. The Computer Within the Prepared Environment

If the decision is made that a computer should be available to the children, its arrangement may follow the same principles as other materials in the prepared environment of the Montessori class. Everything is available to the child and not locked away: The computer may in just the same way be placed somewhere in the classroom, available to children to work at it or to others to observe the ongoing work. It is not a good idea to lock the computer away in a special room, because then the additional problem of supervision arises. If the computer is within the classroom, then the class teacher can supervise the work just the same way as any other work. This also avoids a source of commotion, interrupting the children's concentration and flow of work.

Concerns that children may damage the expensive computer equipment have as little reason as with other materials in the class. Children who are allowed to satisfy their needs of interesting work, movement, and choice of activity develop a positive attitude towards their class environment. And erroneous manipulation can hardly damage the computer, only the software. Sensitive parts are the disk drive and the disks, which may be placed out of reach of the children until they develop the skills to handle them.

Another principle is that only one piece of each kind of material may be around. That way, each piece is unique for the child although the children have to work out a friendly way of getting around each other and managing the priority of who works with which material. This principle will call for one computer per classroom only, which naturally will come about anyway since the computer is an expensive piece of material. There may, however, come the day, when the unique piece of material is no longer the computer itself, but rather the software running on it. So one may consider one computer running Logo as one material and another one running a word processor as another piece of material.

All these questions have to be solved with the needs of the child in mind, which are, of course, not mainly to study the computer, even in the computer age.

b. Health Hazards

As computers increasingly become parts of the workplace in offices, the problems of connected health hazards are discussed. Whether or not these problems are relevant with children depends on how long children are involved in activities with computers. If a child at home spends hours in front of a computer, it may well be worthwhile to consider the design of the workplace and consult an eye doctor, but the use in a class as proposed here involves each single child for short periods of time. All the following remarks[1] are therefore not as significant as with professional workplaces.

The early concern with computer screens was directed towards radiation, similar to television sets. Improved technology seems to have brought this problem under control. But other troubles came up for long-time users, such as eye strain, musculo-sceletal problems, and headaches.

In order to avoid damage, the design of the workplace should satisfy certain objectives:

The position of the screen should allow for an operator's angle of vision from 15 to 30 degrees below horizontal; the typing posture is ideal with the upper arms perpendicular, forearms horizontal and wrists straight. For an individual workplace, this calls for adjustable chair, footrests, and table, the latter adjustable both for the keyboard and screen positions independently. For a classroom workplace with fast-changing users, only a compromise can be achieved. The problem of proper orthopedic posture and accordingly of appropriate chairs and desks is not confined to computer work. Unfortunately, much damage done by inappropriate posture at the desk surfaces only later and is not always traced back to its cause.

For similar reasons a copy holder is recommended, lifting papers to a comfortable reading height.

The screen should be treated with an antiglare coating by the manufacturer. Coating or filters applied after manufacture are not recommended. Recommended screen color is yellow or green, if a color screen is not necessary for other reasons. Word processing or programming in Logo or BASIC does not require a color screen; most software, however, are designed for color display.

Lighting is an important source of trouble, if there is too much light or too much contrast. While lighting standards for usual office space run from 1,000 to 2,000 lux, a mere 300 to 700 lux are recommended for computer

---

[1] These remarks are an excerpt from *Humanizing the VDT Workplace* (Washington, D.C.: The Newspaper Guild and International Typographical Union, 1983.)

work. Indirect light is preferred, or light fixtures that direct the light down vertically without spreading it at a wide angle. This avoids glare at the screen.

Glare in any appearance, from the sun or reflected by glossy surfaces, is especially straining for the eye that is accommodated to the low level of light from a dark computer screen. To avoid both this contrasting glare from the window and glare on the screen itself, the computer should be arranged so that neither operator nor screen are facing the window.

Computer operators with visual defects have special trouble with the different distances of screen and keyboard, which are both different from reading distance. An eye examination by an ophthalmologist is recommended for each person exposed to long-term work in front of a screen. Of course, most children do not yet have vision defects, but it is amazing how many defects with children go undetected. Whenever children work with computers, parents and teachers should be aware of these problems.

c. Schedules

Again, the same principle should be applied as with other activities: There may be as little schedule as possible, in order to give the children a chance for uninterrupted work according to their inner needs and flowing from their own decisions.

Presentations on the computer can be given to a group of two or three, casually integrated into the daily work just as other materials. The same is true for the individualized work at the computer. If there is a rush toward this material, because it is new and exciting, some measures of control may be necessary. Some teachers recommend having "an out of the way place for the computer, limiting use and structuring time. . . . A special computer room, sign-up sheets and the requirement that regular classroom work be current will keep the computer from overshadowing the Montessori curriculum."[2] In many cases, it will be enough, we hope, to have the children work out an organization controlling the access to the computer. In addition, certain guidelines can be established about what work priorities are to be observed.

The rush toward the computer will calm down anyway within a relatively short time. Children are fast to treat a computer as any other part of the learning environment, once it is arranged there in a reasonable way. Watt describes that in his report on the Lamplighter School, which is well equipped with computers: "Computers are accepted by the teachers and students as an integral part of the school, but they are not allowed to dominate it."[3]

In my own class, I observed times when all the children were so interested in certain activities that the computer stood idle. After an initial period of

---

[2] Alan S. Wallace, "Ten Questions and Answers on Computers in the Montessori Elementary Class," (American Elementary Alumni Association Newsletter), Summer 1983, pp. 2-4.

[3] Daniel Watt, "Logo in the Schools," *BYTE, The Small Systems Journal,* August 1982, p. 132.

excitement about the new fascinating instrument, they developed a more relaxed, sober attitude toward it.

d. The Teacher

Computer studies may not become another specialty subject to be scheduled. Montessori teachers are expected to be of professional help in any subject area, but not expected to be professionals in any such area. They are allowed to explore and grow together with their children. They may feel free at any time to give answers like, "Let's explore that together," or, "Let me find out and answer your question later."

Of course, the teacher has to know the rudimentary tools to get the computer going and to keep the child's work afloat so it may not become frustrating. That, however, can be done in a reasonable amount of time. "I learned enough in a few dozen hours over a summer to introduce the computer to my class. There are several of my students (with computers at home) who far surpass my knowledge of computers. I use them as helpers for their classmates freeing me for other work in the classroom."[4]

As for the presentations and exercises given in this chapter, teachers may have to work through these presentations and exercises on their own prior to presenting them to the children.

e. What to Buy

The answer to that question, of course, depends on what uses are planned with the computer in class. Some indications on the necessary equipment are included in Chapter B.

With introduction to programming in BASIC, a $50 computer with a television screen will do, but since a high priority may be given to studying programming, preferably with the Logo language, a computer should be acquired that can handle Logo. For that reason, computers with small memories (below 64K random access memory) may not be suitable. On the other hand, for a long time to come, there will be no need for the capacity of more expensive models. The fastness and compatibility with commercial programs such as high level spreadsheets or bookkeeping routines especially are not necessary for the classroom, nor is the convenience of a filing system. Therefore, a choice between the common brands of Commodore 64, Atari, or Apple and IBM PC Junior may be considered.

Some systems offer a variation of Logo with different kinds of turtles or other additional features, which are nice and interesting but don't make a fundamental difference. Some limit Logo to turtle graphics only. That may suffice for some time for work in the class, and some classes may never go

---

[4] Alan S. Wallace, "Ten Questions and Answers on Computers in the Montessori Elementary Class."

beyond that anyway. But it may be a limitation on future development, which is not recommended.

The components necessary for the classroom are, of course, the computer itself and a screen. A television screen donated by parents may serve the purpose, but a high resolution monitor is preferable for a good picture. If money is of concern, then a green or amber monitor would cover 90% of all purposes. A disk drive is needed, if software such as Logo or a word processor comes on disks (some come on cartridges or tapes, but not all are available on those media). A disk drive is recommended in any case to organize the work in class. A tape recorder, which is much cheaper, would serve the same purpose but would tie up more of the teacher's time if there is not one student who is very handy at handling this machinery.

If word processing is included in the uses of the computer, then a printer is necessary, which, however, is also nice to have to print out the children's products in Logo or BASIC. A very simple dot matrix printer may do for that purpose, but to obtain neat print from word processing, the printer should be able to handle letter-sized paper, and produce readable characters.

If the school intends to run programs for simulation or educational games, it should be considered that each such piece of software runs on a particular type of computer only. Educational software was most numerous for the Apple computer until recently, but meanwhile the more interesting programs have been transcribed or newly written for Commodore 64, Atari, or IBM PC. The computers designed for office use, although usually more powerful and more expensive, often do not have the programs written for them, which the teacher may want to choose.

When considering the place to buy, one should think ahead of problems coming up later. Products with the interesting low prices very often are sold through department stores, where there is little help and counselling in technical and application problems. On the other hand, a knowledgeable parent may be of better help than any salesperson who is trained in selling and not in teaching computers.

f. Materials, Presentations, and Exercises

To implement computer studies in the Montessori classroom, there are not yet materials that would measure up to the high standards of Montessori's scientific approval and development for use in class (see Chapter A, section IIc). These principles on development are based on the concern that the material must serve the needs of the child in a particular level of development rather than just look nice and interesting to the adult.

A few available materials were developed with these needs in mind and are now put to work in classes in order to collect observations. To widen and to speed up this process, some materials are published in the following chapters of this book in the hopes that they may be used in a critical way and that contributions to their further development may come back to the author.

The materials in the following chapters include designs and texts of all necessary drawings and card materials, which may be copied within the copyright, as far as they are used for one's own class. Assembly directions are given in detail of how to derive the final material from those copies.

More development on Montessori materials concerning new math and including computer-related topics, such as numbers on bases other than ten, is done at The Montessori Institute in Bergamo, Italy.[5] One example is a large bead frame suitable to do calculations in binary numbers and numbers in other bases.

II. ELECTRONIC CIRCUITS DOING MATH

a. The Material—Its Goals and Purpose

The presentations and materials provided in this chapter cover the following:

1. Electrons obey certain laws
2. A simple electronic circuit
3. Numbers 0–1,000 represented through wires and switches
4. Symbolic circuits
5. Electronic circuits for adding numbers
6. A "computer" for numbers 0–62.

Goals

This sequence introduces key concepts:

- the laws governing electrons,
- the representation of binary numbers by wires and switches and,
- an adding circuit.

This partial understanding of computing circuits should enable the child to understand computers as an aggregation of basically simple networks.

---

[5] Camillo Grazzini, *Unpublished Lectures on New Math.* Bergamo, Italy: Centro Internazionale Studi Montessoriani, 1983.

Purpose

1. To help the child in exploring and understanding computer hardware. The children are interested in this exploration due to their characteristic at the elementary level to ask the hows and whys of what they find around them in their environment. The factual understanding of computer hardware should also be considered an important part of our approach to computers: There is a need to prevent the build-up of a view of the computer as a magic, humanlike spirit behind the screen.

2. Further purposes of this exploration are studies of the fundamental laws of electronic currents, and arithmetic in binary numbers. (For children not yet studying numbers in other bases, this might be an easy preparation.)

Age

Children six to nine years old.

Method

These lessons should focus on a teaching method adequate to the characteristics of the child at the elementary age: children like personalization, so it is on purpose, that we talk about electrons in a personal way. Children also need impressions: since electrons themselves are not visible, a model (the red bingo chips) may help to give impressions of their behavior. Also in order to build clear impressions, the circuits are not built from wires, tangled around on the table, but from cards with defined, straight conductors. Terms in parentheses may be given later in a more factual repetition or, for older children, right away.

Materials

Cards with real and symbolic conductors, made from copies of Figures C.1 to C.12, see assembly directions; two D size batteries, transformer 120/6 V; four flashlight bulbs 6 V; bingo chips ("bingo markers"), paper fasteners.

b. A Sequence of 6 Presentations

1. *Electrons Obey Certain Laws*

Materials

Electric circuit model, made from Figure C.1; bingo chips (glued together in threes).

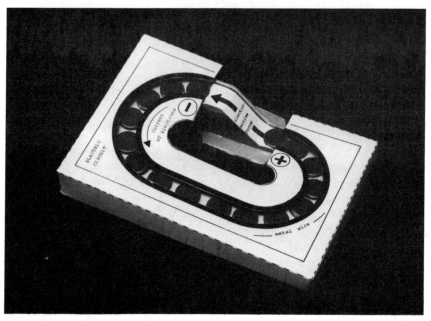

Presentation C.1.

Presentation

"You are interested in computers, aren't you: Computers are often called 'electronic devices.' That means dealing with *electrons.*
So let's first see what electrons are.
Remember the story of God with no hands: We realize that all particles in the universe obey certain laws.
Electrons are very small particles. They are smaller than atoms; actually, they are parts of atoms.
So electrons are everywhere, in all materials.
They also obey certain laws.
In *wood, plastic, glass,* and such materials, they are told: 'You stay *fixed* in your place.'
In *metal,* they are allowed to hop around, they may *move freely.*"

Bring out the materials. Point to the yellow groove describing an oval.

"If this yellow line was a metallic body, like a wire, electrons could move freely along that wire."

Put one chip in the groove and move it along through the circuit.

"One electron would travel quite a while to pass all the wire. But we know it is not only one electron. All materials are full of electrons."

Fill the groove with chips, leaving only one in excess. Put all the rest away.

"Now look: they push each other. So we see another law here; electrons don't like each other. They push each other along through the metal wire.
So the single electron isn't all that fast. But when I push one in here at the beginning of the wire, immediately one comes out at the end."

Do that several times: the one coming out at the plus sign slide up with your finger on the inclined plane labelled "electromotive force" and push it into the groove at the minus sign. Draw attention to the immediate appearance of another electron at the plus sign, since they all push each other along through the "wire."

"We call this flow of electrons through a wire an 'electric *current*.'
One thing puzzles me: these electrons push each other through the wire. But what pushes them into the wire?"

Of course, your finger does, and the children may observe that.

"Well, my finger pushes them. But what does the finger stand for in our model: what do you read here?

Electromotive Force

So there has to be a force pushing electrons up to a 'high potential' labelled 'minus,' so that they may then roll down to the 'low potential' labelled 'plus.' We call that the electromotive force.
That electromotive force can be a chemical reaction, it can be caused by a magnet or by moving bodies.
Would you, Jeannie, like to function as the electromotive force?"
Let the children slide the chip up and into the groove.
Note: Depending on age and interest, you may or may not explain: the symbols 'plus' and 'minus' were chosen by scientists long before they understood the phenomena as we do now. They determined the electric current moving from plus to minus. Unfortunately, the electrons then turned out to be charged what they had defined as minus, so today technicians still talk about the current moving from plus to minus, whereas the real electrons move from minus to plus.

"Realize: Only if one electron returns to the power source can another be pushed into the wire by the electromotive force.

An electric current can *only* move on in a *closed circuit.*

"So what did we realize about electrons?

- They are everywhere.
- They have to stay in their place in plastic, glass, wood, and so forth (insulators).
- They can move freely in metal (conductors).
- They don't like each other; therefore, push each other.
- They can be pushed themselves by an electromotive force.
- An electromotive force is necessary to get an electric current into motion.
- A current of electrons can go on only in a closed circuit, where they come back to the bottom of the power source."

Follow-up Work for Children

- Manipulate the model,
- Draw an electric circuit with labels,
- Write a story about electrons.

2. *A Simple Electronic Circuit*

Materials: Orange power source card made from Figures C.2 and C.3,
two D size batteries,
switch card made from Figure C.4,
lamp card made from Figure C.5,
two connector cards made from Figure C.9 (one elevated, one flat),
all cards with aluminum conductors,
bingo chips, paper fasteners.

Presentation

"Today we will build a working circuit, so that electrons may really push each other round through a metal path.
Remember: To get an electric current going, we need a power source."

Bring out the orange card, (: power source) read the labels, point to the aluminum conductor.

"Now let's provide an avenue for our electrons."

Attach *connectors* with paper fastener.
Bring out the *switch card.*

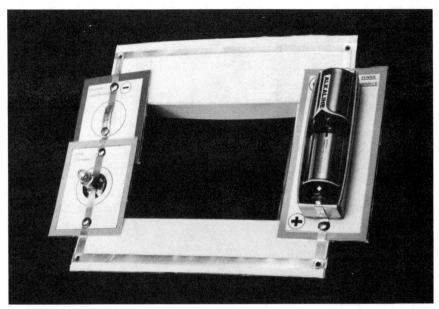

Presentation C.2.

"Here I have a special arrangement that can interrupt our metal avenue. What does the label say?"
"Switch."

Attach the switch card with paper fastener. See that the switch is closed. Bring out the lamp card.

> "Here we have a piece of metal, which is very thin, so when the electrons pass through, it gets very hot."

Take out the *lamp* and show it in detail to the children, how the connection is made to the outer cylinder of the bulb.

> "Inside this cylinder, a connection is provided to one of the thin wires, then through the very thin wire in the middle of the glass bulb to the other wire down to the ball-shaped point at the bottom of the bulb. That point touches our aluminum avenue and there the way is opened back to the power source."

After the circuit is completed, bring out the *two batteries*.

> "As an electromotive force, we use a chemical reaction in these batteries. Inside the batteries, there is a syrup-like substance, which causes a chemical reaction between two metals. This transports the electrons from one metal to the other."

Put the batteries in the orange box: The bulb lights up now.

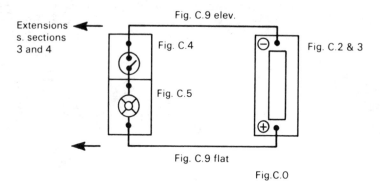

(This and all arrangements are shown the way the child looks at them.)

"If we opened this switch, the metallic cycle is interrupted." Let the child open the switch; let the children open and close it as often as they need.

Take *one red chip.*

"Let's trace where the electrons go."
Move the chip along the conductor, relating the action at each point:

"The electromotive force pushes the electrons to the high potential (labelled " − "). Since even more are pushed that way, they push each other along the metal conductor. If the switch is closed they can pass. They squeeze through this incredibly thin wire inside the bulb and that gets very hot, more than glowing hot so it shines yellow light.
Then the electrons are tired and return to the bottom of the power source (labelled " + ").
Of course, if for any reason they cannot return, the current would stop."

Follow-up Work

Manipulate the material,
Ask questions,
Discuss, draw, and write.

3. *Numbers Represented by Wires and Switches*

Materials: Orange power source card,
two batteries, transformer,
four switch cards,
four lamp cards,
four connectors elevated, Figure C.9,
four connectors flat, Figure C.9.

Presentation

"Today we will use our electric circuits as a part of a computer."

Connect power source with one switch and one lamp *as in section two*.

"This lamp is going to be our screen. You know screens are composed of many, many tiny light dots. This is a very simple screen: only one dot.
It can show only two numbers: *0 and 1*.
Not a big computer, but a beginning.
This switch is going to be our keyboard: If I open the switch, I put a 0 on the screen; if I close the switch, I put a 1 on the screen."

Let the children do this as often as they need according to your or their commanding numbers 0 and 1.

"Well, we would like our computer to handle numbers larger than 1, wouldn't we?
So we need another lamp on our screen,
and another switch on our keyboard."

Attach the *second lamp* and switch with connectors and paper fasteners.

"Since our first lamp could represent 0 and 1, this next lamp has to represent 2."

Switch on second lamp only.

"This shows 2.
But we can now do more than that, since we can show 1 as well.
If we switch on 1 and 2, what does it represent?
Three."

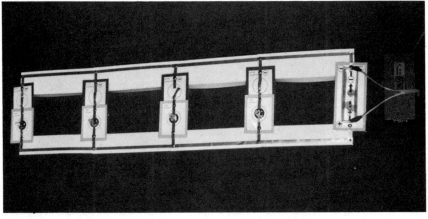

Presentation C.3.

Switch on both lamps.

Let the children switch on numbers between 0 and 3 according to your commands.

At this point, it might be advisable to interrupt the build-up of binary numbers and draw attention to the flow of electrons, since this is now a branching circuit. So, with red chips, they may trace along the aluminum conductors, thus showing the flow of electrons. They may also have questions as to how electrons behave at the branching points on top of the first lamp. The answer: Electrons go wherever they push each other, as long as the avenue leads back to the bottom of the source. So, in this case, they go through both branches.

This may also be the point in time at which to replace the battery with the *transformer.*

To avoid cluttering the arrangement with too many batteries, the lowest number of two batteries was chosen. But they don't work very well with more than two lamps.

Another strong reason to replace them is that they get used up rather fast, while the transformer may be operated for hours.

It may also be interesting to have another type of electromotive force. So take out the batteries and move the transformer next to the orange card and attach the two crocodile clamps to the aluminum strips at "plus" and "minus."

> "Since two lamps are already a heavy load for our batteries, we may as well use another electromotive force. Now our electromotive force sits inside this black box. It is a magnet, which in itself is driven by the power from the wall plug. But we have still a perfect closed circuit."

Move your finger along the aluminum circuit and then along the connecting wire to the black box. Indicate a semicircle over the black box and come back along the other wire to the yellow card where the connection to the aluminum circuit is, and go along the aluminum to the lamp and over the switch. This should be done with a red chip in your hand.

Let these new observations on electronic arrangements sink in, giving the opportunity for questions and discussion.

> "Since we now have a better power source, we may as well go on and build our computer to work with numbers higher than even 3."

Attach the *third lamp* with connectors and paper fasteners.

> "Since the first two lamps could represent numbers 0 to 3, this new lamp will show 4.
> Jeannie, can you switch on 4?"

Only the third lamp should be switched on now.

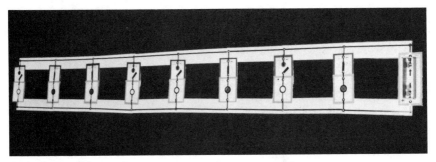

Presentation C.4.

Attach *switch and lamp* with paper fasteners and put out the two units in *vertical order,* since now they are two separate numbers and not just digits for the same number (see control chart Figure C.13).

> "Our *first addend* can include numbers 0 and 1, the same is true for our *second addend.* Let's see what we get if we add two numbers of that kind:" [Put out labels (Fig. C.12) to the right.]

0	0	1	1		first addend
+0	+1	+0	+1		second addend
0	1	1	10	read "two"	sum

Write down for students these four possibilities of additions, and discuss with them, especially the last one:

> "If we add 1 plus 1, then our answer will be 2. But since there is no such numeral as 2 on our computer, we have to represent that with a 1 in the second digit and a 0 in the first digit.
> If we want the computer to perform these additions, then we need a network that provides the right output for either of the four possibilities of the two inputs. This is our network:"

Take out the *red card* (Figure C.6) and discuss it.

> "In this network, we have *new kinds of switches: they are influenced by the electrons themselves.* They have three inputs, two for the switch

> "But since our first two lamps could show numbers from 0 to 3, we can now even go beyond 4.
> What about 4 plus 1?"

Go through numbers 5 to 7 by adding numbers 0 to 3 to number 4 and let the children switch the lights on and off accordingly.

(According to the age of the children, bring in sooner or later the following terms: first, second, third *digit* instead of first, second, third lamp, *place value* 1, 2, 4 being attributed to first, second, third lamp. The fact that these place values are all *powers of 2* may be discovered by the children. At this point, there is no need to help that discovery along.

The same is true for the discovery that this is going to be a number system like our decimal system, but on the *base 2*. It doesn't even matter if that discovery is never made. In that case, the exercise is a preparation for the lessons on number systems with other bases.)

After secure understanding of the 3 digits, so far representing numbers 0 to 7, a *fourth lamp* may be attached to explore numbers 0 to 15.

This may even be left to the children as *follow-up work.*

4. Symbolic Circuits

Materials: Orange power source card,
the following cards with black lines only, no aluminum conductors:
ten switch cards, ten lamp cards,
twenty connectors flat (Figure C.9),
box of bingo chips, paper fasteners.

Presentation

"Since we don't have any more lamps, but want to extend our computer beyond 15, we may as well work with symbolic circuits. That means that now we will use cards with the conductors only printed on, and we will move red chips instead of electrons according to the laws that we already know about electrons."

Build up the circuits with one switch and lamp, put a few red chips into the orange box, and move them along the black lines.

"Let's make up a few rules on how to move the electrons in this game:
- We know that all materials are filled with electrons, but to keep things simple, we will always move only one at a time.
- We move from $\odot$ at the power source.
- We will deposit a red chip wherever the electrons can't pass, especially at the entrance of open switches.
- We will deposit a red chip also whenever a lamp is lighted."

As the children understand the rules and show this by moving the red chips, build up the circuits *as in section three.*

As soon as the children are secure with this arrangement, move beyond 4 digits.

Continuation up to 10 digits, which represents numbers 0 to 1023, may be left as the *follow-up work* to the children.

5. *An Electronic Circuit Adding Numbers*

Materials: All the cards with symbolic black lines:
      two switch cards,
      four lamp cards,
      one red card *half adder* made from Figure C.6,
      one connector made from Figure C.7,
      one connector made from Figure C.10,
      one connector made from Figure C.11,
      three cards   "first addend"
               "second addend"
               "sum" made from Figure C.12
      orange power source card, control chart (Figure C.13).

Presentation

"Our computer that we have built up so far could deal with numbers 0 to 1023. It had a keyboard and a screen so we could input those numbers and the screen could show them. But till now, there was no way of processing these numbers.
Today, let's try to extend our computer so it can add two numbers.
We start again with very small numbers so we have one switch and lamp for the first addend,
and here another switch and lamp for the second addend."
itself and one symbolized by an arrow. The dotted line shows the switch in the rest position.
If an electric potential arrives at the arrow, it pushes the switch out of the rest position."

Move a red electron chip from the input "first addend" to the arrow in the top switch and leave it there. Push the switch into the closed position. Move another red electron chip from input "second addend" across the switch.

"The electron arriving at the arrow causes the switch to close. (This arrangement is called a *transistor*. In reality, it is a tiny crystal with three wires running into it, where the electrons behave just this way. Transistors, therefore, are switches that are operated by the electrons themselves.)
Down here, we have switches that are closed in the rest position and only when an electron arrives at the arrow is the switch opened.
(These switches are really little networks made up from two to four transistors. But at the moment, we consider them as one unit.)
Look, see how our network is going to work."

Attach the second addend to the red card and the first addend with the *connector* from Figure C.7, to the red card (see control chart). Attach the *third lamp* card to the bottom output of the red card.

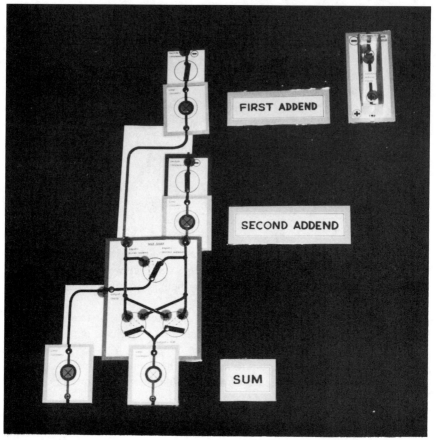

Presentation C.5.

"The lamp on the bottom here is going to be our answer, which is the *sum*."

Have the lamps arranged in one vertical line and the tickets "first addend," "second addend," "sum" on the right side next to each lamp.

Take out the orange power source card and fill in a few red electron chips (place it to the right of the first addend).

"The connections to our power source this time will not be on the table, but we will pretend they are hidden under the table.

Let's now do a little addition of numbers 0 plus 1:"

$$\begin{array}{r} 0 \\ +1 \\ \hline \end{array}$$

Set switch "first addend" to 0, "second addend" to 1; move the red chips from power source along the imaginary connectors to the lamp and to the open switch, respectively; deposit chip there and go on with another chip from the lighted lamp to the input of the half adder, and deposit chip there.

"We have to add a few more rules to our electronic game:
- We will deposit a red electron at any keyboard switch input labelled ⊝, and any input of the half adder where electric power arrives.
- We will also deposit an electron at any arrow within switches wherever electric power arrives.
- An important rule: Move electrons to arrows in switches always prior to ever going across closed switches.

  With these rules we may now work our way through the network of the half adder."

While moving the red chips, repeat the rule that is obeyed at the moment: Move a chip from right input down to the left arrow, opening the switch there; move the chip from right input to the middle transistor, which is still open, so deposit chip there; move chip from right input down to right switch, which is still closed, so move chip across the switch down to the output and further on to the lamp and deposit it there.

"Since our first addend was 0, there is no power at the left input, so our work is done at the moment.
Let's look at the answer:
The answer is 1. Does that comply with our arithmetic?:

$$\begin{array}{r} 0 \\ +1 \\ \hline 1 \end{array}$$

Yes, our network provided the right answer."

Proceed in the same way through the *three adding problems:*

$$0 + 0 = 0$$
$$1 + 0 = 1$$
$$1 + 1 = 10 \ (\text{read "two"})$$

With the answer to the latter problem, you will realize that no output is achieved at the bottom, but an *output "carry"* is achieved at the left side of the red card. Deposit a chip there and discuss the matter:

"Our answer is 0 in the units, but there is a carry. So we need a new digit in our arrangement for the sum, which may display the two."

Connect a *lamp card* with *connector* Figure C.11 to the output "carry" of the red card.
Move down the red chip to that lamp and read the answer—

"What we just investigated here is an adding network, which can add numbers 0 to 1 and will always come up with the right answer."

Take the whole arrangement apart.

Follow-up Work

Students may reassemble the material and redo the four exercises of addition, carefully following the rules of the game moving the red chips through the network.

6. A "Computer" for Numbers 0 to 62

Materials: Orange power source card filled with red chips,
                ten switch cards,
                sixteen lamp cards,
                nine red half adder cards,
                five connectors (Figure C.7)
                four connectors (Figure C.8),
                two connectors (Figure C.10),
                one connector (Figure C.11),
                paper fasteners, labels (Figure C.12),
                control chart (Figure C.13).

Presentation

"Last time, we investigated an adding network for two numbers. Unfortunately, those two numbers could only consist of 0 and 1. So today, let's go beyond that:"

Rearrange the network from *Section Five* and to the left build up the *same* network for the *second digit of addends* (see control chart). Set the switches to the problem

$$\begin{array}{r} 1 \\ +10 \\ \hline \end{array} \quad \text{(read "two")}$$

Let the children work the chips through the network. When the output in the second digit has arrived, make them aware that our arrangement here is not yet perfect:

"Our screen for this sum is not yet arranged correctly: We have one lamp for the first digit here; we have another lamp for the carry of the first digit here, which actually is the second digit of the sum. So, there's

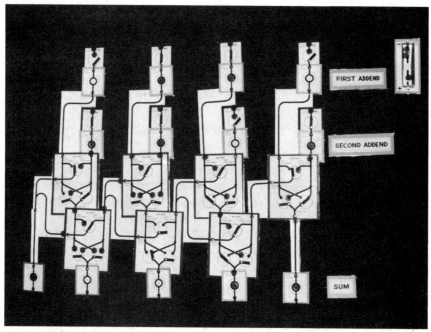

Presentation C.6.

a contradiction, since we also have a second digit for the sum in the output of our second half adder. What are we going to do? For the time being, let's take away the output carry lamp, since there is no output at the moment anyway. So our answer reads: Three. This is according to our arithmetic.":

$$
\begin{array}{r}
1 \\
+\,10 \\
\hline
11
\end{array}
$$

    (read "two")

    (read "three")

Set the switches to the problem

$$
\begin{array}{r}
1 \\
+\,11 \\
\hline
\end{array}
$$

    (read "three")

Let the child work the chips through the networks. When the chip arrives at the output "carry" at the first digit adder, let it stay there for the moment and finish up the second digit.

"Let's look here: We have an output for our second digit in the carry of the first digit and in the adder of the second digit. So what is our second digit going to be? We obviously have to add again these two numbers. This is the same as with all addition: you *add the carried number* to the column of the next digit.":

$$
\begin{array}{r}
1 \\
+1_11 \\
\hline
1\ 0\ 0
\end{array}
$$
    ("three")
    ("four")

If necessary, go through the addition on paper to remind the children that carried numbers are always added together with the next digit. In order to do this, we need a *new half adder.* So, attach a new red card with its left input on the bottom of the red card of the second digit, and with its right input to the carry output of the first digit red card (see Control Chart). Connection between this second red card and the one for the first digit is made with the *connector Figure C.11.* Explain to the children whatever is necessary at this moment.

"This newly added half adder now takes care of adding together the carry output in the first digit and the sum of the second digit."

Let the child do the work with the red chips until he or she arrives at the right answer:

3 + 1 = 4, which complies with our knowledge of arithmetic.

"To represent this answer, we needed already a third digit lamp in the sum, which is connected to the output "carry" from both half adders in the second digit."

Connect the *third digit lamp* to both outputs with *connector Figure C.8* (see control chart).

To get the lamps representing the sum in one straight line, connect digits 1 and 3 with *connector Figure C.10.*

Let the children work through all the possible problems with two addends 0 to 3.

Follow-up Work

Children may extend the "computer" up to 5 digits in the addends and 6 digits in the answer, thus exploring numbers 0 to 62.

c. How to Make the Material

1. Designs Ready to Copy

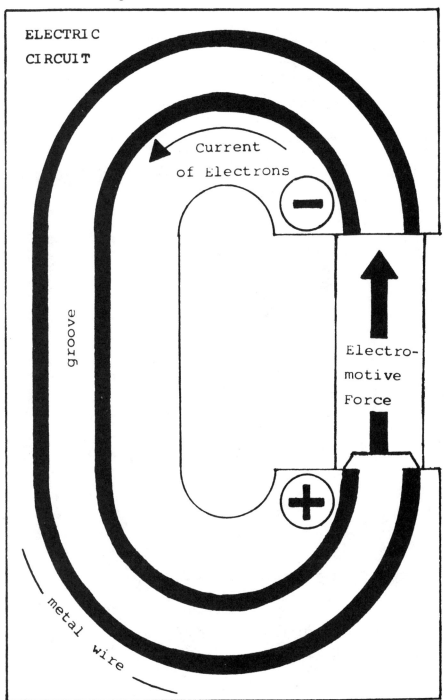

Figure C.1
This figure gives an overall impression of the material.
The material itself is made from assembled copies of
Figures C.1.1 and C.1.2 with C.1a, C.1b and C.1c.

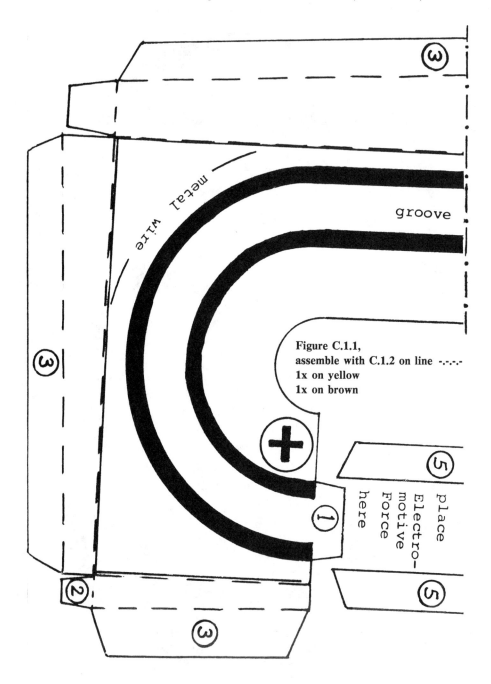

Figure C.1.1,
assemble with C.1.2 on line -.-.-.-
1x on yellow
1x on brown

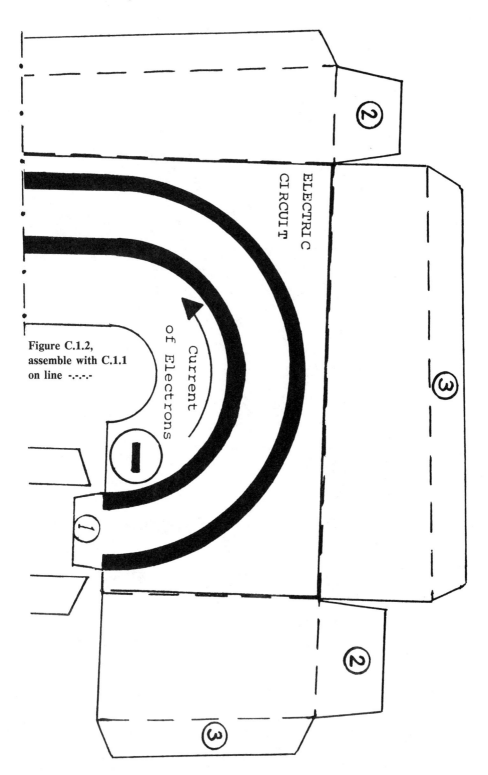

Figure C.1.2,
assemble with C.1.1
on line -.-.-

ELECTRIC
CIRCUIT

Current
of Electrons

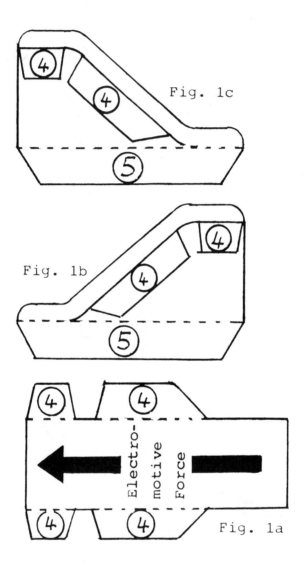

Figures C.1a,b,c 1x on orange

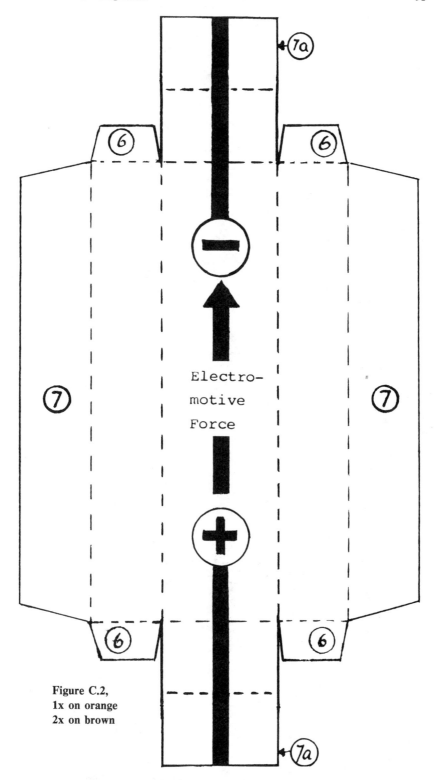

Electro-
motive
Force

Figure C.2,
1x on orange
2x on brown

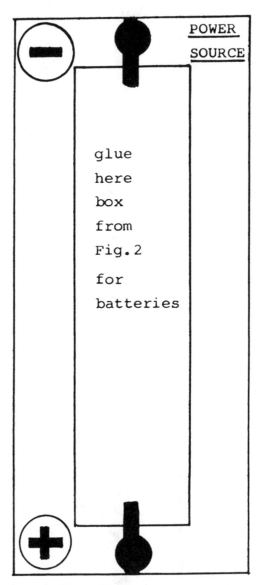

Figure C.3, 1x, on orange

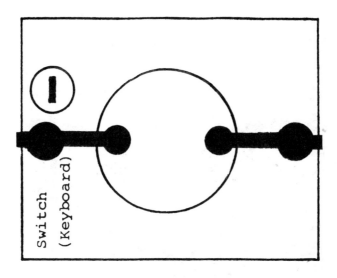

Figure C.4, 14x, on blue

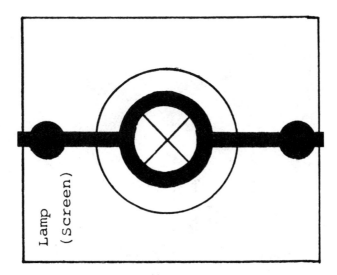

Figure C.5, 20x, on green

Figure C.5a, 4x, on black

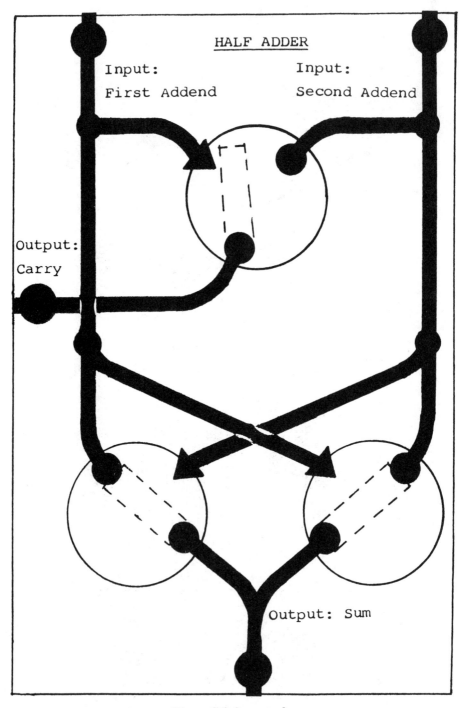

Figure C.6, 9x, on red

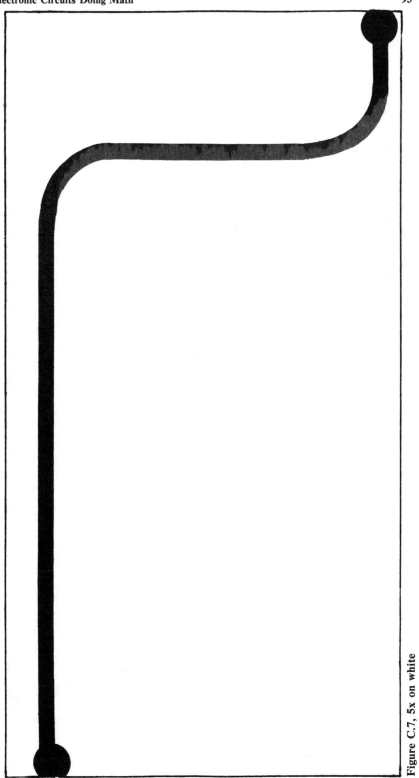

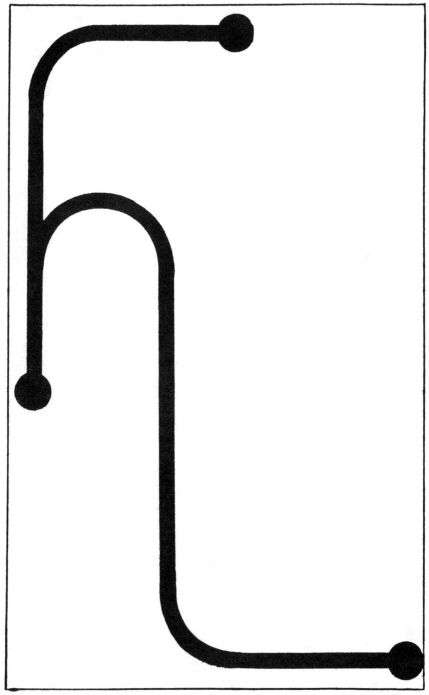

Figure C.8, 4x, on white

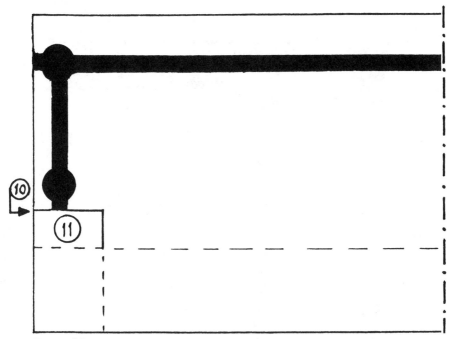

Figure C.9.1,
assemble with 9.2 at line -.-.-

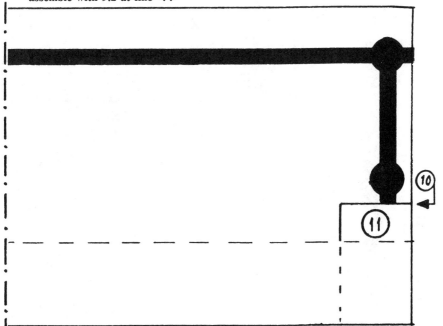

Figure C.9.2,
assemble with C.9.1 at line -.-.-
28x, on white

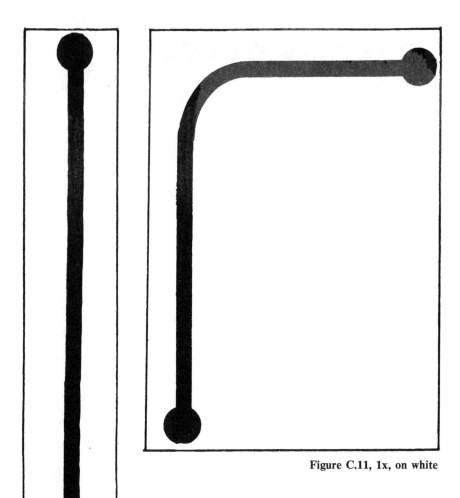

Figure C.11, 1x, on white

Figure C.10, 2x, on white

FIRST ADDEND

SECOND ADDEND

SUM

Figure C.12a,b,c,1x, on green

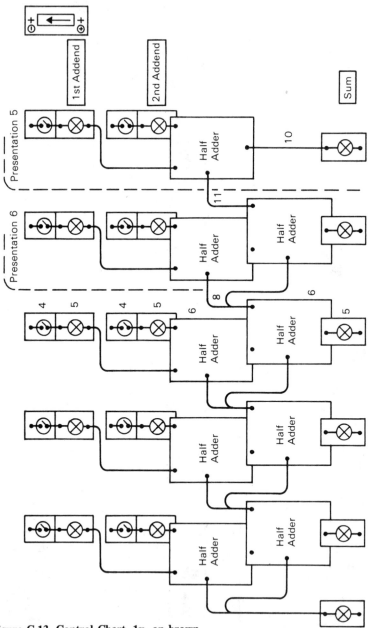

Figure C.13, Control Chart, 1x, on brown

2. *Assembly Directions*

The description of an action is usually more complicated than the action itself (describe how you would climb out of your car!). So don't panic on reading the following, just do it line by line and you will find it simple.

YOU NEED:

- Copies of Figures C.1 to C.13:
  (The number of copies needed is printed next to the number of each figure.)[6]
  Option: You may copy on cardstock of the appropriate color to save pasting on poster board.

Since it was not possible to print Figures C.1 and C.9 on one page, assemble Figure C.1 from Figures C.1.1 and C.1.2 and assemble Figure C.9 from Figures C.9.1 and C.9.2, matching them at the -.-.- line, the line not showing. You may want to copy again after this assembly.

- Poster board (if you didn't choose to copy on colored cardstock):
  1 sheet: brown, yellow, orange, blue, green, black, red
  3 sheets: white

- Contact paper (self-adhesive plastic covering):
  black: 2″
  transparent: 1′ optional

- Glues: glue stick, spray glue, contact cement, clear household cement, and carpet tape.
  (Rubber cement is not recommended, since it will later bleed through the paper and cause brown spots.)

- Hole punch: 3mm (from leather stores or by mail order from Hanover House, Hanover, Pennsylvania 17333)

- 150 red transparent bingo chips ("bingo markers"), about 19 mm diameter (from toy store)

- 120 paper fasteners, 3/4″ (office supply store)
  An alternative to paper fasteners: Take map tacks and pin the cards to foam core board or to other soft material board. In that case you need 70 map tacks and only 50 paper fasteners to fasten the switches to the cards.

- Sheet aluminum about 1 sq. ft. ("oven liner" or pie shells from grocery store)

- 2 D size batteries.

---

[6] These numbers provide a buildup to 4 digits in presentation 3, 10 digits in presentation 4, and 5 digits in 6. If you work with older children, who need the material only for the initial idea and may then prefer to work out more digits on paper, you may save on labor by making smaller sets of material.

The following you may buy in an electric supply store rather than in a hardware store: I found all of them at Radio Shack.

- 1 transformer 120 V input, 6 V output
  (any power supply for a cassette recorder will suffice, with an output of near 6 V and 600 mA. It need not provide DC; AC works as well. Even a transformer with only 200 mA output works with no trouble).

- 4 flashlight bulbs, about 6 V, 150 mA (bulbs "for 4 D size batteries" are for 6 V)

- 2 alligator clips

- Plug for wall outlet with line, if not already attached to transformer.

WHAT YOU DO:

(a). Figures C.7, C.8, C.9, C.10, and C.11:

- Paste on white poster board (if you didn't choose to copy on cardstock).

- Cut outline (cut away black margin line).

- 24 of Figure C.9: Cut a straight line between arrows (10), (these will be the "flat connectors").

- 4 of Figure C.9: Scratch dotted lines (these will be the "elevated connectors").

- Laminate, cut.

- 4 of Figure C.9:
  - Cut solid line round flap (11);
  - Bend at dotted line;
  - Glue (contact cement) flap (11) in back, creating a vertical angle to raise this card about 1″ off the table.

(b). Figures C.3, C.4, C.5, C.6, C.12, and C.13 are made into cards (the white design with a colored margin, if you didn't choose to copy on colored cardstock):

- Cut along outline (cut away the black margin line).

- Cut colored poster board into cards large enough for a colored margin of ¼″ to run around the white figures.

- Paste figures on colored poster board: The appropriate color is printed next to the figure number. If you use glue stick, make sure that glue is put on all spots later to be punched: i.e., all connecting points (big black circles near margin) and all points where switches are going to be attached (black circular end points inside the 1½″ circles).

- Extend thick black lines from connecting points across the colored margin (black felt pen).

- Laminate, cut.

(c). Make the box for 2 D size batteries from Figure C.2:

- Paste on orange poster board (spray glue).

- Scratch dotted line (front or back, whatever works better).

- Laminate.

- Cut outline.

- Bend at dotted lines into a box (design inside box).

- Glue (contact cement) flaps (6) outside.

- Glue flaps (7) inside to show orange.

- Glue flaps (7a) outside to show the black line of the design.

- Glue (contact cement) this box onto Figure 3.

(d). Make boxes from Figure C.2 on brown poster board to store paper fasteners and bingo chips:

- Laminate 2 pieces of brown poster board together (so only one side gets laminated).

- Paste on Figure C.2 (glue stock).

- Cut outline.

- Scratch dotted lines in the back.

- Take off Figure C.2; wipe off glue (option: instead of using a copy of Figure C.2, you may as well just trace Figure C.2 on the board).

- Bend at dotted lines to fold a box (lamination outside).

- Glue flaps (6) inside.

- Glue 1 flap (7) and both flaps 7a inside; the other flap (7) provides the lid of the box.

(e). Figure C.3 and each 4 of Figures C.4, C.5, C.9 elevated and C.9 flat get aluminum strips attached to work with real electric currents:

- Attach carpet tape to aluminum (oven liner), cut into $\frac{1}{4}''$ strips.

- Attach strips on top of all thick black lines.

- Remove carpet tape at places where you want contact: the connecting points (black circles near the margin) in Figure C.9.

- At connecting points, fold strip around margin running back 1″ on the back side for contact with other cards.

(f). 4 Figures C.5 get a bulb attached with help of Figure C.5a:

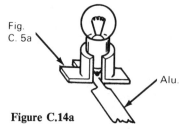

Figure C.14a

- Paste Figure C.5a on black poster board, scratch dotted lines, laminate, attach carpet tape on flaps (9), cut at solid lines.

- Shape Figure C.5a into a cylinder, open on one side.

- Wrap Figure C.5a around the socket of a bulb (black surface outside) (it covers only ¾ of the socket circumference); wrap tight with clear tape.

- Bend flaps (9) to extend on 3 sides like paws.

- Attach aluminum strip to Figure C.5, running from the bottom margin to the center of the X in the inner circle (remove carpet tape from last inch, so strip can spring against bulb (see Figure C.14b)).

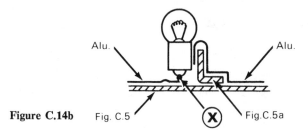

Figure C.14b

- Attach Figure C.5a with lamp on top of that X, so that the aluminum strip runs through the open side under the lamp; fasten flaps (9) with carpet tape on Figure C.5.

- Attach other aluminum strip running from the top margin to the center circle, climbing up the outside of Figure C.5a, and slipping inside Figure C.5a to touch the bulb socket.

(g). Punch 3 mm holes in all connecting points (the black circles near the margin) of both the cards with aluminum attached and those without aluminum.

(h). Attach levers to all switches, i.e., inside the 1½″ circles:

- Cover black poster board with black contact paper.

- Cut strips $1\frac{1}{4}''$ $\times$ $\frac{5}{16}''$ (31×8 mm); you need 41 such strips.

- Punch a 3 mm hole in one end of each strip.

- Attach strips with paper fasteners at the bottom point inside each $1\frac{1}{2}''$ circle (if using a plier-type hole punch, which cannot reach far enough inside the red cards, proceed as follows: Put card on a surface of hardwood or aluminum; turn wheel of hole punch so that the 3 mm punch is outside; place punch on card; hit back of punch with mallet).

- Secure paper fasteners in the back with tape to prevent tangling when stacking the materials.

- For Figure C.4 with aluminum strips: Wrap switch levers in aluminum sheet (bend in a spoon-like arch to provide pressure at the contact point), attach the same way; make sure no clear tape inhibits contact between lever and aluminum strips.

(i). Figure C.1 is made into material that provides an oval groove, inside yellow, where red bingo chips can slide along, pushing each other if the first one is pushed into the groove. Figure C.1 is then folded into a flat box, which has an inclined top surface, providing the image that the electrons travel from high level $(-)$ to a low level $(+)$. Where it says "electromotive force," an inclined plain will be made from Figure C.1a,b,c, to provide the image that the electromotive force pushes the electrons on a higher level of potential. To make this material, follow these steps (S. Figure C.16):

- To get thicker chips, glue each three bingo chips together (with clear household cement). (You need 20 such triple chips.)

- Paste Figure C.1 on brown poster board (spray glue); laminate front only (attach paper when laminating).

- Cut along the solid outline; the part with the flaps (5) will be cut away.

- Scratch dotted lines in back.

- Cut out the white oval labelled, "groove," along the inner margin of the thick black oval lines: You have now 3 pieces:

  - The white-only c-shaped part labelled, "groove," with the flaps (1) attached. Throw this away.

  - Piece a: the inner c-shaped part with the writing "current of electrons" including the inner thick black line.

  - Piece b: the outer part including the thick black line.

(Option: You may choose to cover Figure C.1 with transparent contact paper. If you do so, attach contact paper before cutting and on top surface only.)

- Paste second copy of Figure C.1 on yellow poster board (the purpose here is to have only the oval lines on the board.)

- Laminate.

- Cut out the "groove" but here together with the thick black lines, flaps (1) attached. You get a letter-c-shaped yellow piece, which we will call piece c. The width of piece c equals the diameter of the bingo chips, including some tolerance. If your chips are of different size, adapt piece c accordingly.

- Mount the yellow piece c under pieces a and b with enough distance so that the triple chips can slide inside the groove:

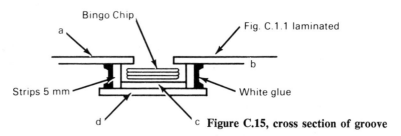

Figure C.15, cross section of groove

- Glue the yellow piece c on a poster board of similar shape, but about $\frac{1}{4}''$ wider (piece d), (contact cement), so the yellow shows.

- Cut strips 5 mm ($\frac{3}{16}''$) wide from heavy cardboard (or 2 layers of poster board glued together). (Check the thickness of your bingo chips, whether 5 mm is right, including 2 mm tolerance.)

- Glue (with contact cement) the 5 mm strip around the yellow piece c. (Don't smear contact cement on the yellow surface; the cement is already on d from prior work.)

- Glue (with contact cement) all this under pieces a and b: The triple chips should now slide easily inside the yellow groove.[7]

- Bend outer flaps of piece b along dotted line into a flat box.

- Glue flaps (2) inside (with contact cement).

- Cut a brown poster board the size of the inner dotted line in Figure C.1 as the bottom of the box.

- Laminate.

- Glue (contact cement) flaps (3) on that bottom.

- Make up the escalator-shaped piece labelled "electromotive force" from Figures C.1a,b,c.

  - Paste Figures C.1a,b,c on orange poster board (spray glue),

---

[7] Pour in white glue between a, b, and d. Let dry (for final stability).

- Cut outline, scratch dotted lines, laminate, cut,

- Bend dotted lines,

- Glue (contact cement) flaps (4) of Figure C.1a ("electromotive force") on places (4) in Figures C.1b and c,

- Glue flaps (5) on brown bottom of box in the places (5) indicated at Figure C.1 (That part of Figure C.1 is cut away, so check with the original for its location.),

- Connect the inclined plain "electromotive force" to the flaps (1) of Figure C.1: at the lower end the flap over, at the upper end under the inclined plain, so that the bingo chips slide without obstacle. Your triple chips may now be pushed by one finger up the inclined plain into the groove and, after travelling around the groove, will reappear at the bottom of the inclined plane.

(j). The transformer is to be prepared for the classroom:

- If it is a closed black box with plug, you need only to solder the alligator chips to the output line,

- If the transformer came without a case, put it into a box:

  - Fold a box from heavy cardboard, covered with black contact paper, a series of holes punched in near bottom and top for ventilation,

  - Fasten transformer inside with screws,

  - Attach plug for wall outlet on input wires,

  - Solder alligator clips on output wires (output wires should be 4"-10" long),

  - Secure wires inside box so if pulled, they will pull the whole box rather than be torn off the transformer.

(k). A box for all the material will depend on how you want it to be on the shelf. A shoe-box-sized box will provide space for the cards in a standing position and everything else in its own place. The four lamp cards with real bulbs need a place where they are protected from damage. The triple chips used in Figure C.1 may stay inside the material except for the first presentation, so usually they would not need an extra box.

d. Four Basic Ideas Make Up a Computer—Guidelines for Further Exploration

After the sequence with this material, the work of the children may extend in several directions: 1) Exploring physical laws of electric currents with wires, batteries, lamps, eventually with kits using transistors, resistors, condensors; 2) Exploring more on the architecture of computers, such as the representation of negative numbers, inversion of numbers, multiplication through shifting categories, division through continuous subtraction with shifting categories, and so forth.

It is not intended to teach all these in more detail, but it should be left to the children to extend their interest and find sources of information.

Careful consideration may come to the conclusion that for an exploration of the computer, more key concepts are necessary. One may consider the following:

• Electric circuits storing the configuration of numbers over certain time (electronic memories), for example, giving the concept of a simple flip-flop;

• Representation of letters through numbers;

• Controlling the cooperation of memory and calculating circuits by transistors, which by themselves are operated through numbers, represented in electric currents;

• Programming those control circuits by sequences of numbers, called a program;

• Replacing the number combinations with letter combinations, which make sense to the human reader as meaningful words, thus arriving at a "computer language."

The exploration also may go into technologies to implement these ideas:

• Instead of connecting transistors with soldered wires, printing these connections with conducting layers on a flat surface;

• Printing even the transistors themselves, which consist of five layers of different materials, together with the printed connections;

• Printing all these in several layers in a microphoto technology on very small surfaces, arriving at "integrated circuits" (IC), which combine on the area of a fingernail several tens of thousands of electronic switches.

The exploring work may also go in the other direction: how the letter combinations controlling the control circuits are combined into programs. This work will then lead into a study of programming computers.

These studies may be organized along the *four basic ideas making up a computer.* These ideas are outlined here in a simplified way. This is not to deny the enormous amount of technical ingenuity and development that has taken place over several years in laboratories and factories. These achievements must be acknowledged, but this is not the place to go into detail of that kind. The basic ideas, however, are easy to understand, and once understood, provide a feeling of security and a better understanding of what the computer can do.

1. *Idea 1: Give Numbers a Physical Representation*

This idea is very old and has been used since ancient times for counting boards and abacuses. Montessorians are well acquainted with it through representing numbers by number rods, counters, beads, stamps. Montessori teachers and children know well that with these materials, they are able to perform arithmetical operations such as plus, minus, times, and division, even powers and roots.

2. *Idea 2: Represent Numbers by Electric Switches*

This idea includes certain improvements over beads or stamps: If you take switches such as relays, electronic tubes, or transistors, then one switch can be connected by wires to the next switch, and one switch representing one number can thus influence another switch. Since electric currents travel nearly as fast as light, this action is rapid and one can accomplish many such actions in a short time. Here is the first characteristic of a computer: Its single action is quite simple, but it accomplishes millions of them in the twinkling of an eye.

The way in which numbers can be represented by switches is studied with the material presented in the previous chapter. Through these presentations and exercises, the child has studied how switches present binary numbers and how a network may provide for addition.

This little investigation did not aim at enabling the student to construct a computer, but rather to give a first idea as to how switches and wires representing numbers can be used to perform math operations. So far we have provided for addition.

Knowing that multiplication is a series of additions, we could use the same network for multiplication. A very similar network could be designed for subtraction, which also could be used for division, since division basically is a series of subtractions.

To this point, we covered the basic operations in arithmetic, which are the basis for everything else in mathematics. This also gives a first example of how a computer, by composing series of simple actions, each of which is performed very rapidly, can build up rather complicated operations. The basic idea for this was to use electric switches to represent numbers and to use a kind of switch that can be operated by electric power provided by other switches.

Of course, we have not answered all the questions. For example, how are the switches operated within the sets representing the two addends? They might be connected to a keyboard so that a person types in the numbers and, after performing the math operation, reads the answer from the lamps in the bottom. Another possibility would be that the sets first and second addend are a part of a larger box containing lots of such sets, and thus function as a memory for numbers. In that case, we would need a few more switches to connect the right set within the memory to the adding circuits. In the same way, the set of lamps representing the answer could be replaced by a set of switches within that memory box, so that the answer is stored away and can be used in another math operation. All these additional ideas are not our concern here. Once the basic idea is understood that numbers are represented by switches, which themselves can be operated by other switches, then it is clear that the switch networks can perform math operations and can store numbers like a memory.

Once this works for numbers, it can also work for letters, since letters can be represented by numbers, as anybody who ever made up a secret code knows, coding each letter with a particular number.[8] Such letters, represented by numbers, can be compared by subtracting the numbers and checking for zero. With this little arrangement, our network can do not only math operations, but also sorting of alphanumeric information and searching for a special item under a lot of words stored in the memory.

3. Idea 3: Numbers Control the Operations

Electric networks are controlled by switches. So, for example, the network in your little hand calculator is controlled by the function switches, choosing the operations of plus, minus, root drawing, percentage, and so forth. On the other hand, numbers in a computer are, as we have learned, represented by switches. So it should be possible to use numbers to control the operation of the networks. That means the set of switches representing that number would operate through a network designed respectively on those switches that control the adding operation. For example, the number 21 fed into the set of switches provided to contain a command would cause an addition to take place. The number 21, therefore, would be the command for addition. If we provide a set of switches to represent a ten-digit number, as many computers do, then the wiring could be done in a way that the first two digits would be used to control the operation; the next four digits would be the number of the location in the memory where the first addend is to be taken (its "address"); and the last four digits could be the number of the location in the memory from where the second addend is to be taken. A command like

$$21 \ \ 2746 \ \ 5314$$

would then be understood by the machine as to perform addition, according to the operational part 21, taking the first addend from the memory location number 2,746 and taking the second addend from the memory location number 5,314. Every time this command was typed into the machine, this operation would be performed.

---

[8] The code used in most American microcomputers is the ASCII, which uses the numbers 32 to 127 to encode the ciphers 0 to 9 as well as the letters of the alphabet in lower case and capitals and a number of punctuation symbols.

The advantage of commands is that many of them can be put together into a program, so that, unlike the hand calculator, each operation does not have to be punched in, but a whole sequence of calculations can be thought out ahead of time, typed into the computer, and the computer can then perform the program in its entirety in a very fast way and, therefore, in a short time. With this ability of free programming, the use of a machine increases almost indefinitely.

Again, the same principle is visible here: a high number of steps, each of which is very simple, can be put together to make up rather complicated operations, which are still performed quickly and in a short time.

The only nuisance remaining is that the programmer has to cope with all these simple steps and the programs will be rather long, with a high chance for error. But once the computer had been developed to this stage, it was only one step further to use the computer itself to manipulate programs. By taking whole chunks of programs, and giving a name to frequently used sequences, a programmed language was created. The programmer now only has to cope with those names, calling for a rather differentiated operation by one name, and the computer itself will find out which commands in its machine language have to be applied to perform this operation.

So far we have looked at the basic ideas leading to a free programmable computer that can do all types of math operations, including comparing numbers or letters, and therefore sorting, and also including plotting characters on a paper or a screen according to given coordinates.

The reader may now wonder how many switches would be necessary to perform all these actions. It should be quite clear that a high number of switches, which means electronic tubes or transistors, are necessary to put together such an electric network. Therefore, computers were initially rather spacious and very costly, running into several millions of dollars.

4. Idea 4: Print Electric Networks Like a Book

A transistor can be seen as a sandwich with five layers: layers one, three and five being a conductor that provides the access of electrons to the system, and layers two and four a semiconductor that provides a particular behavior of the electrons and other particles to the effect that the flow of electric power from layer one to layer five is controlled by the electrical input on layer three.

Other elements of electric circuitry, such as capacitors, diodes, and resistors are sandwich-type structures as well: A capacitor consists of three layers: layers one and three are conductors and layer two an insulator; a diode is a sandwich of three layers: layers one and three are conductors and layer two a semi-conductor controlling the flow of power only one way; a resistor can be seen as a conductor of very little diameter in order to make the resistance higher than a normal wire, so that such a conductor could be represented by a very thin layer of conducting material on any insulator. Even the wires needed to make the connections between the different elements of the circuit

implement Logo in schools. With the educational view of a Montessori teacher, I have looked into some alternatives and made some choices. The following outlines a sequence of lessons and a collection of exploring ideas for implementing Logo in a Montessori class.

The main decisions had to be made based on the following questions:

1. *Free Exploring or Directed Teaching?*

Between these alternatives, I see the Montessori approach as a balanced one: In order to give the child a chance for free exploration that is not frustrating but will lead to satisfying results, it is appropriate for the teacher to make presentations of the necessary tools in considered steps, which build up in sequence to avoid trouble. Connected with each step in this sequence may be proposals for exercises, which are not obligatory for the child, but, rather, provide ideas, which can be done at this level.

2. *Should the Emphasis be on Fast Progress in Programming or on Exhaustive Exploration in Geometry?*

Between these alternatives I opt for dwelling on geometry exploration on each level of programming, rather than pushing for fast acquisition of programming skills, which will be acquired anyway.

Many geometry concepts also need thorough exploration on a lower level of programming in order to be fully understood on a higher one. So, for example, repetitious pattern such as polygons should be explored in a step-by-step way before the REPEAT command is introduced. While this seems to be an unnecessary waste of time for an adult, for a child of six years, it is necessary to build the abstraction of the repetitious pattern.

3. *Define Concepts After Using Them*

One may wonder why angles are studied in section b.3, while they were already used in section b.2. This is due to the principle that permits a sensorial experience prior to any introduction of the concept. Explaining the concept of angle or degree is confusing for children, who had not yet the opportunity to do something with angles. This principle seems contradictory to the logic in mathematics, where a concept has to be defined prior to its proper use. But we forget that those definitions are given to adults who had plenty of opportunity for building a sensorial base. The process is comparable to that in learning a language. It would make little sense to explain a word to babies, but simply using the word while speaking to them helps to build their understanding. Once that has occurred, a more precise definition can be obtained by reading a dictionary.

This approach to concepts works on different levels:

(a) Prior to using any geometry concept in a turtle exercise, a sensorial experience should be provided with physical material, e.g., the geometric cabinet, the box of sticks, and, of course, objects in every day life. The work in turtle geometry should, therefore, run parallel with the classical study of geometry in a Montessori class. We have to remember that turtle geometry on the computer screen is of high abstract level. Whatever concept is implemented on the screen needs the chance to be experienced by the hand with materials or by walking it on the floor or with the toy turtle on paper. There should be a frequent going back and forth between the computer and these body explorations.

(b) Within the sequence of turtle geometry, a more explicit exploration of a geometry or programming concept should be preceded by simple uses. Thus, variables are used long before they are defined as local or public and before their symbols (the quotes and the dots) are explained. The same is true for the terminology: Use the language and only later define the terms. That does not mean, of course, that an unknown word should not get a simple explanation, especially if the child asks.

4. *Tool Procedures*

A tool procedure often is provided to open up facilities at a time where the children are not yet able to create the procedure by themselves, e.g., a procedure to draw a circle may be stored in memory for that reason. However, in doing so, the excitement of the child's own discovery is taken away, which is much more important than having a circle available at any given moment. Developing a circle procedure is one of the beautiful adventures in Logo. It may be achieved through either of three approaches and each of them leads to experiencing an important concept: The circle as a polygon (exercise 4.2 & 4.3), the circle as a collection of points with equal distance from a center point (exercise 4.7) or a circle as a curved line created by infinitesimal small steps and turns (exercise 10.8). Neither of these procedures can be done at the earliest level of programming. So a child who wants to draw a stickman and asks how to do the circle (the head) may as well get the answer: "A circle may still be too difficult for you now, but soon you will discover how to do that." Does it matter if the stickman walks away with a square head for the moment?

The same is true for most tool procedures.

For elementary children, I feel no tool procedures are necessary. All exercises and ideas in the following sequence will be possible with the set of Logo primitives, which is common to most dialects of Logo.

b. Sixteen Presentations through Turtle Geometry

Based on the principles outlined in the previous chapter, a sequence of presentations is supplied here, which leads through the Logo commands and syntax pattern as far as necessary for turtle geometry. The instructional proposals have been reduced to a minimum, in order to save a chance for the child's own discoveries.

The presentations cover the essential parts, but occasional informal help will be necessary to introduce more details, e.g., the use of arithmetic symbols, the use of the cursor and delete keys a.o., which need no formal presentations, or the change of color, HIDETURTLE, NOWRAP a.o., which may be left to the children to discover.

The presentations in this section are followed by a set of exercises in the next section, which are tuned to the sixteen levels. As an additional piece of material, a chart of labels is printed in section d to be used together with the presentations and exercises.

All Logo commands and programs in this chapter are done in "Commodore 64 Logo"[11] which is a Logo dialect very similar to "Terrapin Logo." If a particular class is equipped with another version of Logo, some commands or their formats need some changes, which have to be determined by consulting the respective Logo manual.

It should be mentioned that this section is not meant as an introduction to Logo for the teacher, although one may use it as that. All the most necessary commands for turtle graphics are introduced, the programs included with the presentations show their applications, and the list of programs in section e gives examples of how the exercises may be solved. However, Logo reaches far beyond turtle graphics and for a deeper and wider range of explanations, some books may be recommended:

Daniel Watt's, *Learning with Logo,* is explicit and also suitable for older students;

Harold Abelson's, *Apple Logo,* is more concise and for the adult reader;

Donna Bearden's, *The Turtle Source Book,* brings more examples and teaching suggestions;

Harold Abelson and Andrea diSessa's, *Turtle Geometry,* gives more sophisticated applications especially in geometry,

and of course the manual of whatever Logo program one may use gives instructions relevant to the specific application.[12]

1. *Playing Robot, Commanding the Toy Turtle*

To a group of children, explain briefly that programming a computer means giving instructions to a machine. One piece of such instructions we call a command.

---

[11] Virginia Carter Grammer, E. Paul Goldenberg, and Leigh Klotz, Jr., *The Commodore 64 Logo Tutorial* (Cambridge, Mass.: Terrapin Inc., 1982-3).

[12] Daniel Watt, *Learning with Logo* (New York: McGraw-Hill, 1983). Harold Abelson, *Apple Logo* (New York: McGraw-Hill Byte Books, 1982). Donna Bearden and Jim Muller, *The Turtle Source Book* (Reston, VA: Reston Publishing Co. Inc., 1983). Harold Abelson and Andrea diSessa, *Turtle Geometry: The Computer as a Medium for Exploring Mathematics* (Cambridge, MA: MIT Press, 1981).

"In order to better understand how to perform commands in a precise, narrow-minded way, we may as well try ourselves to follow such commands."

Put a chair a few steps away so you can walk around it.

"In order to direct myself to walk around that chair, I have only two commands: *forward* with a number of steps, and *turn*. Let's try this. I'm going to command myself:

FORWARD 4"

Walk four steps straight forward.

"TURN"

Make a right 90° turn.
In this way, command yourself to walk around the chair.
Let a child do the walking;
Let a child do the commanding.
Have them walk in a rectangle, in a square.

After some exercises, one child commanding, one child doing the walking, introduce the toy turtle on a paper screen:

Materials:

A solid toy turtle (plastic or wood, from toy stores) with a ballpoint pen mounted in the middle;
A sheet of screen-shaped graph paper. (If you make a plastic pouch with a screen-shaped window, you can replace the graph paper to get a clear screen again.)

Introduce the toy turtle drawing a square just as you walked.
Let the children do more exercises.
  Note: At this level TURN is a right 90° turn only.

2. *The Turtle on the Screen, Command Mode*

Commands Introduced

FORWARD n	moves turtle forward n steps.
RIGHT n	turns turtle to the right in an angle n.
DRAW	clears the screen, puts turtle in starting position.
HOME	moves turtle to starting position without clearing the screen.

Presentation:

"Today, we are not commanding ourselves, but a little turtle, which is depicted on our computer screen: this little triangle is supposed to be the turtle, facing in the direction of the top of the triangle."

Introduce FORWARD and RIGHT with exercises 2.1 or 2.2 (see following section). Don't explain that the input of RIGHT is the number of degrees of the angle. This is for the child to explore. Make it a clear rule of the game, that so far no LEFT turn is used (to have them explore the full 360°). Introduce DRAW and HOME as they are needed.

3. *Angles with BACK, Separating Drawings*

New commands:

PENUP	lifts the pen, turtle will not draw.
PENDOWN	puts the pen down, turtle will draw.
BACK n	moves the turtle back n steps.

Presentation:

Start exercises 3.1 and 3.2 by introducing the new commands.

4. *Repetition*

New commands

REPEAT n [ ]	repeats the commands within the bracket n times.
*	multiplies; use as in arithmetic.
/	divides; use as in arithmetic.

Presentation

Introduce the REPEAT command

REPEAT 4 [FORWARD 50 RIGHT 90]

5. *Procedures*

New commands

TO	puts Logo in edit mode, indicates the following as a procedure.
END	indicates the end of a procedure.
CTRL -C	defines the procedure on the screen, puts Logo back in command mode.
CTRL -G	puts Logo back in command mode without defining.

Presentation

"After we have commanded our turtle by typing each command, we now want the computer to store these commands in its memory. Thus,

we will create little sequences of commands that we will call 'a procedure.' A procedure will have a name."

Type the line

TO BOX

Press RETURN (which in the following text will always be understood
without being mentioned).

"Logo has now switched to edit mode. That means whatever we type
on the screen will not be looked at by the computer yet. So we can edit
a few commands, which will not be performed immediately."

Finish the procedure BOX

```
FORWARD 50
RIGHT 90
FORWARD 70
RIGHT 90
FORWARD 50
RIGHT 90
FORWARD 70
RIGHT 90
END
```

"If we want the computer to take this program into its memory, we
have to press
CTRL-C (which means hold the key CTRL down, then the key C)
"Now, after our procedure BOX is defined as the computer tells us,
let's command the computer to perform BOX."

Type the command BOX

Repeat whatever is necessary to help the child to do the following exercises
unassisted.

When introducing procedures, eventually some organization will be necessary to save procedures made up by the children. Without making a big
lesson, casually introduce the usage of the disk drive. Don't bother the children
with the formatting of a disk. That may be done by the teacher according
to your Logo or computer manual. It is also advisable that the children not
handle the disk, such as booting up the computer with Logo and inserting
the disk with the children's procedures, until they are very reliable and
confident in handling the computer.

So the only *new commands* to be introduced here are as follows:

SAVE "name   saves procedures from computer's memory to disk.

	Whatever "name" is given here will be established as the name of that file.
READ "name	reads the file "name" from the disk.
ERASE "name	erases the procedure "name" from the memory.
ERASE ALL	erases all procedures from the memory.
GOODBYE	erases all procedures from the memory and puts the welcome on the screen.

A few rules should be made up for the students, such as how to name their files and how to erase all their procedures after they are saved on the disk, in order to leave the computer empty for the next child. The easiest way of naming the files would be the first name of the child, eventually modified by a one-digit number, if so many procedures are produced that they cannot fit in one file.

With the introduction of procedures, eventually the need will be felt to talk about debugging a procedure. This may be done on occasion of a nasty bug. Some points to make are:

- Show how to bring back a procedure in edit mode by typing
  TO name of procedure,
- Show how to trace the action of this procedure by thinking what Logo does in each step,
- Introduce TRACE and NOTRACE and their use.

6. *Symmetry*

New commands:

LEFT n	turns the turtle to the left in an angle of n.
RIGHT −n	turns the turtle right in a negative angle n, actually meaning the turtle is turned left in an angle n.

This chapter has been left for so long for two reasons: Forcing the child to abide by the rule of the game and not use another turn command than RIGHT means helping him or her to understand the feature of the full angle between 0 and 360°. Furthermore, the introduction now of left angles and negative angles gives an opportunity to explore the realm of symmetry in an explicit way. Symmetry is an important feature throughout geometry and should be carefully explored. We also provide sensorial exercise here for negative numbers.

Presentation:

Introduce the new commands by initializing the exercises 6.1.

7. *Subprocedures*

New programming feature:

No new commands, but the use of procedure names as commands within another procedure.

Presentation 1:

Explain the new feature by initializing any of exercises 7.1.
  Example:

```
TO PINWHEEL
BOX
LEFT 90
BOX
LEFT 90
BOX
LEFT 90
BOX
LEFT 90
END
```

This chapter opens two avenues of work: One is *creative trials,* meaning to try in a creative, playful way, in which new shapes are possibly made by taking procedures recently made and rearranging them or adding them into new shapes. Another avenue, work on *projects,* will start from a clear idea in mind, breaking that down into single procedures. If the children don't come up with a project on their own, it may be introduced through the following presentation:

Presentation 2:

  "Today, let's make up our minds before we start programming. Say we want to produce a house on the screen. So let's type

```
TO HOUSE
```

What is a house made from? The first thing might be the body. So let's type

```
BODY
```

Then, of course, we need a roof. So let's type

```
ROOF
```

That might be enough for today, so let's type

```
END
```

Now we have to work on the parts: first might be the body

```
TO BODY
```

We may take our procedure BOX right here as our body

```
BOX
```

That's all we need, so this is the end of the **BODY** procedure

```
END
```

Now let's work on the roof, which is a triangle

```
TO ROOF
REPEAT 3 [FORWARD 70 RIGHT 120]
END
```

If this is all, let's define it

$\boxed{\text{CTRL}} - C$

After our HOUSE procedure is defined, let's try it

```
HOUSE
```

It turned out that we have a bug here. We obviously need to move the turtle before the roof is attached."

Show how to edit the HOUSE procedure by inserting a MOVE procedure. If necessary, that may be tried out in command mode to find out which moves of the turtle are necessary to get the roof in the right place.

This type of breaking down of a given problem into parts and then working again on the parts in the same way, is called 'top-down programming' or 'structured programming.' Logo is a powerful way to introduce these modern programming techniques without making a big fuss about them.

8. *Variables*

New programming feature:

: The "dots," used in front of a name, will output the value of the variable with that name. When used with a name in the headline of a procedure, it creates a local variable with this name.

At this point, no sophisticated explanation about variables should be given, nor should all the symbols be introduced. This follows the Montessori principles of giving the experience first and only later the name and explanation. This is a well-established teacher's experience, that explanations applied to something that isn't yet experienced are confusing. Just the term 'variable' may be explained as 'a number that has a name.' Later, of course, it will be discovered that it could be any piece of information given a name.

Presentation:

"In order to be more flexible with our numbers, we may give them a name

```
TO BOX :SIZE
```

SIZE is the name for the size of our box. So let's use that in a next BOX procedure

```
REPEAT 4 [FORWARD :SIZE RIGHT 90]
END
```

The :SIZE tells the computer to take the number that we will provide for that name, whatever number it may be."
Define the procedure and call the new BOX

```
BOX 100
```

Try several sizes of boxes.

"When we have a number, to which we have given a name, we call that a variable. Variable is simply a name for a number, such as 'number-of-children-in-our-class' is the name for 24. Yesterday, it was 23 because Jimmy was sick. But that 23 had the same name, which was 'number-of-children-in-our-class.' "

9. *Two and More Variables*

Presentation:

If the child has not yet found out, introduce the possibility of creating more than one variable in the same procedure, as in the following example

```
TO RECTANGLE :LENGTH :WIDTH
REPEAT 2 [FORWARD :LENGTH RIGHT 90 FORWARD :WIDTH
   RIGHT 90]
END
```

10. *Recursion*

New command features:

Usage of a procedure within itself, CTRL G stops whatever Logo is doing.

Presentation:

"Today, we want to explore a particular use of a procedure. So let's just create any simple procedure"

```
TO HOOK
FORWARD 100
RIGHT 120
FORWARD 40
RIGHT 90
END
```

"This creates just a hook. Not a big deal, but let's now try to use this within another procedure"

```
TO SHAPES
HOOK
```

"So far our new 'shapes' procedure will not do anything else other than the 'hook' procedure, making a hook. But now we try something very interesting: We are calling the procedure 'shapes' within itself"

```
SHAPES
END
```

The procedure typed so far should look this way

```
TO SHAPES
HOOK
SHAPES
END
```

After defining, type the command **SHAPES** and let the computer work a while, till you stop it with $\boxed{\text{CTRL}}$ –G.

After some experience, introduce the term "recursion," which is given to a program that calls itself and, if necessary, repeat the characteristics and give some help for understanding: A recursive procedure is like standing between two mirrors. It is also like the label on this cereal box, showing a person holding that same cereal box with the label showing a person holding that same cereal box with the label showing a person holding that same cereal box . . .

11. *Increments*

New commands:

+   adds, use as in arithmetic.
−   subtracts, use as in arithmetic.
Increments of variables in recursive procedures.

Presentation:

"When calling a procedure within a recursive process, we may choose to change the input of that procedure as in this example"

```
TO SPIRAL :SIZE
FORWARD :SIZE
RIGHT 90
SPIRAL :SIZE + 10
END
```

"This procedure is calling itself in a recursive process, but not with the same input, which in the first place is :SIZE, but then with that input increased by 10. Every time this procedure is called again on a new level of recursion, the size is increased by 10. We call that 'an increment of the variable SIZE.' "

Let the turtle draw the spiral. As always, initiate more explanations, repetitions, or discussions only if the child asks and needs them.

12. *Conditional Stops*

New commands:

IF	if the input following the IF command is true, the rest of the line is executed; if the input is false, Logo goes right to the next line.
STOP	makes a procedure stop (the procedure that called this procedure will, however, continue).
HEADING	outputs the turtle's present heading.
SETHEADING *n*	sets the turtle's heading to *n*.

Presentation 1:

"It is cumbersome to stop all these procedures manually by typing $\boxed{\text{CTRL}}$–G. Therefore, let's provide a stop command. Let's assume that we want our spiral to stop when the size reaches the amount of 100:"

Insert in the spiral procedure of Section 11 the following line

```
IF :SIZE > 100 STOP
```

Explore putting this line in different places: after the first (title) line, after the second line, after the third line, and after the fourth line. Discuss the results.

Presentation 2:

"In some cases, as with our polygon procedure, we might want a stop command that depends on the heading of the turtle, because we don't know how often that procedure is to be performed in order to close the polygon."

Take a polygon procedure from exercise 10.2 and insert the following line

```
IF HEADING = 0 STOP
```

Try with several polygons.

"If our turtle was moved prior to calling this procedure, the stop would not work because the original heading wasn't 0. So let's take care of that by turning the turtle to 0 before calling the procedure"

```
SETHEADING 0
```

13. *Random Numbers*

New Commands:

RANDOM n   outputs a random number between 0 and n.
RANDOMIZE   sets the random number generator on a random series. Without this command, the newly powered computer will always come up with the same series of random numbers.
PRINT   prints what follows the command on the screen.

Presentation:

"Our computer can create random numbers, that is, as if throwing a dice. Let's just explore this capacity":

```
TO DICE
PRINT1 RANDOM 7
DICE
END
```

If necessary, introduce the use of random in one of the exercises 13.2. The command RANDOMIZE may be casually introduced at a later time. To prove its necessity, you might run the procedure printing random numbers as the first one every day after booting up the computer and recording the produced numbers on paper. If these records are compared, it should turn out that the first series of random numbers after switching on the computer is always the same. To avoid that, just type the command RANDOMIZE.

14. *Public Variables*

New commands:

MAKE "n m creates a public variable of the name n and assigns it the value m.

"n   outputs the name n itself.

:n   outputs the value of the variable n.

[n] outputs whatever is enclosed as a list.

Presentation:

"So far, our variables were always created in the headline of a procedure and were valid for this procedure exclusively. We call that a 'local variable.' No other procedure will look at it. It might even be possible to take the same name within two different procedures and, in that way deal with two different variables.

Today, we will see a way to create a 'public variable' that is acknowledged by all procedures"

```
TO TRY
MAKE "NAME PETER
PRINT "NAME
PRINT :NAME
PRINT [NAME]
PRINT ["NAME :NAME NAME]
PRINT NAME
END
```

This program will print the following:

```
Name
Peter
Name
" Name :name name
Error message  (Here Logo searched for a procedure "name".)
```

Discuss the results in order to make clear the usage of the different signs.

"In order to try the working of this variable, as opposed to a local variable, let's type and run the following procedure"

```
TO TRY1 :NAME1
PRINT :NAME
PRINT :NAME1
END
```

Now run this by typing TRY1 "HEIDI.

The result will be that both names are printed, because the local variable was called in its own program. To change that, let's try again

```
TO TRY2
PRINT :NAME
PRINT :NAME1
END
```

This time the NAME1 will not be printed, but an error message will come up, since this variable is local to the TRY1 procedure only and is not recognized within the TRY2 procedure. The public variable NAME is recognized and printed.

15. *Full Recursion*

Presentation:

"So far, our recursive programs performed something similar to mere repetition. Since the recursive call was always in the end of the program, each program was finished when it called a new recursive level. However, we are not confined to this. If the recursive call is right in the middle of the program, each program will run to that point, call the new procedure and so on, and only if the last procedure is finished and passes back the initiative to the but-last program, that one will continue and so will all others. Let's try this out"

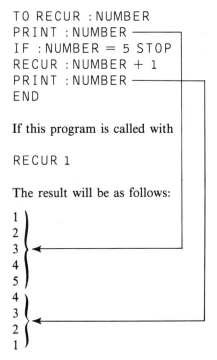

```
TO RECUR : NUMBER
PRINT : NUMBER
IF : NUMBER = 5 STOP
RECUR : NUMBER + 1
PRINT : NUMBER
END
```

If this program is called with

```
RECUR 1
```

The result will be as follows:

```
1
2
3
4
5
4
3
2
1
```

"Each of the recursive levels printed its number before the recursive call came. That accounts for the sequence 1–5 printed. Then, after the last level stopped, it handed back command to the but-last level, which now printed its number after the recursive call, which, of course, was a 4, and then handed back control to the third level, which again performed the print command after the recursive call with the number 3 and so on down to 1."

16. *Coordinates*

New commands:

SETXY x y, moves the turtle to location (x,y).

  x = horizontal coordinate, $-158 < \times < 158$

  y = vertical coordinate, $-128 < y < 128$

Center of screen: (0,0).

SETX x sets x position only.
SETY y sets y position only.
XCOR   outputs turtle's x coordinate.
YCOR   outputs turtle's y coordinate.

This section should not come too early, when the child is still exploring turtle geometry. It opens the realm of analytical geometry and should go parallel with teaching analytical geometry in class.

  Prior to the presentation of the new commands, a procedure should be set up to put the cross of coordinates on the screen.

Presentation of the SET commands may be done with exercises similar to E16.1 or E16.2.

Presentation of the XCOR and YCOR commands may be done by introducing exercise 16.6.

The following procedure COORD with its subprocedures listed below will put the x- and y-axes on your screen:

```
TO COORD
  FULLSCREEN PU
  SETXY (- 160) 0 PD
  DOT 1 0
  MARK - 150 150 1 0
  DOT 1 0
  PU SETXY 0 (- 130) PD
  DOT 0 3
  MARK - 100 100 0 1
  DOT 0 3
  HOME STAMPCHAR "0 HT
END

TO DOT :X :Y
  REPEAT :X [SETY 1 SETY 0 SETX XCOR+10]
  REPEAT :Y [SETX 1 SETX 0 SETY YCOR+10]
END

TO MARK :P :E :X :Y
  IF :P * :P > 0 STAMP :P
  IF :P = :E STOP
```

```
   DOT  :X  *  5  :Y  *  5
   MARK  :P  +  50  :E  :X  :Y
END

TO  STAMP  :N
   SETX  XCOR  +  :Y  *  8
   SETY  YCOR  +  6  SETX  XCOR  −  :X  *  8
   STAMPSUB  :N
   PU  SETX  XCOR  −  :Y  *  8
   SETY  YCOR  −  6  SETX  XCOR  +  :X  *  8  PD
END

TO  STAMPSUB  :N
   IF  :N  =  "  STOP
   PD  STAMPCHAR  FIRST  :N
   PU  SETX  XCOR  +  8  PD
   STAMPSUB  BUTFIRST  :N
   PU  SETX  XCOR  −  8  PD
END
```

Another, simpler program is provided as solution to 16.4 in section e.

c. Logo Exercises Tuned to the Sixteen Levels of Presentations

Each level of these exercises goes hand in hand with a presentation of the previous chapter. The content of presentation is mentioned briefly following the letter P: = presentations. Following the letter E: = exercises, the exercises are then lined up. Each exercise should have the number of level, a period, and a running number of exercises.

The numbers on the right margin relate to the level of the geometry study necessary for this particular exercise. They provide a tool for children to seek out exercises they may be familiar with, without running into some that they cannot yet understand because they lack familiarity with the geometry nomenclature. It is important to remember that all this work should go parallel with the geometry work with the box of sticks and other related math work.

The numbers in parentheses indicate the following level of geometry study:

(0) = no geometry knowledge necessary here
(1) = primary geometry (basic nomenclature)
(2) = nomenclature through lines and angles
(3) = nomenclature through polygons
(4) = nomenclature of circle
(5) = formula of circle circumference

The letter N on the right margin indicates that this exercise is necessary to build on further exercises.

It may be noticed that certain geometric concepts are studied over again in different ways on different levels. One of those examples is the transition from polygons to circles, which should not be taught by the teacher, but left to the child to explore on different levels of programming skills.

Another area closely related to this is the "total turtle trip theorem," which states that the turtle goes through a multiple of 360° when completing any polygon or star. This also should not be taught, but left for the child to explore on several levels of programming skills.

The exercises may be put on command cards and made available for the child to choose from. In order to direct the choice in a reasonable way, the children have to be aware which level of presentation they have had so far and which level of geometry.

It might be a good idea to color code the cards according to the level of geometry, choosing a neutral color if no such level is indicated. A missing indication of geometry level does not mean no geometry is needed, but means that this exercise relates back to other exercises, which in turn call for different geometry knowledge levels.

It should be emphasized that the choice of these exercises stresses geometry, directing the children's attention to ideas they may not come up with on their own. That by no means should lead to a restriction towards geometry only. Quite the opposite—the creative work of the child in Logo is very important and should be encouraged. One reason for including only few ideas of that kind is, not to snap away these ideas and leave it to the children to feel the happiness of developing their own creative ideas.

For the teacher working through these exercises, a sequence of solutions is provided in section e, which is not meant for the child to copy from, but for the teacher to trace these programs and thus pick up ideas which she or he did not come up with on her or his own.

1. *Playing Robot, Commanding the Toy Turtle*

P: Walk according to turtle commands FORWARD, TURN; Move Toy Turtle on paper.

E:	1.1 Walk towards a target.	(0), N
	1.2 Walk around a target.	(0), N
	1.3 Walk a square, a rectangle	(1), N
	1.4 Do as in 1.1 to 1.3 on paper.	N
	1.5 Walk a right angled spiral ⬓	(0)

2. *Turtle on Screen, Command Mode*

P: FORWARD n, RIGHT n, DRAW, HOME.

E:	2.1 Hit a target (use label 0, place target in all directions from home).	(0), N
	2.2 Walk turtle around a target.	(0), N

2.3 Draw irregular polygons (labels 20, 28–33),
      a. close figure with HOME,
      b. do without HOME and bring turtle back into start-
      ing position.   (1), N

2.4 Draw different squares (label 21).   (1)

2.5 Draw different rectangles (label 22).   (1)

2.6 Create simple drawings from these shapes.

3. Angles with BACK, Separating Drawings

P: PENUP, PENDOWN, BACK n.

E: 3.1 Draw lines (labels 1–7).   (2)

3.2 Draw different angles (labels 8–12),
      a. use BACK for the first leg of the angle,
      b. use FORWARD for both legs.   (2), N

3.3 Draw regular polygons with turns 40;72;120;36;60;
 90;45;180; always bring turtle back into starting position, label the polygons (labels 21,13,34–39) add up the
 angles turned.   (3), N

3.4 Draw stars (that is polygons with turns 144;
 135;160;150), always bring turtle back into starting position, add up the total of angles turned, keep record
 of the number of full cycles.   (3), N

3.5 Draw regular quadrilaterals (labels 21–27),
 position them in different ways: (3)

3.6 Draw triangles (labels 13–19),
      a. close figure with HOME,
      b. position the isosceles triangles in
      different ways:
      c. try without HOME bringing turtle
      back in starting position,   (3)

3.7 Create drawings from the shapes 3.1 to 3.6 such as a
 house, a stickman, a table . . .   (0)

4. Repetition

P: REPEAT n [. . .] , * , /

E: 4.1 Draw regular polygons according to labels 34-39,
      a. find the correct angle by trying,
      b. let Logo calculate the angle.   (3), N

4.2 Draw polygons with ever higher number of sides.   (3), N

4.3 Draw a circle. Draw different sized circles.   (3), N

4.4   Draw a circle starting at the bottom point,
      a. starting from home,
      b. starting from any place at the screen.   (3), N

4.5   Draw a circle with a given radius.   (5)

4.6   Draw a circle around a given center point with a given
      radius.   (5)

4.7   Draw a circle as a collection of points equally distant
      from a center point.   (1), N

4.8   Draw a circle around a given center other than home
      with a given radius as in 4.7.   (1), N

4.9   Draw parts of a circle (labels 40-47).   (4)

4.10 Draw a line and a circle (labels 48-50).   (4)

4.11 Draw 2 circles (labels 51-56).   (4)

4.12 Draw spirals built from semicircles or quartercircles
      with increasing radius.   (4)

4.13 Draw a pentacle, a five-pointed
      star, find the angle by trying: (3)

4.14 Draw stars with 8;9;10;12;15;20 points,
      a. find the angles by trying,
         add up the total of angles,
         keep a record of the number of full cycles;
      b. let Logo calculate the angle.   (3)

4.15 Create your own stars.

4.16 Create designs with the shapes 4.1 to 4.15.

5. Procedures

P: Edit Mode, TO, END; recordkeeping of all procedures
      created;
E: 5.1 Program any of the shapes 3.2–4.16 as procedures, save
      them for future use, print them on hardcopy, keep an
      inventory of all your procedures.   N

6. Symmetry

P: LEFT n, RIGHT –n;
E: 6.1 Take any of the procedures 5.1 and create a mirror
      image, that is, the symmetric figure,   N
         a. with LEFT turns,
         b. with RIGHT turns having negative angles,
         c. draw the symmetry line, representing the mirror,
            between the two figures.

7. *Subprocedures*

P: Use of procedures within procedures; top-down pro-
       gramming;

E: 7.1   Assemble any of the procedures 5.1 as subprocedures
       into a superprocedure, such as creating designs built
       from basic shapes (like a window assembled of 4
       squares).   N

   7.2   Take any of the procedures created in 7.1 and assemble
       them again into more polymorphic designs. Try what
       you can create.   N

   7.3   Program a project, that is, have a final design in mind
       and develop the procedures and subprocedures, try a
       house, a face, a truck, a flower, a stickman . . . try your
       own projects.   N

8. *Variables*

P: Local Variables, symbol:

E: 8.1   Draw squares in different sizes.   (1)

   8.2   Draw rectangles in different sizes.   (1)

   8.3   Draw regular polygons with the number of sides being
       a variable, (labels 13, 21, 34–39).   (3)

   8.4   Draw chinese boxes, such as: ▣   ◬   ◎

   8.5   Find a procedure for a circle with the radius being a
       variable.   (5)

   8.6   Define procedures of semicircles and quartercircles with
       variable radius.   (5)

   8.7   Draw rhomboi with different angles:

   8.8   Draw isosceles triangles with different angles, let Logo
       calculate the angles from one variable: (close with
       HOME)

   8.9   Take your projects from 7.3 and change them, so that
       the size becomes a variable. Then assemble them in
       different sizes:
       a village, a crowd of people, a flower garden . . .   N

9. *Two and more variables*

P: Procedures with 2 and more variables;

E: 9.1   Draw polygons with different size and number of sides.   (3)

   9.2   Draw rhomboi with different angles and sides: (3)

   9.3   Draw a Christmas tree with isosceles triangles
       with different heights and bases: (3)

9.4 Draw stars with a procedure providing the number of points and the number of full cycles as variables. Find out which values of these variables make stars and which don't.

9.5 Draw flowers with variable leaf-radius, number of petals, and size of flower.

9.6 Draw houses with variable height, width, but fixed size of windows and doors.

10. *Recursion*

P: call a procedure within itself, [CTRL]–G.

E: 10.1 Draw any repetitious designs from 4. now without REPEAT

10.2 Make a recursive procedure to draw polygons or stars with variable angle, explore the number of repetitions necessary.   N

10.3 Explore recursive designs with HOOK = FORWARD, RIGHT, FORWARD, RIGHT.

10.4 Take procedures from 10.3, make lengths and angles as variables and try several values.

10.5 Draw rosettes: Take any shape from your work so far and repeat them after turning the turtle a bit.

10.6 Create rosettes by turning and walking the turtle between recursions, as in 10.5.

10.7 Create laces: Just walk the turtle a bit between recursions as in 10.5.

10.8 Draw a circle as a recursion of its basic step and turn pattern. (Pre-exercise: Walk a circle and observe your step and turn pattern.)

11. *Increments*

P: +, −, increments in variables.

E: 11.1 Draw chinese boxes.   N

11.2 Draw the pink tower.

11.3 Draw a spiral as a polygon with increasing sidelength. try spirals from regular polygons with 3;4;5;6;8;9;10 sides.   N

11.4 Draw spirals with angles close to but not exactly those in regular polygons.

11.5 Make in the spirals (11.3) the increase itself a variable.

11.6 Draw spirals as in 11.3 with "geometric" increments, that is, increase the sidelength by multiplying, try *2; *1.1; *0.8 . . .

11.7 Draw Inspirals: Polygons with increasing angles.

12. *Conditional Stops*

P: IF, STOP, HEADING, SETHEADING n.

E: 12.1 Take any of the recursive procedures from 11. and provide it with an appropriate stop.   N

12.2 Take any of the recursive polygon procedures and provide it with a stop by introducing a count down variable.   N

12.3 Take any of the recursive star procedures and provide it with a stop depending on the heading of the turtle,   N
a. starting at home,
b. starting anywhere on the screen by setting heading to 0.
c. starting anywhere by introducing a variable for the start heading, (f.e.:
            TO PROCEDURE   :START
               IF HEADING = :START STOP
                        . . .

and calling that procedure by giving that variable the value of the present heading:
            PROCEDURE HEADING   )

12.4 Make a recursive procedure, which does nothing, except decrease a number, use this procedure for slowing down other procedures.   N

12.5 Create rosettes (s. 10.5 and 10.6) from spirals or (and) chinese boxes.

12.6 Create laces (s.10.7) from spirals and chinese boxes.

13. *Random Numbers*

P: RANDOMIZE, RANDOM n, PRINT, PRINT1.

E: 13.1 Let the computer print random numbers.

13.2 Take any procedures from 8.9, 9.5 and 9.6 and assemble them in random sizes:
a flower garden with random size flowers,
a town with random size houses . . .

13.3 Create designs from random size circles, squares . . .

14. *Public Variables*

P: Difference of local variables, created in TO procedure definitions and public variables created with MAKE.

E: 14.1 Take any exercise from 6.1 and create the symmetric figure by multiplying all turn-inputs (angle numbers) by a variable, which you can call SYM, then draw the right image with MAKE "SYM 1 and draw the left image with MAKE "SYM (−1)

14.2 With the technique from 14.1, create symmetric pictures including lots of procedures.

14.3 Take any of your pictures from 8.9 and 9.5 and 9.6 and enlarge them to scale: Multiply all size numbers by a variable, which you can call SCALE,
then draw the original picture with

	MAKE "SCALE	1
or draw it to scale 3 with	MAKE "SCALE	3
or draw it smaller with	MAKE "SCALE	1/3
or " "	MAKE "SCALE	0.5

15. *Full Recursion*

P: Study of problems, where the recursive call comes not at the end of the procedure but when the calling procedure is not yet done.

E: 15.1 Draw a tree with the following procedure:

```
TO TREE :SIZE            Run it: TREE 40.
IF :SIZE <5 STOP         Run it several times,
RIGHT 45                 watch the tree grow,
FORWARD :SIZE            study the procedure.
TREE :SIZE/2
BACK :SIZE
LEFT 90
FORWARD :SIZE
TREE :SIZE/2
BACK :SIZE
RIGHT 45
END                                              N
```

15.2 Build your slowing procedure from 12.4 into the tree procedure, so you can watch slowly and carefully what your program does.

15.3 Go through the tree program (with size 40) by putting on graph paper, whatever the turtle does in each step. Take a separate paper for each procedure call and write the procedure called with the corresponding values of SIZE.

Check off every program line dealt with.

15.4   Draw different sizes of trees.

15.5   Change the stop line, so it will draw until the branches are only 2 steps long.

15.6   Change the divisor from 2 to 3; to 1.5 ...

15.7   Change the angle.

15.8   Change the tree procedure, so that left and right branches have different branch lengths.

15.9   Draw a square with a smaller square attached to each corner, with a smaller square attached to each corner, and so on.

15.10 Draw as 15.9 with pentagons.

15.11 Draw as 15.9 with pentacles.

16. Coordinates

P: SETXY, SETX, SETY, XCOR, YCOR

E: 16.1 Draw the triangle A (23,12), B (65,12), C (51,73).

16.2   Draw the quadrilateral A $(-33,-15)$, B $(54,-8)$, C (46,38), D $(-52, 65)$.

16.3   Draw the square with the base A (10,20) and B (50,20).

16.4   Draw the lines x = 0 and y = 0 (the x- and y-axes) and let the turtle mark every 10 with a one-step dot and every 50 with three-step dots. Use this procedure together with all other procedures in this section 16, in order to place all the created drawings in the co-ordinate system.

16.5   Draw a stick man (plot it on graph paper to find the coordinates).

16.6   Walk the turtle through all points y = x (it is rec-ommended to create a recursive subprocedure to run x from 0 to the maximum value and another one to run x in the minus direction to the minimum value).

16.7   Walk the turtle through all points y = 2 * x.

16.8   Walk the turtle through all points y = m * x. Try several values such as m = 3, 4, 10, 0.5, 0.25 ...

16.9   Walk the turtle through all points y = x + b. Try several values such as b = 10, 30, 100, -10, -30, -100 ...

16.10 Walk the turtle through all points $y = m * x + b$.

16.11 Walk the turtle through all points $y = x^2$.

16.12 Walk the turtle through all points $y = m * x^2$. Try several values such as $m = 0.1, 0.02 \ldots$

16.13 Walk the turtle through all points
$y = m * (x - a)^2 + b$.

16.14 Rescale your coordinate system so that $x = 1$ and $y = 1$ will be the 50 mark on your x- and y-axes. This could be done by creating a new command SETXY50 :X :Y. Do exercises 16.11 to 16.13 with this rescaling command.

16.15 Walk the turtle through all points $y = 1/x$.

16.16 Walk the turtle through all points $y^2 + x^2 = r^2$ that may be converted into $y = \pm \sqrt{r^2 - x^2}$.

d. Labels for Logo Exercises

1. *Purpose*

One purpose of these labels is to make the connection between the geometry work with Logo and the same work with other Montessori materials such as the box of sticks. The exploration of geometry with Logo is not meant to replace any other studies, but rather to complement them due to the principle of "repetition through variety." The Montessori exercises in many cases will be necessary to introduce the nomenclature and the basic properties of geometric figures, which are then applied in the Logo exercises.

2. *Assembly Directions*

The attached label chart is to be assembled into

- a chart
- individual labels with sticking part, which may be placed on the computer screen or on the chart. (The chart is the place to store the labels and to take them from it.)

You need:

2 copies of the chart
colored posterboard.

What you do:

- Paste chart on posterboard.

0 Target	20 Common Quadrilateral	40 Semicircle
1 Horizontal Line	21 Square	41 Quartercircle
2 Vertical Line	22 Rectangle	42 Sector
3 Oblique Line	23 Rhombus	43 Segment
4 Parallel Lines	24 Parallelogram	44 Arc
5 Divergent Lines	25 Scalene Trapezoid	45 Chord
6 Convergent Lines	26 Isosceles Trapezoid	46 Diameter
7 Perpendicular Lines	27 Right Angled Trapezoid	47 Radius
8 Acute Angle	28 Pentagon (Irregular)	48 Tangent Line
9 Right Angle	29 Hexagon (Irregular)	49 Secant Line
10 Obtuse Angle	30 Heptagon (Irregular)	50 External Line
11 Straight Angle	31 Octagon (Irregular)	51 2 Circles: Internal
12 Whole Angle	32 Nonagon (Irregular)	52 2 Circles: External
13 Equilateral Triangle	33 Decagon (Irregular)	53 2 Ci.:Internal Tangent
14 Isosceles Triangle	34 Regular Pentagon	54 2 Ci.:External Tangent
15 Scalene Triangle	35 Regular Hexagon	55 2 Circles: Secant
16 Right Angled Triangle	36 Regular Heptagon	56 2 Circles: Concentric
17 Obtuse Triangle	37 Regular Octagon	57
18 Acute Triangle	38 Regular Nonagon	58
19 Isosceles Right A.Tri.	39 Regular Decagon	59

Figure C.16

- In the back, paste this advice:

> Labels for Logo Exercises
>
> _____
>
> Always "park" labels back in their proper "garage" with their number!

- Laminate the chart.
- Laminate the second copy.
- Cut into three columns, (vertical lines).
- Attach clear tape to the left margin of each column, so that half of the tape stands out beyond the laminated material.
- Cut horizontal lines to obtain individual labels, each having a sticky piece of tape standing out.
- Assemble the labels according to their numbers on the chart.

e. Program Ideas to Solve the Exercises

This section contains Logo procedures, which respond to the exercises in section c. They are not meant for the child to copy from, but for the teacher working through the exercises. If any one of them poses problems, the teacher could go back to these solutions and find programming ideas there which he or she may then include in counseling the students.

The procedures' names are numbers rather than names, although that is not in line with the Logo usage. The reason is that in that way they are directly related to the numbers of the exercises. Of course, procedures on exercises levels 2 to 4 reflect work that is supposed to be done in command mode. To program them as procedures was done only to have the possibility of keeping them in the computer's memory.

The procedures are written in "Commodore 64 Logo," which is very similar to "Terrapin Logo."[13]

```
TO E2.3A
  FORWARD 50
  RIGHT 70
  FORWARD 30
  RIGHT 50
  FORWARD 100
  RIGHT 40
```

---

[13] Virginia Carter Grammer, E. Paul Goldenberg and Leigh Klotz, J., *The Commodore 64 Logo Tutorial* (Cambridge, Mass.: Terrapin Inc., 1982, 1983).

```
  FORWARD 25
  HOME
END

TO E2.3B
  FORWARD 40
  RIGHT 50
  FORWARD 60
  RIGHT 110
  FORWARD 85
  RIGHT 73
  FORWARD 30
  RIGHT 55
  FORWARD 53
END

TO E2.4
  FORWARD 70
  RIGHT 90
  FORWARD 70
  RIGHT 90
  FORWARD 70
  RIGHT 90
  FORWARD 70
  RIGHT 90
END

TO E2.5
  FORWARD 40
  RIGHT 90
  FORWARD 70
  RIGHT 90
  FORWARD 40
  RIGHT 90
  FORWARD 70
  RIGHT 90
END

TO E3.1
  RIGHT 90
  FORWARD 60
  PENUP
  FORWARD 30
  RIGHT 270
  PENDOWN
```

```
    FORWARD 80
    PENUP
    FORWARD 30
    RIGHT 50
    PENDOWN
    BACK 70
    PENUP
    BACK 40
    PENDOWN
    RIGHT 270
    FORWARD 80
    RIGHT 90
    PENUP
    FORWARD 20
    PENDOWN
    RIGHT 90
    FORWARD 80
END


TO E3.2A
    FULLSCREEN
    BACK 40
    RIGHT 60
    FORWARD 40
    PENUP
    FORWARD 70
    PENDOWN
    BACK 40
    RIGHT 90
    FORWARD 40
    PENUP
    FORWARD 70
    PENDOWN
    BACK 40
    RIGHT 120
    FORWARD 40
    PENUP
    FORWARD 150
    PENDOWN
    BACK 40
    RIGHT 180
    FORWARD 40
END
```

```
TO E3.2B
  FULLSCREEN
  FORWARD 40
  RIGHT 120
  FORWARD 40
  PENUP
  FORWARD 30
  PENDOWN
  FORWARD 40
  RIGHT 90
  FORWARD 40
  PENUP
  FORWARD 30
  PENDOWN
  FORWARD 40
  RIGHT 60
  FORWARD 40
  PENUP
  FORWARD 30
  PENDOWN
  FORWARD 40
  RIGHT 0
  FORWARD 40
END

TO E3.3
  FORWARD 35
  RIGHT 40
  FORWARD 35
  RIGHT 40
  FORWARD 35
  RIGHT 40
  FORWARD 35
  RIGHT 40
  FORWARD 35
  RIGHT 40
  FORWARD 35
  RIGHT 40
  FORWARD 35
  RIGHT 40
  FORWARD 35
  RIGHT 40
  FORWARD 35
  RIGHT 40
END
```

```
TO E3.4
  FORWARD 70
  RIGHT 144
  FORWARD 70
  RIGHT 144
  FORWARD 70
  RIGHT 144
  FORWARD 70
  RIGHT 144
  FORWARD 70
  RIGHT 144
END

TO E3.5.23
  RIGHT 330
  FORWARD 65
  RIGHT 60
  FORWARD 65
  RIGHT 120
  FORWARD 65
  RIGHT 60
  FORWARD 65
  RIGHT 150
END

TO E3.5.24
  FORWARD 75
  RIGHT 70
  FORWARD 55
  RIGHT 110
  FORWARD 75
  RIGHT 70
  FORWARD 55
  RIGHT 110
END

TO E3.5.25
  RIGHT 90
  FORWARD 100
  RIGHT 70
  FORWARD 30
  RIGHT 110
  FORWARD 135
  HOME
END
```

```
TO E3.6A
  FORWARD 70
  RIGHT 130
  FORWARD 85
  HOME
END

TO E3.6B1
  FORWARD 100
  RIGHT 140
  FORWARD 100
  HOME
END

TO E3.6B2
  PENUP
  FORWARD 100
  RIGHT 90
  PENDOWN
  FORWARD 25
  HOME
  PENUP
  FORWARD 100
  RIGHT 270
  PENDOWN
  FORWARD 25
  HOME
END

TO E4.1B
  REPEAT 5 [FORWARD 20 RIGHT 360/5]
END

TO E4.3
  REPEAT 20 [FORWARD 5 RIGHT 360/20]
END

TO E4.4A
  RIGHT 270
  REPEAT 20 [FORWARD 10 RIGHT 360/20]
END

TO E4.4B
  PENUP
  FORWARD 20
```

```
RIGHT 270
FORWARD 30
PENDOWN
REPEAT 20 [FORWARD 10 RIGHT 360/20]
END

TO E4.5
  REPEAT 20 [FORWARD 30*3.14/20 RIGHT 360/20
    FORWARD 30*3.14/20]
END

TO E4.6     (R = 30)
  FORWARD 1
  PENUP
  BACK 30
  RIGHT 270
  PENDOWN
  REPEAT 20 [FORWARD 2*30*3.14/20 RIGHT 360/
    20]
  RIGHT 90
  FORWARD 29
END


TO E4.7
  FORWARD 1
  PENUP
  REPEAT 360 [FORWARD 30 PENDOWN FORWARD 1
    PENUP BACK 31 RIGHT 1]
END


TO E4.7A
  FORWARD 1
  PENUP
  REPEAT 360 [FORWARD 30 PENDOWN RIGHT 90
    FORWARD 1 BACK 1 RIGHT 270 PENUP BACK 30
    RIGHT 1]
END

TO E4.9.40
  REPEAT 10 [FORWARD 30*3.14/20 RIGHT 360/20
    FORWARD 30*3.14/20]
END

TO E4.9.41
  REPEAT 5 [FORWARD 30*3.14/20 RIGHT 360/20
    FORWARD 30*3.14/20]
END
```

```
TO E4.9.42
  REPEAT 60 [FORWARD 30 BACK 30 RIGHT 1]
END

TO E4.9.43
  REPEAT 5 [FORWARD 30*3.14/20 RIGHT 360/20
    FORWARD 30*3.14/20]
  HOME
END

TO E4.9.45
  REPEAT 20 [FORWARD 30*3.14/20 RIGHT 360/20
    FORWARD 30*3.14/20]
  RIGHT 30
  FORWARD 30
END

TO E4.9.46
  REPEAT 20 [FORWARD 30*3.14/20 RIGHT 360/20
    FORWARD 30*3.14/20]
  RIGHT 90
  FORWARD 30 * 2
END

TO E4.9.47
  BACK 30
  RIGHT 270
  BACK 2 * 30 * 3.14 / 20 / 2
  REPEAT 20 [FORWARD 2*30*3.14/20 RIGHT 360/
    20]
END

TO E4.10.48
  REPEAT 20 [FORWARD 2*30*3.14/20 RIGHT 360/
    20]
  BACK 50
  FORWARD 100
END

TO E4.10.49
  REPEAT 20 [FORWARD 2*30*3.14/20 RIGHT 360/
    20]
  RIGHT 60
  BACK 50
  FORWARD 150
END
```

```
TO E4.10.50
  REPEAT 20 [FORWARD 2*30*3.14/20 RIGHT 360/
    20]
  PENUP
  FORWARD 30
  RIGHT 45
  PENDOWN
  BACK 50
  FORWARD 120
END

TO E4.11.51
  REPEAT 20 [FORWARD 2*30*3.14/20 RIGHT 360/
    20]
  RIGHT 90
  PENUP
  FORWARD 10
  RIGHT 270
  PENDOWN
  REPEAT 20 [FORWARD 2*15*3.14/20 RIGHT 360/
    20]
END

TO E4.11.52
  REPEAT 20 [FORWARD 2*30*3.14/20 RIGHT 360/
    20]
  PENUP
  FORWARD 70
  PENDOWN
  REPEAT 20 [FORWARD 2*15*3.14/20 RIGHT 360/
    20]
END

TO E4.11.53
  REPEAT 20 [FORWARD 2*30*3.14/20 RIGHT 360/
    20]
  REPEAT 20 [FORWARD 2*15*3.14/20 RIGHT 360/
    20]
END

TO E4.11.54
  REPEAT 20 [FORWARD 2*30*3.14/20 RIGHT 360/
    20]
  REPEAT 20 [FORWARD 2*15*3.14/20
    RIGHT 360-360/20]
END
```

```
TO E4.11.55
  REPEAT 20 [FORWARD 2*30*3.14/20 RIGHT 360/
    20]
  RIGHT 270
  PENUP
  FORWARD 10
  RIGHT 90
  PENDOWN
  REPEAT 20 [FORWARD 2*15*3.14/20 RIGHT 360/
    20]
END

TO E4.11.56
  REPEAT 20 [FORWARD 2*30*3.14/20 RIGHT 360/
    20]
  RIGHT 90
  PENUP
  FORWARD 30 − 15
  RIGHT 270
  PENDOWN
  REPEAT 20 [FORWARD 2*15*3.14/20 RIGHT 360/
    20]
END

TO E4.12
  REPEAT 36/2 [FORWARD 30*3.14/36 RIGHT 360/
    36 FORWARD 30*3.14/36]
  REPEAT 36/2 [FORWARD 35*3.14/36 RIGHT 360/
    36 FORWARD 35*3.14/36]
  REPEAT 36/2 [FORWARD 40*3.14/36 RIGHT 360/
    36 FORWARD 40*3.14/36]
  REPEAT 36/2 [FORWARD 45*3.14/36 RIGHT 360/
    36 FORWARD 45*3.14/36]
END

TO E4.13
  REPEAT 5 [FORWARD 70 RIGHT 2*360/5]
END

TO E4.14.8
  REPEAT 8 [FORWARD 100 RIGHT 3*360/8]
END

TO E4.14.9
  REPEAT 9 [FORWARD 100 RIGHT 4*360/9]
END
```

```
TO E4.14.10A
  REPEAT 10 [FORWARD 100 RIGHT 3*360/10]
END

TO E4.14.10B
  REPEAT 10 [FORWARD 100 RIGHT 7*360/10]
END

TO E4.14.12
  REPEAT 12 [FORWARD 100 RIGHT 5*360/12]
END

TO E4.14.15A
  REPEAT 15 [FORWARD 100 RIGHT 4*360/15]
END

TO E4.14.15B
  REPEAT 15 [FORWARD 100 RIGHT 7*360/15]
END

TO E4.14.20A
  REPEAT 20 [FORWARD 100 RIGHT 7*360/20]
END

TO E4.14.20B
  REPEAT 20 [FORWARD 100 RIGHT 9*360/20]
END

TO E6.1A
  REPEAT 5 [FORWARD 50 RIGHT 360/5]
  REPEAT 5 [FORWARD 50 LEFT 360/5]
END

TO E6.1B
  REPEAT 5 [FORWARD 70 RIGHT 2*360/5]
  REPEAT 5 [FORWARD 70 RIGHT -2*360/5]
END

TO E6.1C
  REPEAT 5 [FORWARD 70 RIGHT 2*360/5]
  PENUP
  LEFT 90
  FORWARD 30
  RIGHT 90
  PENDOWN
  FORWARD 100
```

```
  BACK 100
  PENUP
  LEFT 90
  FORWARD 30
  RIGHT 90
  PENDOWN
  REPEAT 5 [FORWARD 70 RIGHT -2*360/5]
END

TO E7.1
  REPEAT 5 [FORWARD 70 E4.6 RIGHT 2*360/5]
END

TO E7.2
  E7.1
  BACK 70
  E4.9.41
  RIGHT 90
  E4.9.41
  E4.9.41
  RIGHT 90
  E4.9.41
END

TO E8.1 :SIDE
  REPEAT 4 [FORWARD :SIDE RIGHT 90]
END

TO E8.2 :LENGTH
  REPEAT 2 [FORWARD :LENGTH/2 RIGHT 90
    FORWARD :LENGTH RIGHT 90]
END

TO E8.3 :NUMBER
  REPEAT :NUMBER [FORWARD 30 RIGHT 360/
  :NUMBER]
END

TO E8.4
  E8.1 30
  MOVE.E8.4
  E8.1 50
  MOVE.E8.4
  E8.1 70
  MOVE.E8.4
  E8.1 90
END
```

```
TO MOVE.E8.4
  PENUP
  BACK 10
  RIGHT 90
  BACK 10
  LEFT 90
  PENDOWN
END

TO E8.4A
  E8.4A.SUB 30
  MOVE.E8.4
  E8.4A.SUB 50
  MOVE.E8.4
  E8.4A.SUB 70
END

TO E8.4A.SUB :SIDE
  REPEAT 6 [FORWARD :SIDE RIGHT 60]
END

TO E8.5 :RADIUS
  FORWARD 1
  PENUP
  BACK :RADIUS
  RIGHT 270
  PENDOWN
  REPEAT 36 [FORWARD :RADIUS*3.14/36
    RIGHT 360/36 FORWARD :RADIUS*3.14/36]
  RIGHT 90
  PENUP
  FORWARD :RADIUS - 1
  PENDOWN
END

TO E8.4B
  E8.5 30
  E8.5 50
  E8.5 70
  E8.5 90
END

TO E8.6A :RADIUS
  FORWARD 1
  PENUP
  BACK :RADIUS
  RIGHT 270
  PENDOWN
```

```
  REPEAT 18 [FORWARD :RADIUS*3.14/36
    RIGHT 360/36 FORWARD :RADIUS*3.14/36]
  RIGHT 90
  PENUP
  FORWARD :RADIUS + 1
  PENDOWN
  RIGHT 180
END

TO E8.6B :RADIUS
  REPEAT 18 [FORWARD :RADIUS*3.14/36
    RIGHT 360/36 FORWARD :RADIUS*3.14/36]
END

TO E8.6C:RADIUS
  REPEAT  9  [FORWARD   :RADIUS*3.14/36   RIGHT
    360/36 FORWARD :RADIUS*3.14/36]
END

TO E8.7 :ANGLE
  LEFT :ANGLE / 2
  REPEAT 2 [FORWARD 70
    RIGHT (180-(360-2*:ANGLE)/2)
    FORWARD 70 RIGHT 180-:ANGLE]
  RIGHT :ANGLE / 2
END

TO E8.7A
  E8.7 60
  E8.7 80
  E8.7 100
  E8.7 130
END

TO E8.8 :ANGLE
  RIGHT :ANGLE - 90
  FORWARD 50
  RIGHT 360 - 2 * :ANGLE
  FORWARD 50
  HOME
END

TO E8.8A
  E8.8 100
  E8.8 115
```

```
    E8.8 130
    E8.8 160
END

TO E9.1 :NUMBER :SIDE
   REPEAT :NUMBER [FORWARD :SIDE
     RIGHT 360/ :NUMBER]
END

TO E9.2 :ANGLE :SIDE
   LEFT :ANGLE / 2
   REPEAT 2 [FORWARD :SIDE
     RIGHT (180-(360-2* :ANGLE)/ 2)
     FORWARD :SIDE RIGHT 180- :ANGLE]
   RIGHT :ANGLE / 2
END

TO E9.2A
   E9.2 70 40
   E9.2 100 55
   E9.2 130 80
END

TO E9.3 :HEIGHT :BASE
   PENUP
   BACK :HEIGHT
   RIGHT 90
   PENDOWN
   FORWARD :BASE / 2
   HOME
   PENUP
   BACK :HEIGHT
   LEFT 90
   PENDOWN FORWARD :BASE / 2
   HOME
END

TO E9.3A
   E9.3 20 50
   E9.3 40 60
   E9.3 60 70
   E9.3 90 80
END

TO E9.4 :NUMBER :CYCLES
   REPEAT :NUMBER [FORWARD 50
     RIGHT :CYCLES*360/ :NUMBER]
END
```

```
TO E10.2 :ANGLE :SIDE
  FORWARD :SIDE
  RIGHT :ANGLE
  E10.2 :ANGLE :SIDE
END

TO E10.3 :ANGLE :HOOK
  FORWARD 50
  RIGHT :ANGLE
  FORWARD :HOOK
  RIGHT :ANGLE / 2
  E10.3 :ANGLE :HOOK
END

TO E10.3A :ANGLE :HOOK
  FORWARD 50
  RIGHT :ANGLE
  FORWARD :HOOK
  RIGHT :ANGLE
  E10.3A :ANGLE :HOOK
END

TO E10.5
  E4.3
  E4.13
  LEFT 60
  E10.5
END

TO E10.5A
  E4.3
  LEFT 25
  E10.5A
END

TO E10.6
  E4.3
  LEFT 90
  FORWARD 10
  RIGHT 30
  E10.6
END

TO E10.6A
  E4.13
  LEFT 50
```

```
     FORWARD 50
     E10.6A
END

TO E10.7
     E4.12
     FORWARD 30
     E10.7
END

TO PENTAGON
     REPEAT 5 [FORWARD 50 RIGHT 360/5]
END

TO E10.7A
     PENTAGON
     FORWARD 20
     E10.7A
END

TO E10.7B
     LEFT 90
     E10.7A
END

TO E10.7C :NUMBER
     E8.3 :NUMBER
     FORWARD 20
     E10.7C :NUMBER
END

TO E11.1 :SIDE
     FULLSCREEN
     E8.1 :SIDE
     PENUP LEFT 90 FORWARD 10 RIGHT 90 BACK 10
     PENDOWN
     E11.1 :SIDE + 20
END

TO E11.2
     DRAW
     FULLSCREEN
     PENUP BACK 120 PENDOWN
     SUB.E11.2 42
END
```

```
TO SUB.E11.2 :SIDE
  E8.1 :SIDE
  FORWARD :SIDE RIGHT 90 FORWARD 4.2 / 2
  LEFT 90
  SUB.E11.2 :SIDE - 4.2
END

TO E11.3 :SIDE
  FORWARD :SIDE RIGHT 360 / 5
  E11.3 :SIDE + 5
END

TO E11.4 :SIDE
  FORWARD :SIDE RIGHT 69
  E11.4 :SIDE + 1
END

TO E11.5 :SIDE :INCR
  FORWARD :SIDE RIGHT 360 / 5
  E11.5 :SIDE + :INCR :INCR
END

TO E11.6 :SIDE
  FORWARD :SIDE RIGHT 360 / 5
  E11.6 :SIDE * 1.1
END

TO E11.6A :SIDE
  FORWARD :SIDE RIGHT 360 / 5
  E11.6A :SIDE * 0.9
END

TO E11.7 :ANGLE
  FULLSCREEN
  FORWARD 20 RIGHT :ANGLE
  E11.7 :ANGLE + 10
END

TO E12.1
  DRAW
  FULLSCREEN
  PENUP BACK 120 PENDOWN
  SUB.E12.1 42
  HIDETURTLE
END
```

```
TO SUB.E12.1 :SIDE
  E8.1 :SIDE
  FORWARD :SIDE RIGHT 90 FORWARD 4.2 / 2
  LEFT 90
  IF :SIDE < 4.2 STOP
  SUB.E12.1 :SIDE - 4.2
END


TO E12.2
  DRAW
  FULLSCREEN
  SUB.E12.2 10
  HIDETURTLE
END


TO SUB.E12.2 :COUNT
  IF :COUNT = 0 STOP
  FORWARD 30
  RIGHT 36
  SUB.E12.2 :COUNT - 1
END


TO E12.3A :ANGLE
  FORWARD 100
  RIGHT :ANGLE
  IF HEADING = 0 STOP
  E12.3A :ANGLE
END


TO E12.3B :ANGLE
  CLEARSCREEN
  FULLSCREEN
  SETHEADING 0
  E12.3A :ANGLE
  HIDETURTLE
END


TO E12.3C :ANGLE
  CLEARSCREEN
  FULLSCREEN
  E12.3C.SUB :ANGLE HEADING
  HIDETURTLE
END
```

```
TO E12.3C.SUB :ANGLE :START
  FORWARD 100
  RIGHT :ANGLE
  IF HEADING = :START STOP
  E12.3C.SUB :ANGLE :START
END

TO E12.4 :COUNT
  IF :COUNT = 0 STOP
  E12.4 :COUNT - 1
END

TO E13.1
  PRINT1 RANDOM 7
  E13.1
END

TO E13.2
  E8.5 RANDOM 50
  PENUP
  RIGHT RANDOM 360
  FORWARD 40 + RANDOM 30
  PENDOWN
  E13.2
END

TO E14.1A
  REPEAT 9 [FORWARD 40*3.14/36  RIGHT  :SYM*
    360/36 FORWARD 40*3.14/36]
END

TO E14.1
  REPEAT 5 [FORWARD 70 RIGHT (2*360/5)*:SYM]
END

TO E14.2
  MAKE "SYM 1
  REPEAT 2 [E14.1 BACK 50 E14.1A PENUP HOME
    MAKE "SYM ( — 1 ) PENDOWN]
END

TO E14.3B
  REPEAT 9 [FORWARD 20*:SCALE
    RIGHT (2*360/9)*:SYM]
END
```

```
TOP E14.3A
  REPEAT 7 [FORWARD 20*:SCALE
    RIGHT (2*360/7)*:SYM]
END

TO E14.3
  REPEAT 5 [FORWARD 20 *:SCALE
    RIGHT (2*360/5)*:SYM]
END

TO E14.3C
  LEFT 90 PENUP FORWARD 120 RIGHT 90 BACK 125
  PENDOWN FULLSCREEN
  MAKE "SYM 1
  MAKE "SCALE 1
  REPEAT  3  [E14.3  PENUP  FORWARD  27*:SCALE
    PENDOWN
    E14.3A   PENUP   FORWARD   33*:SCALE   PENDOWN
    E14.3B
    PENUP BACK 60*:SCALE RIGHT 90
    FORWARD 60*:SCALE LEFT 90 PENDOWN
    MAKE "SCALE :SCALE+1]
END

TO SUB.E14.4 :ANGLE
  FORWARD 100
  RIGHT :ANGLE
  IF HEADING = :START STOP
  SUB.E14.4 :ANGLE
END

TO E14.4 :ANGLE
  MAKE "START HEADING
  SUB.E14.4 :ANGLE

TO E15.1 :SIZE
  IF :SIZE < 5 STOP
  RIGHT 45
  FORWARD :SIZE
  E15.1 :SIZE / 2
  BACK :SIZE
  LEFT 90
  FORWARD :SIZE
  E15.1 :SIZE / 2
  BACK :SIZE
  RIGHT 45
END
```

```
TO E15.2 :SIZE
  IF :SIZE < 5 STOP
  RIGHT 45
  FORWARD :SIZE
  E12.4 50
  E15.2 :SIZE / 2
  BACK :SIZE
  LEFT 90
  FORWARD :SIZE
  E12.4 50
  E15.2 :SIZE / 2
  BACK :SIZE
  RIGHT 45
END

TO E15.9 :SIDE
  IF :SIDE < 10 STOP
  REPEAT 4 [FD :SIDE LT 90 E15.9 :SIDE/2 RT
  180]
END

TO E15.10
  BK 35 LT 90 FD 60 RT 90 CS FULLSCREEN
  SUB.E15.10 71
  HT
END

TO SUB.E15.10 :SIDE
  IF :SIDE < 3 STOP
  REPEAT 5 [FORWARD :SIDE LEFT 110
    SUB.E15.10 :SIDE/2.5 RIGHT 110+72]
END

TO E15.11
  DRAW
  BK 35 LT 90 FD 60 RT 90 CS FULLSCREEN
  SUB.E15.11 71
  HT
END

TO SUB.E15.11 :SIDE
  IF :SIDE < 9 STOP
  REPEAT 5 [FORWARD :SIDE LEFT 40
    SUB.E15.11 :SIDE/2.5 RIGHT 40+144]
END
```

```
TO E16.1
  PENUP
  SETXY 23 12
  PENDOWN
  SETX 65
  SETXY 51 73
  SETXY 23 12
END

TO E16.2
  PENUP
  SETXY ( - 33 ) ( - 15 )
  PENDOWN
  SETXY 54 ( - 8 )
  SETXY 46 38
  SETXY ( - 52 ) 65
  SETXY ( - 33 ) ( - 15 )
END

TO E16.3
  PU SETXY 10 20 PD
  SETX 50
  SETY YCOR + ( 50 - 10 )
  SETX XCOR - ( 50 - 10 )
  SETXY 10 20
END

TO E16.4
  FULLSCREEN
  PENUP
  SETXY ( - 160 ) 0
  PENDOWN
  DOTX 1
  REPEAT 6 [MARKX DOTX 5]
  MARKX DOTX 1
  PENUP
  SETXY 0 ( - 130 )
  PENDOWN
  DOTY 3
  REPEAT 4 [MARKY DOTY 5]
  MARKY DOTY 3
  HOME HT
END

TO MARKX
  SETY - 3
```

```
   SETY 3
   SETY 0
END

TO MARKY
  SETX - 3
  SETX 3
  SETX 0
END

TO DOTX :N
  REPEAT :N [SETY 1 SETY 0 SETX XCOR +10]
END

TO DOTY :N
  REPEAT :N [SETX 1 SETX 0 SETY YCOR +10]
END

TO E16.6
  CALL [:X]
END

TO CALL :Y
  DRAW
  E16.4
  PLOT 0 1
  PENUP
  HOME
  PENDOWN
  PLOT 0 ( - 1 )
END

TO PLOT :X :F
  IF :X * :F > 158 STOP
  IF (RUN :Y)*(RUN :Y) > 128*128 STOP
  SETXY :X ( RUN :Y )
  PLOT ( :X + :F ) :F
END

TO E16.8 :M
  CALL [:M*:X]
END

TO E16.9 :B
  CALL [:X+:B]
END
```

```
TO E16.10 :M :B
  CALL [:M*:X+:B]
END

TO E16.11
  CALL [:X*:X]
END

TO E16.12 :M
  CALL [:M * :X * :X]
END

TO E16.13 :M :A :B
  CALL [:M * (:X — :A)*(:X — :A) + :B]
END

TO E16.14
  CALL50 [:X*:X]
END

TO CALL50 :Y
  DRAW
  E16.4
  PLOT50 0 1
  PENUP
  HOME
  PENDOWN
  PLOT50 0 ( - 1 )
END

TO PLOT50 :X :F
  IF :X * 50 * :F > 158 STOP
  IF (RUN :Y)*(RUN :Y)*2500 > 128*128 STOP
  SETXY50 :X ( RUN :Y )
  PLOT50 ( :X + :F / 50 ) :F
END

TO SETXY50 :X :Y
  SETXY :X * 50 :Y * 50
END

TO E16.15
  DRAW
  E16.4
  PENUP
  PLOT.15 ( 50 / 128 ) 1
```

```
  PENUP
  PLOT.15 ( - 50 / 128 ) ( - 1 )
END

TO PLOT.15 :X :F
  IF :X * :F * 50 > 158 STOP
  SETXY50 :X ( 1 / :X ) PD
  PLOT.15 ( :X + :F / 50 ) :F
END

TO E16.16 :R
  DRAW
  E16.4
  PLOT.16 0 1
  PLOT.16 0 ( - 1 )
END

TO PLOT.16 :X :F
  IF ( :R * :R - :X * :X ) < 1 STOP
  SETXY :X ( SQRT ( :R * :R - :X * :X ) )
  PLOT.16 ( :X + :F ) :F
  SETXY :X ((-1)*SQRT(:R*:R - :X*:X))
END
```

IV. BASIC AND COMPUTER ARCHITECTURE WITH PACS

a. Idea and Purpose of the Material

The Paper Computer Simulator (PACS) is designed to give the student an experience of "how a computer works inside." It has many purposes: Living in a world where computers are so omnipresent, it is necessary that we understand what they do, that they are no magic, that they are normal machines set to action by man.

To understand their capacities and limits, one must understand their functioning, rather than just how to push the buttons.

That cannot be done with the real computer from the beginning because it works too fast and the important part of the process is hidden within the black box. Just explaining how it works inside is of little help for a child. Children need to understand by doing.

The basic idea with this material is to put the children into the role of being the computer, to give them the opportunity to experience step by step the functioning of that machine. Thus, it also is based on the principle of avoiding confronting students with tasks they cannot yet handle, but rather providing preparing exercises—a principle applied in many Montessori materials.

While working through certain programs, students experience what sequence of steps the computer has to perform with each command and which functions the different parts have, such as ROM, RAM, the calculator, the central processing unit, and the screen.

The material then provides suggestions for producing one's own little programs at the keyboard, and thus guides students to the point where they can program according to their own ideas.

The material also uses the fascination of computing to teach other basic skills, such as

—practicing and improving reading and writing
—comprehending written information with precision
—following directions precisely
—practicing arithmetic skills
—understanding priorities in math terms ($+$ after $\times$, after $(\ )$.)
—understanding the concept of variables (preliminary introduction for later algebra studies)
—using x and y coordinates
—understanding the functions of the parts of a computer, such as the different memories, the calculator, the central processing unit, and last but not least,
—programming a computer.

The PACS uses BASIC computer language. BASIC was developed under J. Kemeny and T. Kurtz at Dartmouth College. Today, modified versions are used in most personal computers. PACS mostly uses original BASIC in its simplest version, thus, the programs in this material should run on real computers. Some commands need adaptation to the system on hand. Not all BASIC commands are introduced. The emphasis is placed on understanding of the basic pattern of programs. Therefore, f.e. loops are programmed initially by really counting up a variable and going back after an IF decision. More commands and more convenient ways of programming may be introduced in the level II of this manual.

b. Teacher's Manual

The Levels of the Work with the Student:

Level I   a) Introducing the material (lesson of the teacher).
          b) Working through Programs 1 to 27 (with occasional help from the teacher).
          c) Working on assignments, creating own programs, on a real computer if available. This step may also be done on paper, but then it needs frequent checking by the teacher and is less stimulating.

Level II: Introducing further commands and techniques, such as READ-DATA, FOR-NEXT, ON-GOTO, subscripted variables, subroutines, and so forth. This is done by introducing each on the PACS with an extended ROM card set, and then practicing with assignments on a real computer.

Introduction of the Material by the Teacher:

1. A Simple Introduction to Computers

"A computer deals with numbers and letters. It represents numbers with help of wires and switches.[14] (Letters are coded as numbers inside the computer, just as you set forth a secret code.)"

I go to the lightswitch, which in our classroom has two switches for two sets of ceiling lights. I switch on one set of lights: "Let's assume this represents the number 1."

I turn off this set and on the other one:
"This may represent the number 2."
"What would this be then?"
I switch on both.
"1 + 2 = 3!, so we can represent four numbers here (including the 0) and we can do simple math operations.
What then would this represent?"
(I turn all lights off).
"It is 0." I repeat and practice a little, adding and subtracting with numbers 0 to 3.

"A computer has many more switches, so it can represent and handle many and higher numbers. The switches are not mechanical like these, but are transistors, which can be turned on and off by other switches."

(This may be discussed on other occasions with a logical model of a wire-switch-adding network. But at this moment, I don't go into more details. The objective of this introduction is to understand that a computer represents numbers and letters by switches and wires, and that it builds up sophisticated actions by adding many very simple elements to each other.)

2. Introducing the Material

While the previous short presentation may be given to a group of children, the following introduction of the material (sections 2 through 5) is given to one child. We assume that child is Jenny:
"This material simulates a computer. It has all the important parts:

- The ROM (Read Only Memory) holds the commands. They are built in and cannot be changed, only read.
- The RAM (Random Access Memory) stores numbers or statements. (We will see later what a statement is.)

---

[14] Relate to the study with the "Electronic Circuits" material, see section II this chapter.

- The calculator, to perform math calculations, will be explained when it is to be used.
- The screen is the device that either the computer may 'print' on or the operator may 'type' on, each of them using a single box for each character.
- And the most important: The Central Processing Unit (CPU), which will be YOU, Jenny."

I give Jenny the sign to hang around her neck.

"The CPU is not smart, as you are, but it is very precise! It does not remember procedures, therefore, it has to look them up in the ROM. But it performs them precisely as written there, without thinking ahead or thinking at all."

3. Let's Start

I write the Program 1 on the screen and place the card ENTER in front of Jenny.

"ENTER is the first command for the computer to perform. Go to the ROM where all the commands are stored in alphabetical order; there you find ENTER. Read and do what it says!" (See ROM cards in section c.4)

I stay with the student and help along with this first program, but only tying her down to reading one sentence at a time, considering it and performing accordingly.

Now, a few words of advice for the teacher in a bit more detail: It looks confusing when written, but when done step by step, it will become clear and easy.

First, a word of clarification: There are two papers saying ENTER: the small card (ticket) ENTER represents the key on a computer keyboard and is used by the operator. The ROM card ENTER explains what the computer should do and is used by the computer only. When the student reads the ROM card ENTER, this explanation is necessary:

"A line number is the number in front of a program line. The program lines (= statements) are stored in the order of their line numbers. The purpose of a line number is to be a means of identification that the computer can use in searching for and then finding a certain program line."

When coming to the end of the ROM card ENTER, the student places the prompt (the sign)) on the screen. This sign is drawn on purpose on the back of the ticket ENTER:

"The ENTER key (which is represented by the ticket in PACS) or the 'prompt' makes all the difference: If the ENTER key is pushed (ticket shows the word ENTER), it's the *computer's turn*. The operator cannot do anything then. If the prompt is on the screen (ticket shows the sign)), it's the *operator's turn;* the computer does nothing."

4. Let's RUN Program 1

"The program is now in the computer's memory. We will now make it execute that program:"

I write RUN on the screen and turn the ticket to show ENTER.

I expect the student (or help her) to get the ENTER card from the ROM and to decide, per instruction on the card, that she then has to get the card RUN.

"We cannot have two cards out at the same time. The computer would never do that. In fact, it would not even remove any storage element, but only look at it. However, it cannot look at two commands at a time. Now we need to work on RUN before we have finished with ENTER. Therefore, let's mark ENTER: Since we are working on 2B on the card ENTER, we mark that on the upper right corner, where it says 'working on 2B' with paperclip 1."

(The clips should have numbers or colors indicating a sequence. The clips are referred to as "markers" in the command texts.)

"In the same way, if you work on a command card and you have to come back to it after working on other cards, then you should mark that card with the next clip (the computer has a special memory to know where it has to come back to)."

"Now go from the card ENTER in the ROM to the card RUN."

There, Jenny will discover that she now has to pull out the first statement from the RAM and, according to that, has to get the card CLS from the ROM. But before the child can do that, she will need to mark the place on the card RUN with clip 2 and return that card to the ROM in the same way with the card ENTER. I will have to watch that the child, after finishing the CLS statement and having returned that card to the ROM, goes back to the unfinished card RUN.

With the first use of the PRINT command 1, explain the following: "Printing for PACS always means printing on the screen. Our paper simulator has some slips to write on, but in the real computer, there are only wires and switches. So printing never means writing within the computer, but printing on the screen for the operator to read."

At the end of a PRINT statement, there may be no sign. The directions on the card PRINT say "move for next print item to the beginning of the next line." Here I suggest:

"We don't know when the next PRINT will come about. So let's just mark the next line with a dot. The real computer puts a little dash where it will print text. That dash is called the 'cursor.' "

Occasionally, I show the cursor on the real computer.

After finishing the PRINT statement, the student will be advised by card RUN now to pull the next statement from the RAM. At the same time, she should put back the statement just finished.

The last statement in Program 1 is END. Sometimes it is necessary to mention that this does not mean to stop working, but is a command of its own. Therefore, the child has to get out the ROM card END and carry out what it says.

This first program is in fact the most important step in understanding the computer's way of working: to rely on the memory in ROM or RAM only and therefore be forced to look up each step and bit of information, even if the same step was executed just minutes ago. So, for example, the card RUN has to be pulled and looked at each time a statement is done, just to learn from that card that now you have to take the next statement.

After working through this first program, Jenny may go to the real computer, type in the same program and RUN it.[15] I make her aware that now the roles are reversed: she acts as the operator while the computer's performance is hidden inside and completed in an instant. She may run other programs on the real computer after working them through on PACS; but may not make program changes yet. That is to come only after a solid experience is gained through the 27 programs.

5. *Points to be Introduced During the Further Work*

a) Repeat:

"A computer is not smart. It only follows step-by-step commands, but does that precisely without understanding more than the present step."

(Especially with PRINT, check the correct interpretation of the comma and semicolon.)

"If you were Jenny, as you used to be, we know you were pretty smart. But now you are the CPU. The CPU has no memory but has to look up everything in the ROM and RAM. (In fact, the CPU does have a few memory elements, but just enough to keep one sentence from a ROM card and one statement from the RAM, and only for the time it works on it. Therefore, the CPU must look up each sentence again in the ROM.) It's the rule of this game that you have to act like that."

b) With Program 2, explain:

"A variable is a number that has a name in order to identify it and to find it in the memory. We use single letters as names for such variables. The number itself is called 'the value of the variable.' A variable may change its value: If the number of students in our class is the variable N, it may have the value 25 today. Tomorrow, if 2 are absent, it would have the value 23, but still be the number N."

c) "It says on the ROM card, LET 'assign value to variable.' That is really a heading for all that you do there: You must *find* that value (#2 on the card), then *write* it on a RAM variable card and thus *store* it in the RAM

---

[15] PAC's Dialect of BASIC is closest to the TRS 80's. Other systems need replacements in certain program lines, which the teacher should prepare ahead of time.

(#3). Use different cards for string variables, subscripted variables, and simple variables (those for numbers only)."

d) With any entry into cards, the rule is to erase first any old entries:

"The computer doesn't clean up after its work is done, but before working in a certain part. The reason is that something may have been messing up since the last work and therefore the cleaning job has to be done anyhow before entering any new information. So we may do the same; not erasing after our work, but during the work before doing any new entry."

e) Program 3 cannot be stored in the RAM because it includes a five-digit-line number, while only 4 boxes are provided on the RAM statement card. Emphasize on this occasion:

"The boxes on the slips are absolutely the only places to write on! This is to emphasize that in a computer a number or letter can only be placed where there is a place provided by switches and wires. In our PACS, we have boxes instead."

If Jenny does not find the solution to program 3, help her. "Since a five-digit number cannot be stored, we have to perform ERROR. Get the card ERROR from the ROM and do what it says there."

With programs 4 and 5, the students then should discover the need to perform ERROR on their own by following the directions on the card RUN.

f) Occasionally introduce the commands BREAK and CONT (meaning continue): Jenny should never leave her work while working through a program. If there is any need to do so, place the ticket BREAK in front of her and insist that the card BREAK be looked up in the ROM and executed. After she comes back to the work, write CONT on the screen and push ENTER.

g) With a short program, introduce LIST (which is not used in any of the program cards): If there is a mistake in the student's RAM statement cards, push BREAK and after she has turned the prompt up, write LIST and push ENTER. But even without having introduced that, LIST is learned fast with the work on assignments.

h) "The calculator works just like the little electronic calculators you use. Our simulator uses paper cards instead, providing the boxes for the operations $+$, $-$, $\times$, $\div$, which are carried out on these slips as usual."

Direct the student to follow ROM card $\boxed{+ - */=}$

"Unfortunately, computer engineers decided to use other signs for math operations than the ones we use in school. The simple reason is to prevent confusion (x for "ex" or for "times", 0 for "zero" or for the "letter 0"), and to use normal keyboards, which have no division sign ($\div$). Thus, the times sign is the starlet (*); the division sign is the oblique fraction line (/); and the zero has a diagonal line in it (∅)."

i) With more than one math sign (as in long math terms), we suggest a compromise: Develop the expression as usual on a separate notepaper, line by line, but do all single calculations on the provided cards in the calculator section. The real computer would store away the partial answers as variables, but that turned out to be confusing for the student.

j) With the first IF command (program 7), check on the correct use of the card $\boxed{\langle\ \rangle\ =}$ in the calculator. Here, as in all calculator cards, the boxes are filled, as the information flows: the variable values, after they are looked up in the RAM; the answer after the operation is carried out; (with the IF card, the answer is to check either box "true" or "false").

k) Program 8 prints a wrong birth year (line 12o), if the birthday of the current year is still to come. Be ready to explain that. Also, line 16o should use the past tense, if a person is older than 21. Changes would be a nice task for older students, with lots of IF commands.

l) Program 21 says "ask for the story!" A short account of the "Story of the Checkerboard" is included as Section 9. It may be embellished during the telling of the story.

m) Each program shows a certain basic pattern. After working through a program, some patterns should be discussed and brought to consciousness: the different branches after IF commands, the three elements of a loop (counting, doing, and going back), and so forth. The programs and assignments should be done in numerical order. Some of the math programs 11 to 13 are not absolutely necessary for understanding program patterns, but rather use the fascination of "computering" to practice arithmetic.

n) After certain steps of the work have been completed, shortcuts may be taken:

- First, programs are to be worked precisely as introduced.
- Shortcut after program 2—The teacher doesn't write the program on the screen, but the student may consider the printed program as written on the screen.
- Shortcut after program 14 or earlier—The student doesn't copy the program on the slips in the RAM, but takes the printed card and slides it into the RAM (pretending it has been loaded from a cassette).
- Shortcut after program 13—Simple additions, like $A = A + 1$, may be done without calculator card in the mind only. But make sure the result is stored as the new variable in the RAM.

o) With several variables used in loops such as programs 19 and 20, variable values may be noted on one paper in a way that makes it easier to trace the

flow of the program: Each variable has a column; each line represents one
work through the loop. In program 18, that would appear as follows:

D	R	A	C	(= names of variables)
8	3	0	0	
		8	1	LOOP 1
		16	2	LOOP 2
		24	3	LOOP 3

This technique may always be used in tracing other programs, even one's
own programs if they need tracing when hunting for bugs.

p) If the programs are typed into a real computer, little changes may be
necessary:

- Loops are very short for PACS, because it takes so much time to perform
  them. The real computer may run them more often;
- The screen has other measures; the limits for X and Y can therefore be
  larger;
- In RND, numbers used in the PACS may be too large;
- The final print READY may destroy the graphic that the program produced; in that case, replace the END command by a GOTO to the own
  line number.

q) When working on the real computer with assignments, there has to be
an organization to save half-finished programs on cassettes or disk. Details
depend on the used system.

r) Working with diagrams may be explained with assignment 6. Rectan-
gular boxes contain actions in the program, diamond boxes contain IF questions. One box in the diagram may need several statements in the program.
The purpose of the diagram is to free you from writing statements in the
first level of work. The diagram focuses on the given problem. Its realization
in program statements is then a second step.

s) "When working on assignments, make it a habit to keep notes on what
variables you used. Otherwise, in long programs you may use the same variable
twice."

6. Level II

a) You may now bring out the ROM cards of DATA, DIM, FOR, GOSUB,
INT, NEXT, READ, RETURN, ON-GOTO, the subscripted variables cards,
and the programs and assignments with No. II. In this step, each program
on PACS is followed by an assignment on the real computer.

b) The PACS material is open ended. In level II, you may add on more commands, programs, and assignments. The BASIC version of your system may offer possibilities you may want to introduce if the student's own program ideas call for it. The use of external memories (tape, disc) has to be taught according to your system. You may also have realized that some commands are not explained with all their possibilities. You might want to extend in that respect, too.

7. *Training the Teacher*

Workshop experience shows that the same material can be used by teachers without any computer experience to introduce themselves to programming. Be aware of this.

a) In working alone with the PACS, you combine both the operator's and the computer's work in yourself. Keep clear and precise in your mind which function you are performing. The ENTER ticket is your signal: If ENTER is up, you are the computer; if the prompt is up (⟩), you are the operator. (For the children, this difficulty does not exist, because they are always the computer, which is told step-by-step what to do!).

b) Adults have more difficulties in merely following the step-by-step routine. Be very precise in the beginning. Take out the ROM card, even if you think you know what it says; perform each line on it; do not think ahead.

c) You might want to take shortcuts earlier. Be sure at least to visualize all steps in detail, especially those you are not doing with your hands. The first four programs should really be done without shortcuts.

d) Be patient with yourself: None of the new information is really difficult. Only the amount of new concepts may need certain time until you feel comfortable with it.

c) Working to the end of the PACS material should enable you to read and understand the manual of your computer and thus expand your skills beyond PACS.

f) For the work in the classroom, no perfect computer specialist is needed. The teacher does not need to know very much beyond the PACS material, except the usage of cassette tapes or disc memories.

g) For further studies, Herbert Peckham's "BASIC"[16] and "Computer Literacy,"[17] both hands-on approaches, were found helpful.

---

[16] Herbert D. Peckham, *BASIC, a Hands-on Method,* (New York: McGraw-Hill Book Co, 1981).

[17] Arthur Luehrmann-Herbert Peckham *Computer Literacy, a Hands-on Approach,* (New York: McGraw-Hill Book Co, 1980).

8. *Reference List of Commands*

BASIC comes in dialects, so not all commands are the same or have the same format in each computer. Check your manual!

Commands used in PACS are as follows:

a) the same in most machines (although some commands may have additional features):

		Examples:
CONT	continues the program after a break.	—
DIM	specifies the size of an array, represented by a subscripted variable.	DIM X$(15)
END	marks the end of a program, stops execution.	
FOR	starts a loop.	FOR X=1 TO 9
NEXT	checks and goes back to last FOR.	NEXT X
GOSUB	goes to subroutine.	GOSUB 2oo
RETURN	returns from subroutine to main progr.	RETURN
GOTO	goes to other line.	GOTO 30
IF – THEN	conditional branch.	IF X=9 THEN 30
INPUT	waits for input from keyboard.	INPUT X$
INT	takes the integer part of a number.	INT (19/3)
LET	assigns a value to a variable.	LET X=9
LIST	displays the program.	—
ON – GOTO	goes to different lines, according to the number after ON.	ON X GOTO 30,40,50
PRINT	prints on the screen: Values of variables, whatever is in " ", results of math operations.	PRINT "Hello";X$
print dividers:	Semicolon: next print item in same line, comma: next print item in next column, nothing: next print item in next line.	
READ	assigns next DATA to given variable.	READ A$,A,B$
DATA	holds data to be read by READ.	DATA Tom,9,May
REM	performs nothing, informs the programmer.	—
RUN	starts the program to run.	

b) mostly different in other computers:

BREAK	a key to stop a running program.	
CLS	clears the screen.	
ENTER	a key, enters the previously typed line into the memory and returns the cursor to the beginning of the next line; causes commands to be executed.	

(Some computers call this key RETURN)

ERROR	an output, if the computer cannot execute a command.	
RND(X)	generates a random number between 0 and X.	RND(6)
SET(X,Y)	colors the square indicated by X and Y.	SET(12,23)
RESET(X,Y)	clears the square indicated by X and Y.	RESET(12,23)

c) As an example; when running PACS programs on Commodore 64, use these replacements:

Commands in PACS	For Commodore 64, replace by:	
BREAK key	RUN/STOP key	
CLS	PRINT "{CLR/HOME}"	(instead of {} press these keys: SHIFT – CLR/HOME)
ENTER key	RETURN key	
RND(X)	INT(X * RND(1) + 1)	
SET(X,Y)	POKE 1024 + X + 40*Y , 160	{X may run 0 to 39
RESET(X,Y)	POKE 1024 + X + 40*Y , 32	{Y may run 0 to 24
replace line numbers in program 3:		
9999	63999	
10000	64000	

9. The Story of the Checkerboard

This is the story mentioned in Program 21:

When Sissa Ibn Dahir had invented the checkerboard game for his king, the king was so delighted that he said: "Ask for any favor; whatever you ask shall be granted."

Sissa Ibn Dahir modestly said, "Mighty King! Give me one wheat kernel for the first square of my checkerboard, two kernels for the second square, four kernels for the third square, and so on. Always double the amount for the next square. That wheat shall be my reward."

The king was angry because he felt that Sissa Ibn Dahir didn't hold the royal riches in very high esteem. Nevertheless, he called the vizir and told him to hand over the wheat to Sissa Ibn Dahir. The vizir, however, returned, pale as he stuttered, "Mighty King! All the wheat in the kingdom would not be enough to cover even *half* of that checkerboard."

This is the story. PACS will figure out Sissa Ibn Dahir's reward. The student may then explore the weight of these wheat kernels and compare it to wheat production in the modern world.

How many years would it take to fill that checkerboard? The answer should be approximately 1000 years. Probably that much wheat has never been produced on earth. The checkerboard game was surely the highest paid invention ever—*if* the story is true!

c. The Material
  Designs ready to copy

  1. Screen

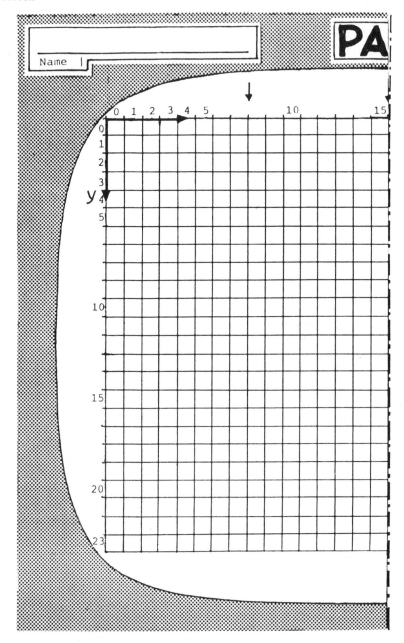

Figure C.17a.

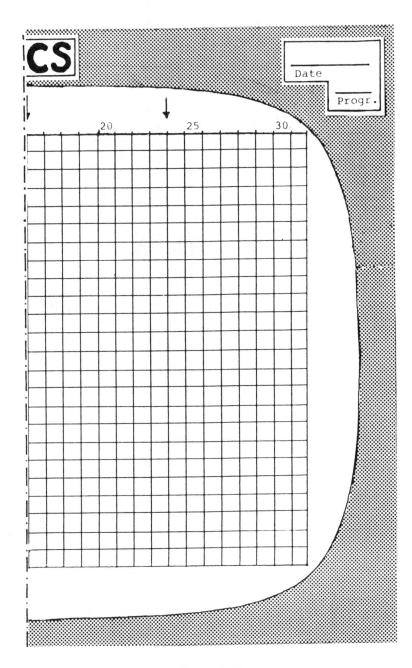

Figure C.17b.

```
.YKEYKEYKEYKEYKEYKEYKEYK.
YKEYKEYKEYKEYKEYKEYKEYKEY
KEYKE ┌─────────────┐ YKEYK
EYKEY │    ENTER    │ KEYKE
YKEYK └─────────────┘ EYKEY
KEYKEYKEYKEYKEYKEYKEYKEYK
`YKEYKEYKEYKEYKEYKEYKEYK`
```

```
.YKEYKEYKEYKEYKEYKEYKEY.
CYKEYKEYKEYKEYKEYKEYKEYKE
YKEYK ┌─────────────┐ EYKEY
KEYKE │    BREAK    │ YKEYK
EYKEY └─────────────┘ KEYKE
YKEYKEYKEYKEYKEYKEYKEYKEY
`CYKEYKEYKEYKEYKEYKEYKEY`
```

```
rACSPACSPACSPACSPACSPAC.
CSPACSPACSPACSPACSPACSPAC
ACSPA ┌─────────────┐ ACSPA
PACSP │    PACS     │ PACSP
SPACS └─────────────┘ SPACS
CSPACSPACSPACSPACSPACSPAC
CSPACSPACSPACSPACSPACSP`
```

Figure C.18.

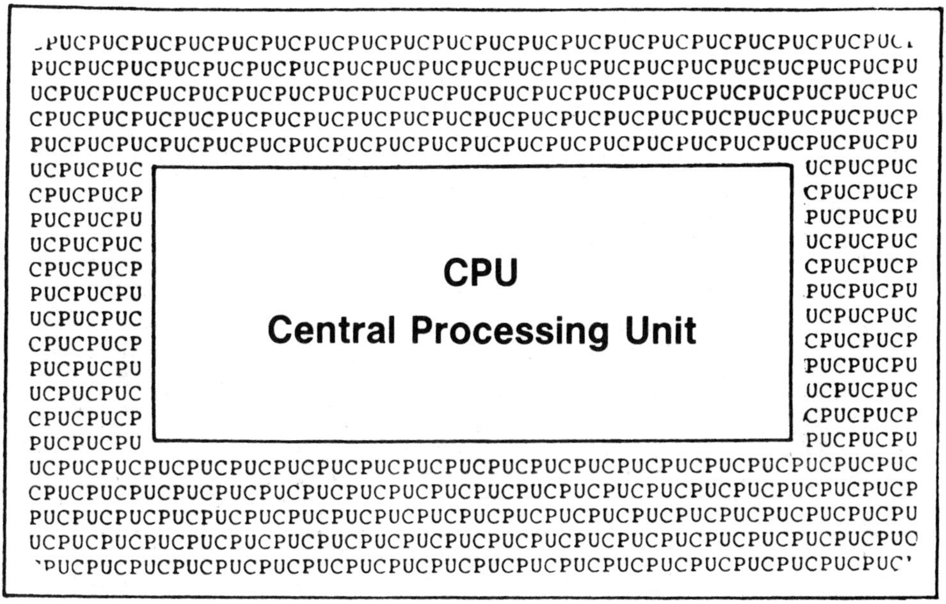

Figure C.19.

Figure C.20.

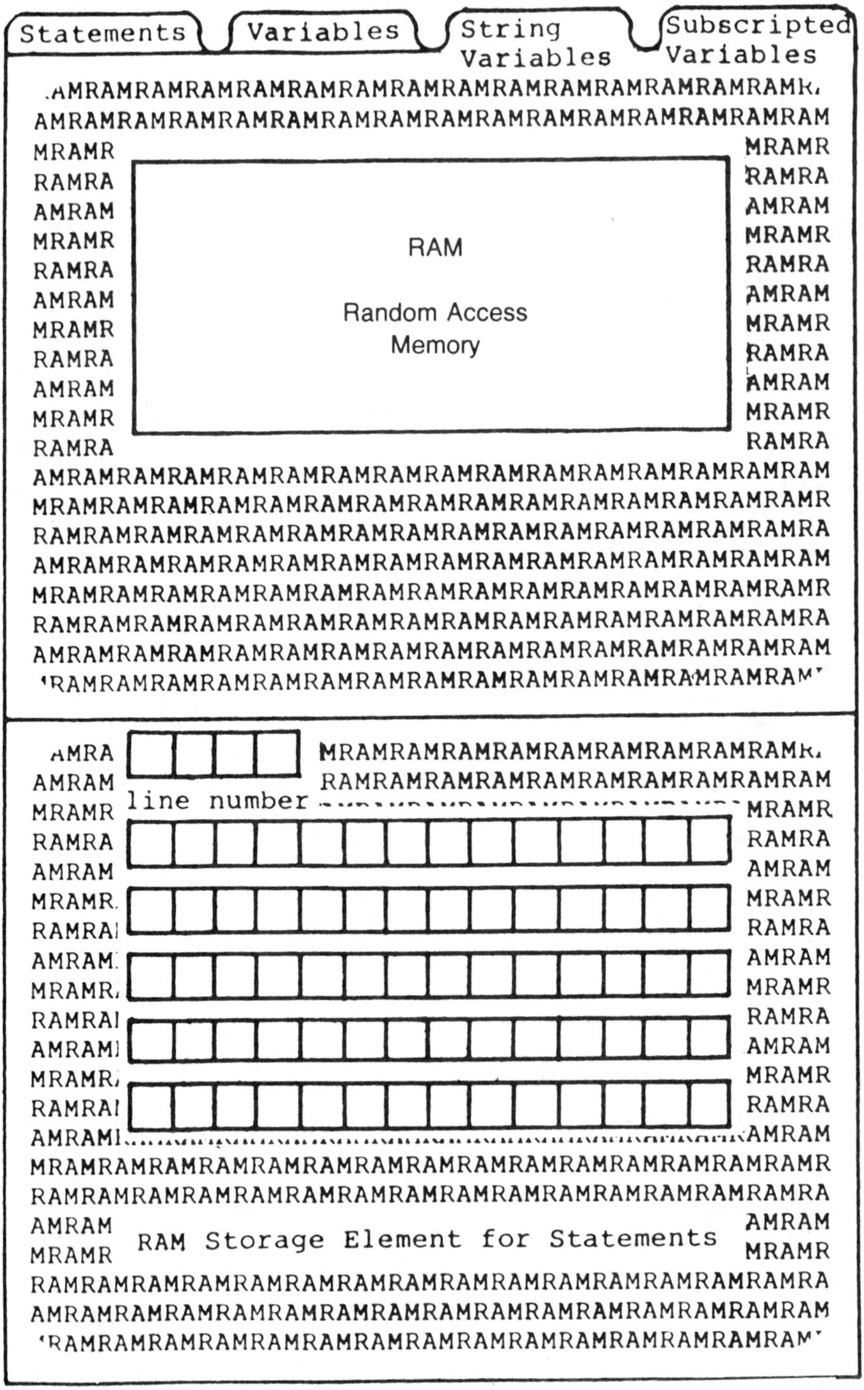

Figure C.21.

Figure C.22.

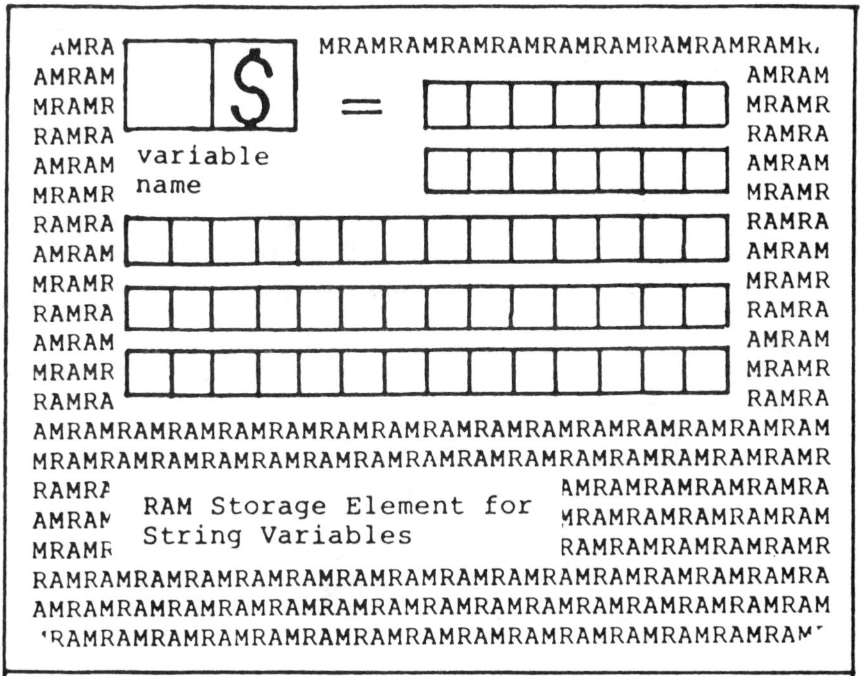
$
=
variable
name
RAM Storage Element for
String Variables

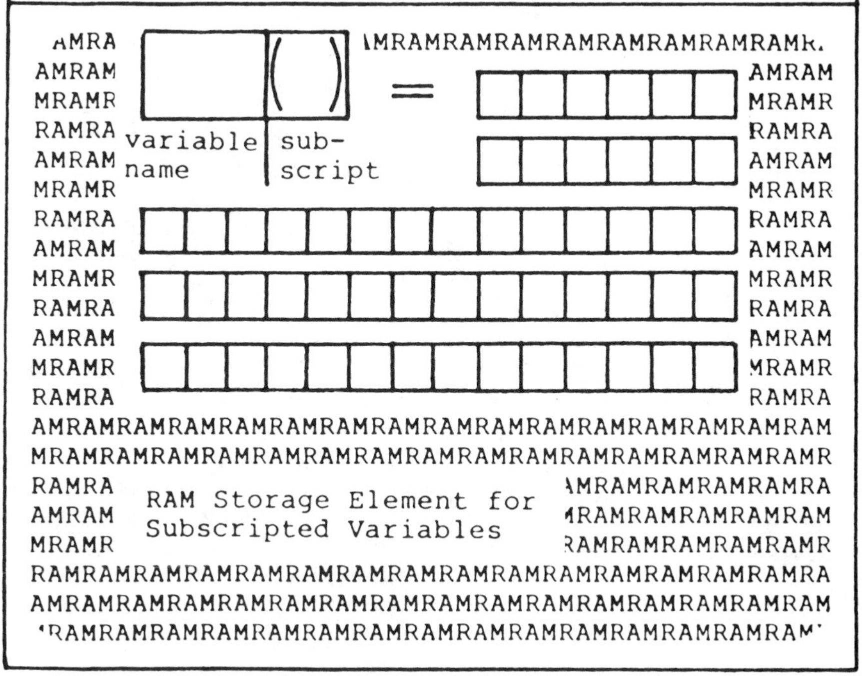
( )
=
variable
name
sub-
script
RAM Storage Element for
Subscripted Variables

Figure C.23.

Figure C.24.

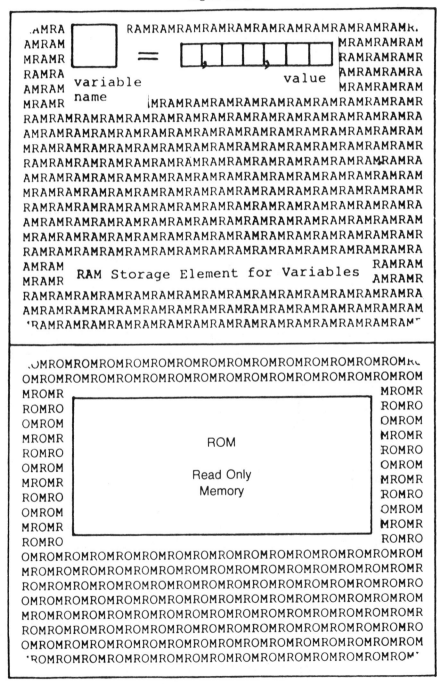

Figure C.25.

BREAK

```
ՍMRO   ┌─────────┐                                    ROMRᵤ
OMROM  │ BREAK │                                       OMROM
MROMR  └─────────┘                                     MROMR
ROMRO    1. Print "break at . . ." (give line number where the   ROMRO
OMROM       break occurred)                            ᎧMROM
MROMR    2. Print "Ready"                              MROMR
ROMRO    3. After putting everything in place (including this   ROMRO
OMROM       card), turn your control to the keyboard by show-   ᎧMROM
MROMR       ing the prompt >.                          ᎧMROMR
ROMRO                                                   ᎧROMRO
OMROM                                                   OMROM
MRᴏMRᴏMRᴏMRᴏMRᴏMRᴏMRᴏMRᴏMRᴏMRᴏMRᴏMRᴏMRᴏMRᴏMRᴏMRᴏMᎡ
RᴏMRᴏMRᴏMRᴏMRᴏMRᴏMRᴏMRᴏMRᴏMRᴏMRᴏMRᴏMRᴏMRᴏMRᴏMRᴏMRᴏ
OMRᴏMRᴏMRᴏMRᴏMRᴏMRᴏMRᴏMRᴏMRᴏMRᴏMRᴏMRᴏMRᴏMRᴏMRᴏMRᴏM
MRᴏMRᴏMRᴏMRᴏMRᴏMRᴏMRᴏMRᴏMRᴏMRᴏMRᴏMRᴏMRᴏMRᴏMRᴏMRᴏMᎡ
RᴏMRᴏMRᴏMRᴏMRᴏMRᴏMRᴏMRᴏMRᴏMRᴏMRᴏMRᴏMRᴏMRᴏMRᴏMRᴏMRᴏ
OMRᴏMRᴏMRᴏMRᴏMRᴏMRᴏMRᴏMRᴏMRᴏMRᴏMRᴏMRᴏMRᴏMRᴏMRᴏMRᴏM
MRᴏMRᴏMRᴏMRᴏMRᴏMRᴏMRᴏMRᴏᎡᴏMRᴏᎡᴏMᎡᴏMRᴏMRᴏMRᴏMRᴏMᎡ
RᴏMRᴏMRᴏMRᴏMRᴏMRᴏMRᴏMRᴏM.ᎡᴏMRᴏMRᴏMRᴏMRᴏMRᴏMRᴏMRᴏ
OMRᴏMRᴏMRᴏMRᴏMRᴏMRᴏMRᴏMRᴏMRᴏMRᴏMRᴏMRᴏMRᴏMRᴏMRᴏMRᴏM
ᎡᴏMRᴏMRᴏMRᴏMRᴏMRᴏMRᴏMRᴏMRᴏᎡᴏMRᴏMRᴏMRᴏMRᴏMRᴏMᴿᴼᴹ˙
```

Figure C.26.

Figure C.27.

```
     CLS

 .UMRC   ┌──────┐                          ROMRL
 OMROM   │ CLS  │                          OMROM
 MROMR   └──────┘                          MROMR
 ROMRC                                     ROMRO
 OMROM    Clear the screen.                OMROM
 MROMR                                     MROMR
ROMROMROMROMROMROMROMROMROMROMROMROMROMROMROMRO
OMROMROMROMROMROMROMROMROMROMROMROMROMROMROMROM
MROMROMROMROMROMROMROMROMROMROMROMROMROMROMROMR
ROMROMROMROMROMROMROMROMROMROMROMROMROMROMROMRO
OMROMROMROMROMROMROMROMROMROMROMROMROMROMROMROM
MROMROMROMROMROMROMROMROMROMROMROMROMROMROMROMR
ROMROMROMROMROMROMROMROMROMROMROMROMROMROMROMRO
OMROMROMROMROMROMROMROMROMROMROMROMROMROMROMROM
MROMROMROMROMROMROMROMROMROMROMROMROMROMROMROMR
ROMROMROMROMROMROMROMROMROMROMROMROMROMROMROMRO
OMROMROMROMROMROMROMROMROMROMROMROMROMROMROMROM
MROMROMROMROMROMROMROMROMROMROMROMROMROMROMROMR
ROMROMROMROMROMROMROMROMROMROMROMROMROMROMROMRO
OMROMROMROMROMROMROMROMROMROMROMROMROMROMROMROM
'ROMROMROMROMROMROMROMROMROMROMROMROMROMROMROM'
```

```
      CONT

 .UMRC   ┌───────┐                         ROMRL
 OMROM   │ CONT  │                         OMROM
 MROMR   └───────┘                         MROMR
 ROMRO    1. Look up the last line number after BREAK;   ROMRO
 OMROM    2. Continue Program performance at that line num-   OMROM
 MROMR       ber.                          MROMR
 ROMRC                                     ROMRO
OMROMROMROMROMROMROMROMROMROMROMROMROMROMROMROM
MROMROMROMROMROMROMROMROMROMROMROMROMROMROMROMR
ROMROMROMROMROMROMROMROMROMROMROMROMROMROMROMRO
OMROMROMROMROMROMROMROMROMROMROMROMROMROMROMROM
MROMROMROMROMROMROMROMROMROMROMROMROMROMROMROMR
ROMROMROMROMROMROMROMROMROMROMROMROMROMROMROMRO
OMROMROMROMROMROMROMROMROMROMROMROMROMROMROMROM
MROMROMROMROMROMROMROMROMROMROMROMROMROMROMROMR
ROMROMROMROMROMROMROMROMROMROMROMROMROMROMROMRO
OMROMROMROMROMROMROMROMROMROMROMROMROMROMROMROM
MROMROMROMROMROMROMROMROMROMROMROMROMROMROMROMR
ROMROMROMROMROMROMROMROMROMROMROMROMROMROMROMRO
OMROMROMROMROMROMROMROMROMROMROMROMROMROMROMROM
'ROMROMROMROMROMROMROMROMROMROMROMROMROMROMROM'
```

Figure C.28.

Figure C.29.

```
        ┌─────  DATA  ─────┐
```

| DATA |

Do nothing.
This line is not a command.
It contains numbers or words, which are to be read
according to the command READ.

```
        ┌─────  DIM  ─────┐
```

| DIM |

1. Take as many RAM storage elements for subscripted variables+) as the number in parentheses indicates,
2. Fill in the name given in the statement and the
   subscripts 1, 2, ..., up to the number given in
   parentheses.
   (that is, set aside that space in the memory, that
   is, Dimension the memory!)

   _____

+) A "subscript" is a number attached to a variable's name, that can be changed. The subscript
   is written in parentheses and attached to the
   name, for example, A(1), A(1), A(3).
   The subscript can also be a variable itself (like
   A(N)), or a math operation (like A(N+1)).
   Both normal variables for numbers as well as
   string variables can become subscripted.

Figure C.30.

Figure C.31.

```
                         END
.OMRO                                              ROMRu
OMROM    [ END ]                                   OMROM
MROMR    1. Print "READY",                         MROMR
ROMRO    2. Remove all markers.                    ROMRO
OMROM    3. After putting all cards in place (including this   OMROM
MROMR       one), turn control to the keyboard by showing      MROMR
ROMRO       the prompt > on the screen.            ROMRO
OMROM                                              OMROM
MROMROMROMROMROMROMROMROMROMROMROMROMROMROMR
ROMROMROMROMROMROMROMROMROMROMROMROMROMROMRO
OMROMROMROMROMROMROMROMROMROMROMROMROMROMROM
MROMROMROMROMROMROMROMROMROMROMROMROMROMROMR·
ROMROMROMROMROMROMROMROMROMROMROMROMROMROMRO
OMROMROMROMROMROMROMROMROMROMROMROMROMROMROM
MROMROMROMROMROMROMROMROMROMROMROMROMROMROMR
ROMROMROMROMROMROMROMROMROMROMROMROMROMROMRO
OMROMROMROMROMROMROMROMROMROMROMROMROMROMROM
MROMROMROMROMROMROMROMROMROMROMROMROMROMROMR
ROMROMROMROMROMROMROMROMROMROMROMROMROMROMRO
OMROMROMROMROMROMROMROMROMROMROMROMROMROMROM
'ROMROMROMROMROMROMROMROMROMROMROMROMROMROM'
```

```
                                 ENTER
.OMRO                                              ROMRu
OMROM    [ ENTER ]        [ Working on | 2A | 2B ] OMROM
MROMR                                              MROMR
ROMRO    1. Look at the screen:                    ROMRO
OMROM    2.   A. If there is a statement (with a line number),  OMROM
MROMR                                              MROMR
ROMRO          • copy it into the RAM,*)           ROMRO
OMROM          • do so with all statements, *)     OMROM
MROMR         B. If there is a command (without a line num-     MROMR
ROMRO          ber),                               ROMRO
OMROM          • get it from the ROM,*)            OMROM
MROMR          • perform it,*)                     MROMR
ROMRO    3. Perform END                            ROMRO
OMROM    _____                         OMROM
MROMR    * If any of this cannot be executed, perform ER-       MROMR
ROMRO    ROR.                                      ROMRO
OMROM                                              OMROM
MROMROMROMROMROMROMROMROMROMROMROMROMROMROMR
ROMROMROMROMROMROMROMROMROMROMROMROMROMROMRO
OMROMROMROMROMROMROMROMROMROMROMROMROMROMROM
'ROMROMROMROMROMROMROMROMROMROMROMROMROMROM'
```

Figure C.32.

Figure C.33.

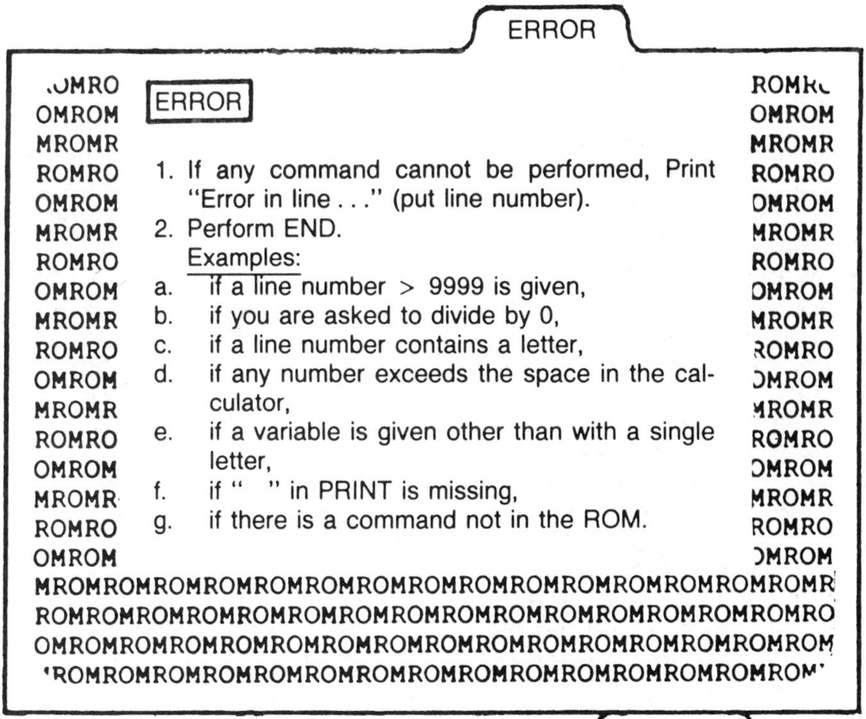

ERROR

| ERROR |

1. If any command cannot be performed, Print "Error in line . . ." (put line number).
2. Perform END.
   Examples:
   a. if a line number > 9999 is given,
   b. if you are asked to divide by 0,
   c. if a line number contains a letter,
   d. if any number exceeds the space in the calculator,
   e. if a variable is given other than with a single letter,
   f. if " " in PRINT is missing,
   g. if there is a command not in the ROM.

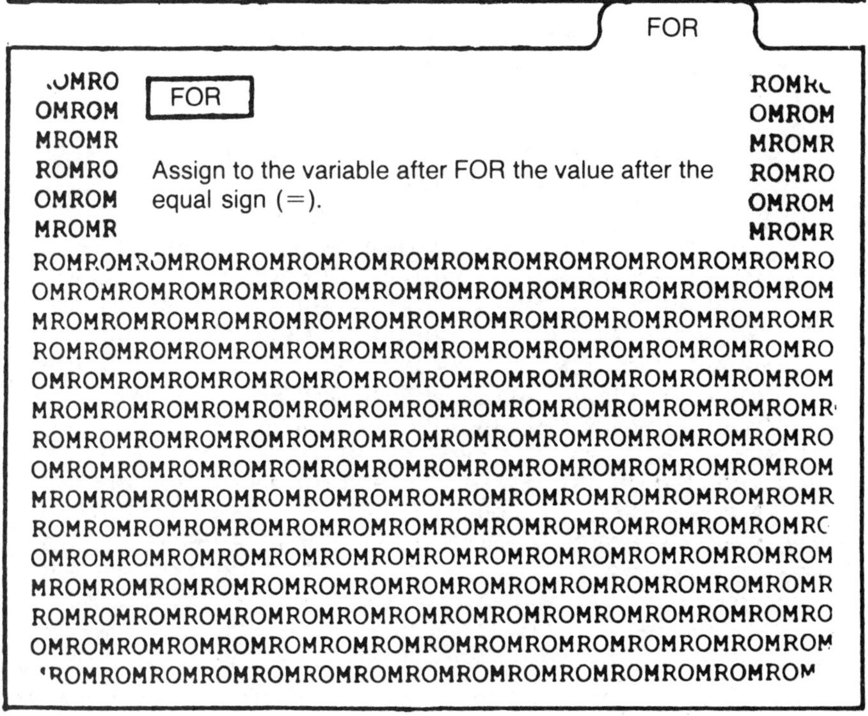

FOR

| FOR |

Assign to the variable after FOR the value after the equal sign (=).

Figure C.34.

Figure C.35.

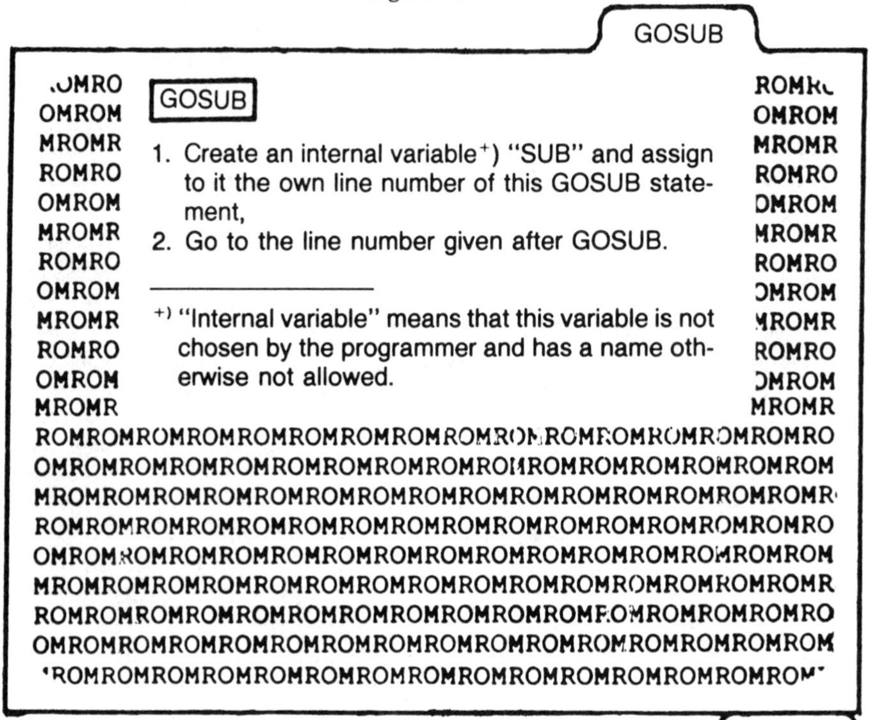

```
                                              GOSUB
```

ROM (decorative border text)

GOSUB

1. Create an internal variable⁺⁾ "SUB" and assign to it the own line number of this GOSUB statement,

2. Go to the line number given after GOSUB.

─────────────

⁺⁾ "Internal variable" means that this variable is not chosen by the programmer and has a name otherwise not allowed.

```
                                              GOTO
```

GOTO

Do not take the next line number, but go to the line number given in this statement.

Figure C.36.

Figure C.37.

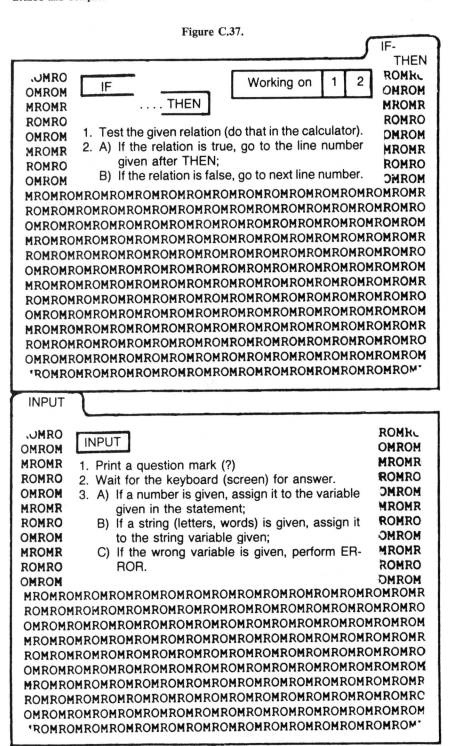

IF-THEN

1. Test the given relation (do that in the calculator).
2. A) If the relation is true, go to the line number given after THEN;
   B) If the relation is false, go to next line number.

INPUT

1. Print a question mark (?)
2. Wait for the keyboard (screen) for answer.
3. A) If a number is given, assign it to the variable given in the statement;
   B) If a string (letters, words) is given, assign it to the string variable given;
   C) If the wrong variable is given, perform ERROR.

Figure C.38.

Figure C.39.

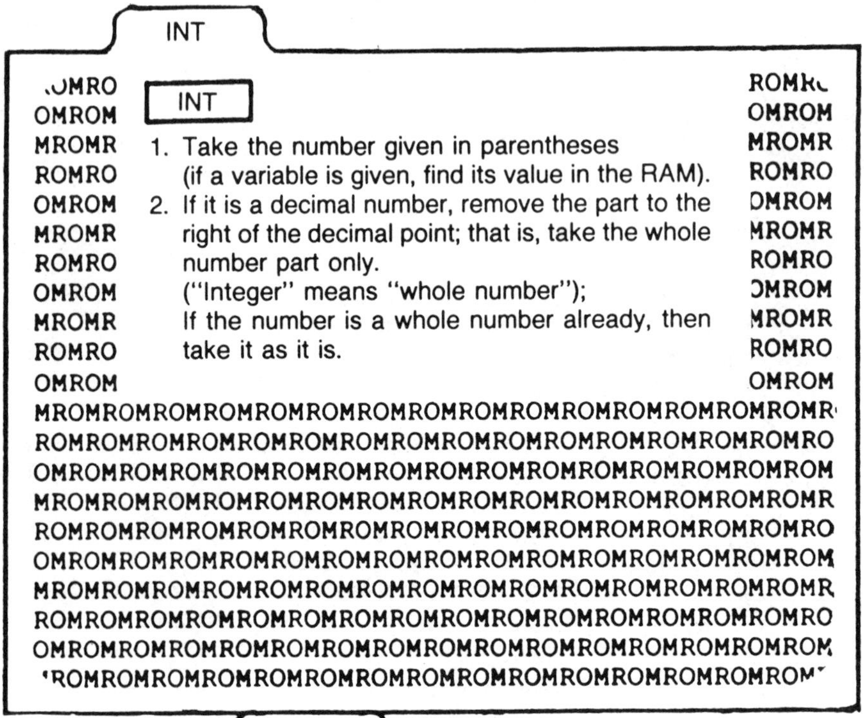

INT

```
INT
```

1. Take the number given in parentheses
   (if a variable is given, find its value in the RAM).
2. If it is a decimal number, remove the part to the
   right of the decimal point; that is, take the whole
   number part only.
   ("Integer" means "whole number");
   If the number is a whole number already, then
   take it as it is.

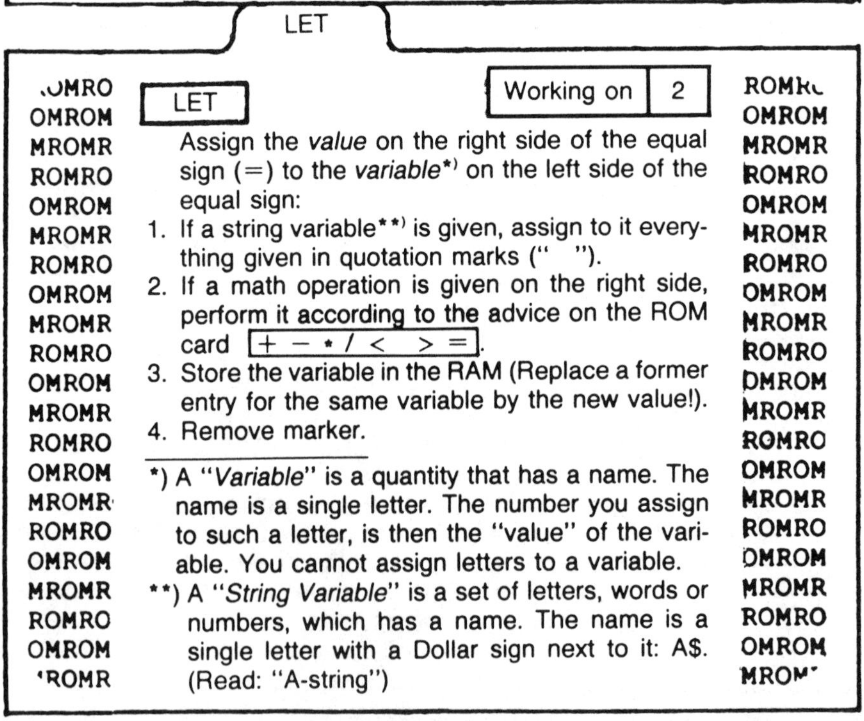

LET

```
LET
```

Working on | 2

Assign the *value* on the right side of the equal
sign (=) to the *variable*[*] on the left side of the
equal sign:

1. If a string variable[**] is given, assign to it everything given in quotation marks (" ").
2. If a math operation is given on the right side,
   perform it according to the advice on the ROM
   card $\boxed{+ - * / < \quad > =}$.
3. Store the variable in the RAM (Replace a former
   entry for the same variable by the new value!).
4. Remove marker.

[*] A "*Variable*" is a quantity that has a name. The
name is a single letter. The number you assign
to such a letter, is then the "value" of the variable. You cannot assign letters to a variable.

[**] A "*String Variable*" is a set of letters, words or
numbers, which has a name. The name is a
single letter with a Dollar sign next to it: A$.
(Read: "A-string")

Figure C.40.

Figure C.41.

LIST

LIST

1. Take the first statement.
2. Print that statement.
3. Do the same with all statements until you hit END.

Figure C.42.

NEXT

NEXT

1. Find the most recent FOR line with the same variable.
2. Compare the value given there after TO with the variable in this NEXT statement (use the calculator for comparing).
3. A. If the variable in this statement is still smaller, then
      a) add 1 to its value (counting !),
      b) GOTO the line number following that FOR line you found in 1;
   B. If both values are equal, then take the next line number.

Figure C.42.

Figure C.43.

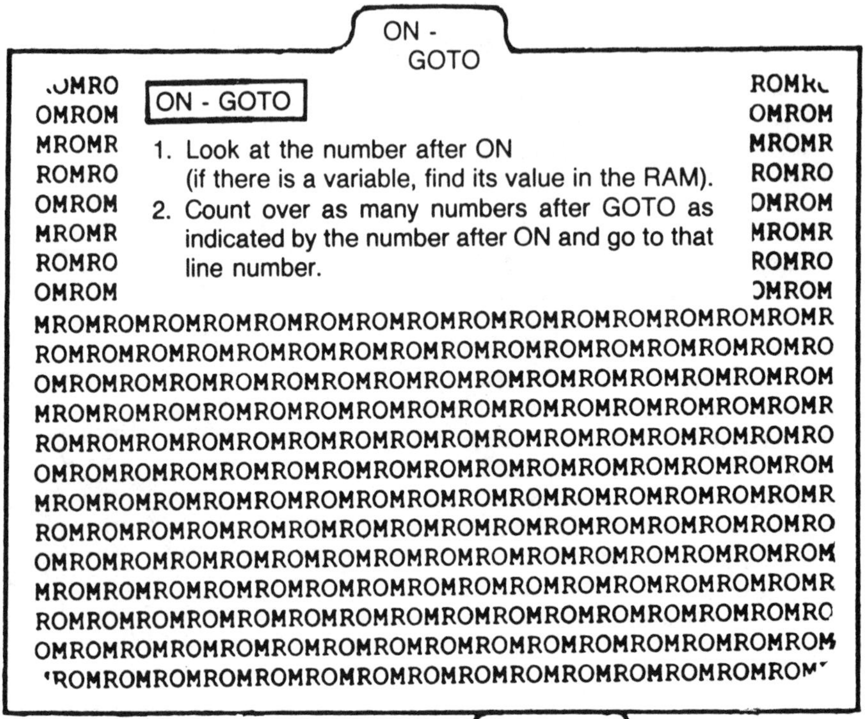

```
              ON -
                 GOTO
```

ON - GOTO

1. Look at the number after ON
   (if there is a variable, find its value in the RAM).
2. Count over as many numbers after GOTO as
   indicated by the number after ON and go to that
   line number.

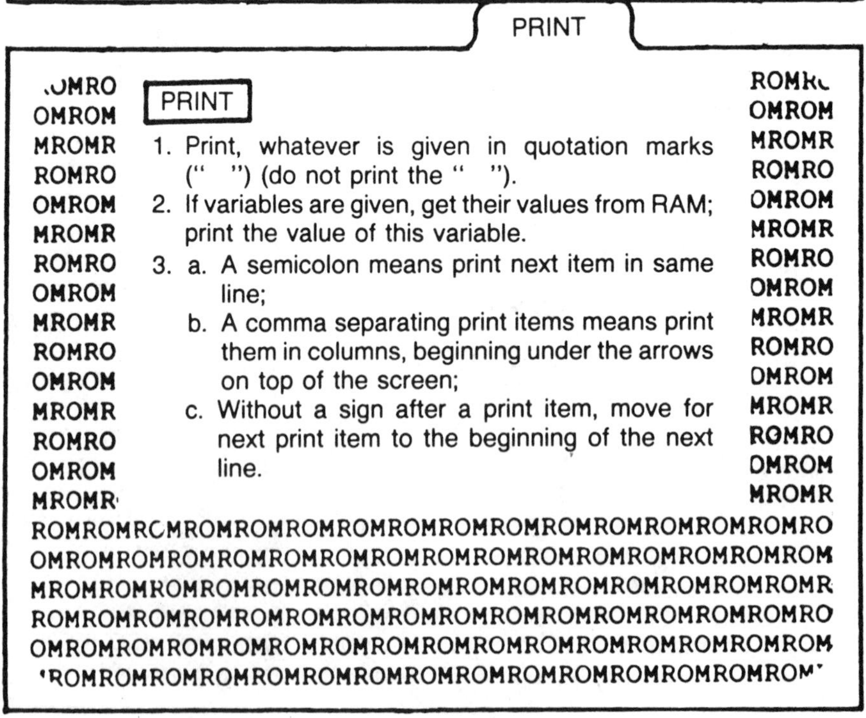

PRINT

PRINT

1. Print, whatever is given in quotation marks
   (" ") (do not print the " ").
2. If variables are given, get their values from RAM;
   print the value of this variable.
3. a. A semicolon means print next item in same
      line;
   b. A comma separating print items means print
      them in columns, beginning under the arrows
      on top of the screen;
   c. Without a sign after a print item, move for
      next print item to the beginning of the next
      line.

Figure C.44.

Figure C.45.

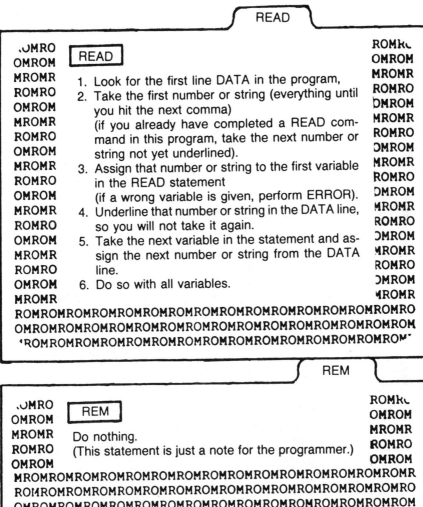

READ

READ

1. Look for the first line DATA in the program,
2. Take the first number or string (everything until you hit the next comma)
   (if you already have completed a READ command in this program, take the next number or string not yet underlined).
3. Assign that number or string to the first variable in the READ statement
   (if a wrong variable is given, perform ERROR).
4. Underline that number or string in the DATA line, so you will not take it again.
5. Take the next variable in the statement and assign the next number or string from the DATA line.
6. Do so with all variables.

REM

REM

Do nothing.
(This statement is just a note for the programmer.)

Figure C.46.

Figure C.47.

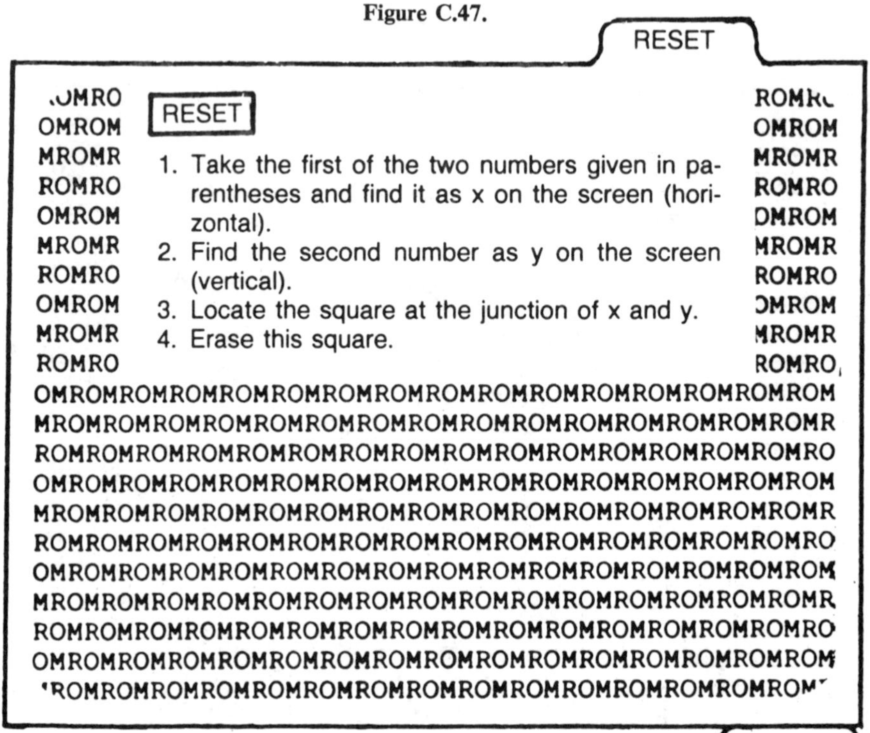

RESET

RESET

,OMRO
OMROM
MROMR
ROMRO
OMROM
MROMR
ROMRO
OMROM
MROMR
ROMRO

1. Take the first of the two numbers given in parentheses and find it as x on the screen (horizontal).
2. Find the second number as y on the screen (vertical).
3. Locate the square at the junction of x and y.
4. Erase this square.

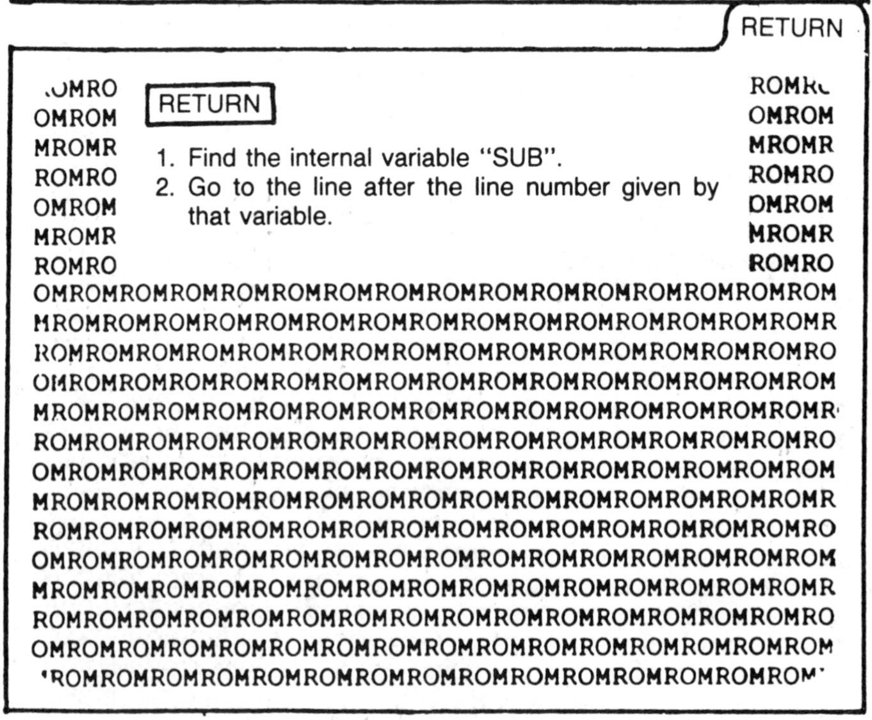

ROMRu
OMROM
MROMR
ROMRO
OMROM
MROMR
ROMRO
OMROM
MROMR
ROMRO,

OMROMROMROMROMROMROMROMROMROMROMROMROMROMROM
MROMROMROMROMROMROMROMROMROMROMROMROMROMROMR
ROMROMROMROMROMROMROMROMROMROMROMROMROMROMRO
OMROMROMROMROMROMROMROMROMROMROMROMROMROMROM
MROMROMROMROMROMROMROMROMROMROMROMROMROMROMR
ROMROMROMROMROMROMROMROMROMROMROMROMROMROMRO
OMROMROMROMROMROMROMROMROMROMROMROMROMROMROM
MROMROMROMROMROMROMROMROMROMROMROMROMROMROMR
ROMROMROMROMROMROMROMROMROMROMROMROMROMROMRO
OMROMROMROMROMROMROMROMROMROMROMROMROMROMROM
'ROMROMROMROMROMROMROMROMROMROMROMROMROMROM'

RETURN

RETURN

,OMRO
OMROM
MROMR
ROMRO
OMROM
MROMR
ROMRO

1. Find the internal variable "SUB".
2. Go to the line after the line number given by that variable.

ROMRu
OMROM
MROMR
ROMRO
OMROM
MROMR
ROMRO

OMROMROMROMROMROMROMROMROMROMROMROMROMROMROM
MROMROMROMROMROMROMROMROMROMROMROMROMROMROMR
ROMROMROMROMROMROMROMROMROMROMROMROMROMROMRO
OMROMROMROMROMROMROMROMROMROMROMROMROMROMROM
MROMROMROMROMROMROMROMROMROMROMROMROMROMROMR'
ROMROMROMROMROMROMROMROMROMROMROMROMROMROMRO
OMROMROMROMROMROMROMROMROMROMROMROMROMROMROM
MROMROMROMROMROMROMROMROMROMROMROMROMROMROMR
ROMROMROMROMROMROMROMROMROMROMROMROMROMROMRO
OMROMROMROMROMROMROMROMROMROMROMROMROMROMROM
MROMROMROMROMROMROMROMROMROMROMROMROMROMROMR
ROMROMROMROMROMROMROMROMROMROMROMROMROMROMRO
OMROMROMROMROMROMROMROMROMROMROMROMROMROMROM
'ROMROMROMROMROMROMROMROMROMROMROMROMROMROM'

Figure C.48.

Figure C.49.

RND

| RND |

,UMRO
OMROM
MROMR
ROMRO
OMROM
MROMR
ROMRO

Grab a random number between 0 and the number given in parentheses (if the number is 7, use dice); (Make sure, the number is *random*. Random numbers seldom repeat digits!)

ROMK
OMROM
MROMR
ROMRO
OMROM
MROMR
ROMRO

RUN

| RUN |

Working on | 2 |

,UMRO
OMROM
MROMR
ROMRO
OMROM
MROMR
ROMRO
OMROM
MROMR
ROMRO
OMROM

1. Take the first statement from the RAM and read it.
2. Get the command from the ROM and perform it
   (if that is not possible, perform ERROR);
3. Take the statement with the next line number.
4. Perform again line 2 of this card.
5. After the last statement, perform END.

ROMK
OMROM
MROMR
ROMRO
OMROM
MROMR
ROMRO
OMROM
MROMR
ROMRO
OMROM

Figure C.50.

Figure C.51.

SET

SET

.OMRO
OMROM
MROMR
ROMRO
OMROM
MROMR
ROMRO
OMROM
MROMR
ROMRO

1. Take the first of the two numbers given in parentheses and find it as x on the screen (horizontal).
2. Find the second number as y on the screen (vertical).
3. Locate the square at the junction of x and y.
4. Light up this square (that is, color it in).

ROMRO
OMROM
MROMR
ROMRO
OMROM
MROMR
ROMRO
OMROM
MROMR
ROMRO

OMROMROMROMROMROMROMROMROMROMROMROMROMROMROM
MROMROMROMROMROMROMROMROMROMROMROMROMROMROMR
ROMROMROMROMROMROMROMROMROMROMROMROMROMROMRO
OMROMROMROMROMROMROMROMROMROMROMROMROMROMROM
MROMROMROMROMROMROMROMROMROMROMROMROMROMROMR
ROMROMROMROMROMROMROMROMROMROMROMROMROMROMRO
OMROMROMROMROMROMROMROMROMROMROMROMROMROMROM
MROMROMROMROMROMROMROMROMROMROMROMROMROMROMR
ROMROMROMROMROMROMROMROMROMROMROMROMROMROMRO
OMROMROMROMROMROMROMROMROMROMROMROMROMROMROM
'ROMROMROMROMROMROMROMROMROMROMROMROMROMROM'

+ − * / = < >

Math. Operations

A) Performing is done in the calculator as follows:
1. Take the card with the respective sign.
2. Erase all former entries on it.
3. Write into this card the given numbers; if variables are given, get their values from the RAM.
4. Perform the operation on the card.

B) If more than one math operation is asked for, follow this sequence:
first perform operation within parentheses( ),
then perform * and / from left to right,
after this perform + and − from left to right.

Figure C.52.

Figure C.53.

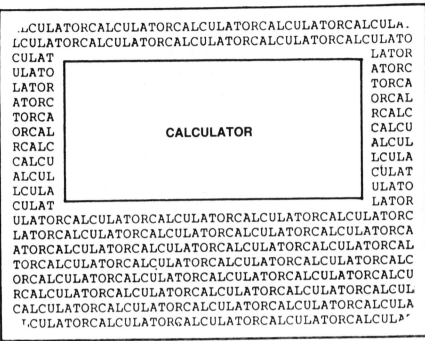

Figure C.54.

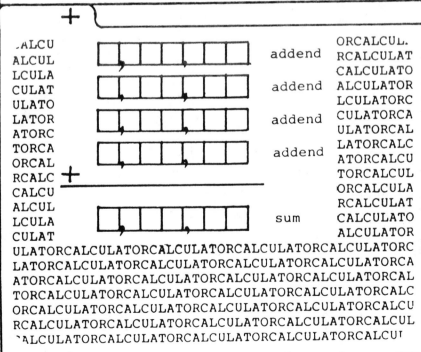

Figure C.55.

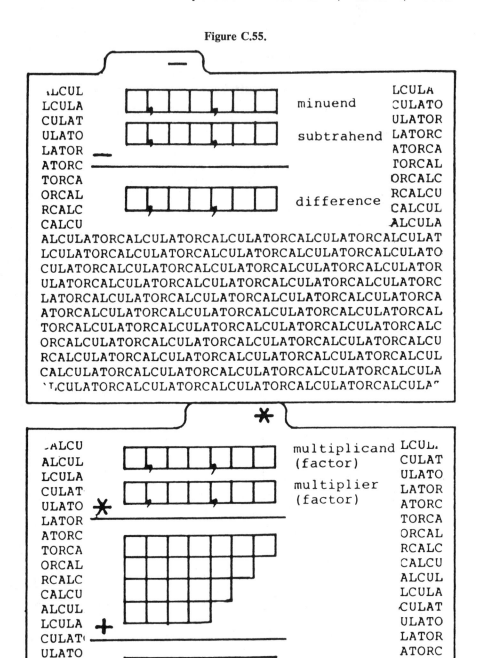

Figure C.56.

Figure C.57.

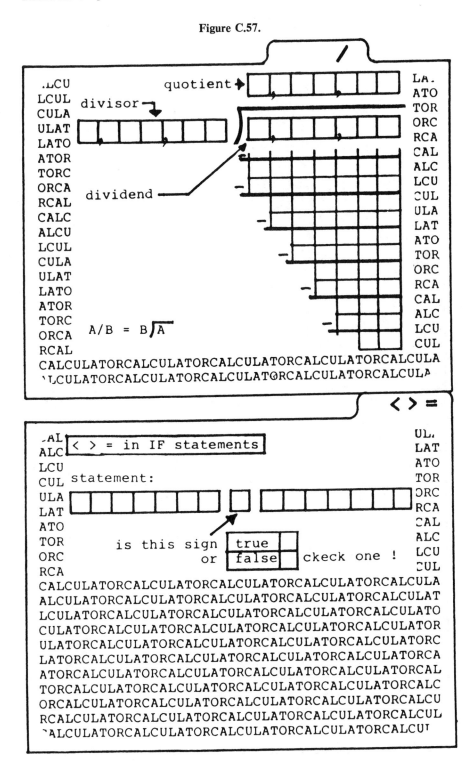

Figure C.58.

PROGRAMS FOR THE PACS

```
 1 : PRINT
 2 : PRINT VARIABLES
 3 : Watch out
 4 : ERASE
 5 : Long math terms
 6 : Working with Variables
 7 : Practicing Timetables
 8 : Strings
 9 : Playing Dice
10 : Multiplication
11 : Addition, Subtraction with check
12 : +, −, / with check
13 : Multiplication with check
14 : Yes or No
15 : "or" decisions
16 : "and" decisions
17 : Do Loop
18 : What is multiplication
19 : Powers
20 : Grocery Store (lists)
21 : Checkerboard (lists)
22 : Graphics
23 : Draw a Line
24 : Nested Loops
25 : Rectangle
26 : Move a Point
27 : Move diagonally
```

Figure C.59.

PROGRAM 1

```
10 CLS
20 PRINT "Good morning!"
30 END
```

Figure C.60.

PROGRAM 3

```
8000  REM Watch out!
9000  PRINT "I AM O. K."
9999  PRINT "I am still O. K."
10000 END
```

Figure C.62.

PROGRAM 2

```
10 CLS
20 LET A = 2
30 LET B$ = "PACS"
40 PRINT "My name is  ";B$;"  the Paper Computer Simulator."
50 PRINT "This is Program number  ";A
60 END
```

Figure C.61.

PROGRAM 5

```
5 CLS
10 REM Long math terms
20 LET A = 28 - 3
30 PRINT "The answer is A="; A
40 LET B = 28 - 3 * 5
50 PRINT "The answer is B="; B
60 LET C = 28/7
70 PRINT "The answer is C="; C
80 LET D = 28/(7 - 3)
90 PRINT "The answer is D="; D
100 LET E = 12 - 4 * 2 - (1 + 3)
110 PRINT "The answer is E="; E
120 LET F = 4 + 20/5 + 2 * 2
130 PRINT "The answer is F="; F
140 LET G = 51/(7 - 2 * 3)
150 PRINT "The answer is G="; G
160 LET H = 31/(8 - 2 * 4)
170 PRINT "The answer is H="; H
180 END
```

Figure C.64.

PROGRAM 4

```
10 PRINT "This is fun"
20 PRINT "This is still fun"
30 ERASE
40 END
```

Figure C.63.

```
PROGRAM 7

 5 REM Practicing timetables
10 CLS
20 PRINT "What timetable do you want";
25 INPUT D
30 LET R = RND (10)
40 LET A = D * R
50 PRINT R; "x"; D; "=";
60 INPUT B
70 IF A = B THEN 100
80 PRINT "No. Try again!"
90 GO TO 50
100 PRINT "RIGHT!"
110 GO TO 30
120 END
Operator: Stop program with BREAK.
```

Figure C.66.

```
PROGRAM 6

 5 REM Working with variables
 7 CLS
10 LET A = 14
20 LET B = 8
30 LET C = 2
40 LET D = 3
41 LET X = A − B
42 PRINT "X="; X
43 LET Y = C * D
44 PRINT "Y="; Y
45 LET Z = A/C
46 PRINT "Z="; Z
47 LET V = A/(C + C + D)
48 PRINT "V="; V
50 LET W = A + B/C + (B * D)
60 PRINT "The answer is W="; W
70 LET U = C/(B − D * C)
80 PRINT "The answer is U="; U
90 END
```

Figure C.65.

PROGRAM 9

```
10 CLS
20 PRINT "Playing dice"
30 LET X=RND (7)
40 IF X < 6 THEN 70
50 PRINT "I won! It's 6!"
60 END
70 PRINT "Only"; X "I try again"
80 GOTO 30
90 END
```

Figure C.68.

PROGRAM 8

```
10  CLS
20  PRINT "What is your name";
30  INPUT N$
40  PRINT "How old are you in years";
50  INPUT A
60  PRINT "What year do we have now";
70  INPUT Y
80  CLS
90  PRINT "Hello ";N$;" I like you."
100 PRINT "You are now"; A; "years old."
110 LET B=Y- A
120 PRINT "You were born in"; B; "."
130 LET N=A + 1
140 PRINT "We are looking forward to your"; N; "th birthday."
150 LET T=Y + (21 - A)
160 PRINT "In"; T; "you will be 21 years old."
170 LET X= 2000 - B
180 PRINT "In the year 2000 you will be"; X; "years old."
190 PRINT "Good luck ";N$;" Bye, bye."
200 END
```

Figure C.67.

PROGRAM 11

```
1   REM Addition, Subtraction
6   CLS
10  LET H = RND (2 000 000)
20  LET G = RND ( 300 000)
30  LET J = G + H
40  LET K = J − H
60  IF K = G Then 120
65  LET L = J − G
70  IF L = H Then 100
80  PRINT "Sorry, J is wrong."
90  GOTO 30
100 PRINT "not so bad, only K is wrong."
110 GOTO 40
120 PRINT "you got it right!"
130 PRINT "H", "G", "J", "K"
135 PRINT H, G, J, K
140 GOTO 10
150 END
```

Operator: Stop run with BREAK.

Figure C.70.

PROGRAM 10

```
5   REM Multiplication
10  CLS
15  PRINT "What is the multiplicand";
20  INPUT D
25  PRINT "What is the multiplier";
30  INPUT R
40  LET A = D * R
50  PRINT D; "*",R; "=",; A
60  GO to 15
70  END
```

Operator: Stop program with BREAK

Figure C.69.

PROGRAM 13

```
  1 REM Multiplication with checks
  5 CLS
 10 LET A = RND (3 000)
 20 LET B = RND ( 999)
 30 LET C = A * B
 40 LET D = C/B
 50 IF D = A THEN 80
 60 PRINT "mistake, I do it again."
 70 GOTO 30
 80 PRINT "Hurrah!" "The answer is"; A; "*"; B; "="; C
 90 PRINT C; "/"; B; "="; D
100 END
```

Figure C.72.

PROGRAM 12

```
 20 REM Addition, Subtraction, Division
 30 CLS
 40 LET A = RND (2 000 000)
 50 LET B = RND ( 900 000)
 60 LET C = A + B
 70 LET D = C + B
 80 LET E = D + B
 90 LET F = E + B
100 LET G = F - A
110 LET H = G/4
120 IF H = B THEN 160
130 PRINT "sorry"
140 GOTO 60
160 PRINT "right!!"
170 PRINT "A="; A, "B="; B, "C="; C,
    "D="; D, "E="; E, "F="; F,
    "G="; G, "H="; H
180 END
```

Figure C.71.

```
PROGRAM 14
10 REM Yes or No!
20 CLS
30 PRINT "answer questions with YES or NO only!"
50 PRINT "Do you like candy";
60 INPUT C$
70 IF C$= "Yes" THEN 110
80 IF C$= "No" THEN 130
90 PRINT "answer with either 'Yes' or 'No', dummy!"
100 GO TO 50
110 PRINT "Sorry for your poor teeth!"
120 END
130 PRINT "You are smart! I haven't got one any way."
140 END
```

Figure C.73.

PROGRAM 15

```
10 REM Logical "or" Decisions
20 CLS
45 PRINT "The long sound of a vowel."
46 PRINT
50 PRINT "choose a one syllable word!"
55 PRINT "is the vowel e, a, o, u at the end of the syllable";
65 INPUT S$
70 PRINT "is there a magic e in the end";
75 INPUT E$
80 IF S$= "Yes" THEN 120
90 IF E$= "Yes" THEN 120
100 PRINT "the vowel may have its short sound"
110 END
120 PRINT "the vowel has its long sound"
130 END
```

Figure C.74.

PROGRAM 16

```
10 REM Logic "and" decision
20 CLS
21 PRINT
22 PRINT "A birthday party!"
23 PRINT
30 PRINT
40 PRINT "answer YES or NO only."
50 PRINT "Do you have birthday";
55 INPUT S$
60 PRINT "Do you want a party";
65 INPUT P$
70 PRINT, "Do your parents agree";
75 INPUT A$
80 JF B$ <  > "Yes" THEN 130
90 JF P$ <  > "Yes" THEN 130
100 JF A$ <  > "Yes" THEN 130
110 PRINT "Hurrah, there will be a birthday party."
120 END
130 PRINT "Sorry, no birthday party."
140 END
```

Figure C.75.

PROGRAM 18

```
 10 REM What is Multiplication
 20 PRINT "Choose a multiplicand";
 30 INPUT D
 40 PRINT "Choose a one digit multiplier";
 50 INPUT R
 60 LET A = 0
 70 REM A will be the answer
 80 LET C = 0
 90 REM C is the loop counter
100   LET C = C + 1
110   LET A = A + D
120   JF C < R THEN 100
130 PRINT D; " * "; R; "="; A
140 END
```

Figure C.77.

PROGRAM 17

```
10 REM Simple do-loop
20 CLS
25 PRINT
26 PRINT
27 PRINT
30 PRINT "I'll do 5 runs."
35 PRINT
40 LET A=0
50   LET A= A+1
60   PRINT "run"; A
70   If A < 5 THEN 50
80 PRINT "I'm done"
90 END
```

Figure C.76.

PROGRAM 19

```
10 REM Powers
20 PRINT "Choose a one-digit number as the basis";
30 INPUT B
40 PRINT "Choose a one-digit number as the exponent";
50 INPUT E
60 LET A = 1
70 REM A will be the answer
80 LET C = 0
90 REM C is the loop counter
100  LET C = C + 1
110  LET A = A * B
120 JF C < E THEN 100
130 PRINT B; "to the"; E; "Power="; A
140 END
```

Figure C.78.

PROGRAM 20

```
10 REM At the grocery store
15 CLS
20 LET A= 60
25 REM A is the price in cents of 1 pound of apples
30 LET P= 25
35 REM P is the price in cents of 1 pound of potatoes
40 PRINT
50 PRINT "Price Chart"
60 PRINT
80 PRINT "Weight", "Apples", "Potatoes"
85 PRINT
90 LET X=0
100 LET X=X+1
110 REM X is the weight in pounds
115 LET B=A*X
120 LET Q=P*X
130 PRINT X; "lb", B; "cents", Q; "cents"
140 IF X < 5 THEN 100
150 PRINT "We sell only best quality"
160 END
```

Figure C.79.

PROGRAM 21

```
10 REM the reward for the checkerboard (ask for the story!)
20 CLS
25 PRINT
30 PRINT "chart of wheat kernels"
40 PRINT
50 PRINT, "number", "amount", "sum"
51 PRINT, "of", "of"
52 PRINT, "this", "kernels", "kernels"
53 PRINT, "square", "on this", "so far"
54 PRINT, " ", "square"
55 PRINT
60 LET Q=1
62 LET S=1
64 LET A=0
66 REM A is the number of the square,
       Q is the quantity of the kernels,
       S is the sum of the kernels so far
70 LET A=A+1
80 PRINT, A, Q, S
90 LET Q=Q*2
100 LET S=S+Q
110 IF A < 64 THEN 70
120 PRINT "Take these kernels as your reward"
130 END
```

Figure C.80.

PROGRAM 22

```
5 REM graphics
10 CLS
20 SET (14, 9)
30 SET (15, 9)
40 SET (16, 9)
50 SET (14, 10)
60 SET (15, 10)
70 SET (16, 10)
80 SET (15, 11)
90 SET (15, 12)
100 SET (15, 13)
110 SET (15, 14)
120 SET (12, 12)
130 SET (13, 12)
140 SET (14, 12)
150 SET (16, 12)
160 SET (17, 12)
170 SET (18, 12)
180 SET (16, 15)
190 SET (17, 16)
200 SET (18, 17)
210 SET (19, 18)
220 SET (14, 15)
230 SET (13, 16)
240 SET (12, 17)
250 SET (11, 18)
260 END
```

Figure C.81.

PROGRAM 24

```
10 REM Draw a line
20 CLS
30 LET X=0
40   SET (X, 10)
50   LET X=X+1
60 IF X < 32 THEN 40
70 END
```

Figure C.83.

PROGRAM 23

```
10 REM nested loops
20 CLS
21 PRINT
22 PRINT
30 LET L=0
40   LET L=L+1
50   PRINT "Loop L"; L
60   LET M=0
70     LET M=M+1
80     PRINT, "Loop M"; M
90   IF M < 3 THEN 70
100 IF L < 2 THEN 40
110 PRINT "loops are fun"
120 END
```

Figure C.82.

```
PROGRAM 26   10 REM Moving a point
             20 CLS
             30 LET X=0
             40 SET (X, 10)
             50 LET X=X+1
             60 SET (X, 10)
             70 RESET (X−1, 10)
             80 IF X < 32 THEN 50
             90 RESET (X, 10)
            100 END
```

Figure C.85.

```
PROGRAM 25   10 REM Draw a rectangle
             20 CLS
             30 LET L=0
             40 LET L=L+1
             50 LET H=0
             60 LET H=H+1
             70 SET (10+L, 5+H)
             80 IF H < 4 THEN 60
             90 IF L < 3 THEN 40
            100 END
```

Figure C.84.

```
PROGRAM 27
10  REM Move diagonally
20  CLS
30  LET X= 10
40  LET Y= 5
50  SET (X, Y)
60  LET A=0
70   LET A=A+1
80   SET (X+A, Y+A)
90   RESET (X+A−1, Y+A−1)
100  IF A < 7 THEN 70
110  RESET (X+A, Y+A)
120  END
```

Figure C.86.

Assignments

1 PRINT statements
2 loops
3 practicing timetables
4 " × problems
5 " + problems
6 " − problems
7 " ÷ problems
8 " divisibility
9 Yes or no
10 choosing +, −, × or ÷
11 moving a figure horizontally
12 Space Shuttle
13 moving diagonally
14 moving a rectangle

II. Programs and Assignments:

II,1 ÷ with remainder
II,2 rounding numbers
II,3 subroutines
II,4 drawing with DATA
II,5 ON-GOTO
II,6 sorting with subscripted variables

Figure C.87.

Assignment 1
- Type in Pr. 1,
- Run it,
- Change it (and run it each time):
  - to print: hello, dear friend!
  - to print: hello,
    dear friend.
  - to print in columns:

    A B C D
    E F G H
    J K L M

  - to clear the screen before printing.
- List the last program, show to teacher.

Figure C.88.

Assignment 2

Assignment 2

- Type in Program 17
- Run it,
- Change it (and run it each time)
  - to do 7 loops instead of 5;
  - to do 10 loops instead;
  - to create another loop, which prints "second loop, run 1", "second loop, run 2". . .
  - to ask the operator, how many runs he wants for loop 1;
  - to do the same for loop 2.
- Show it to the teacher

Figure C.89.

Assignment 3

Assignment 3

- Type in Program 7
- Run it, several times and try to get all the possible answers,
- Change it (and run each time as above)
  - to go back only 10 times, then END;
  - not to end after 10 times, but to repeat the question "What timetable do you want?"
  - to let the answer "correct" stay a short time, and then print the next problem.
  - not to leave all the previous problems on the screen, but to clear them off each time.
- Save the program. Use it for math practicing.

Figure C.90.

Assignment 4

• Type in Pr. 10,
• Run it,
• Change it (and run it each time):

  • to ask the operator how many runs he wants to do, and to stop after that number of runs;
  • before stopping to ask: "How many more runs do you want?", and to stop only if 0 is answered;
  • instead of printing the answer, to ask the operator for the answer; (printing "right" for correct answer and "wrong" for incorrect);*
  • to repeat the same problem after an incorrect answer;*) to include a 3-second time delay before repeating the next question for the multiplicand; (a loop doing nothing);
  • instead of asking for the value of multiplicand and multiplier to choose random values for them;
  • to ask for the largest preferred multiplicand and multiplier and to choose them accordingly;
  • to repeat this question after the chosen number of runs is done.
  • Instead of asking for the largest multiplicand, ask "How many digits shall have the multiplicand?" and make up a random number accordingly. (Remember: $10^3 - 1$ is a 3-digit number! Check for other powers of 10!, for program pattern look at Program 19).

• Save the program (use it as math-practicing tool!).

* See Pr. 7 for pattern

Figure C.91.

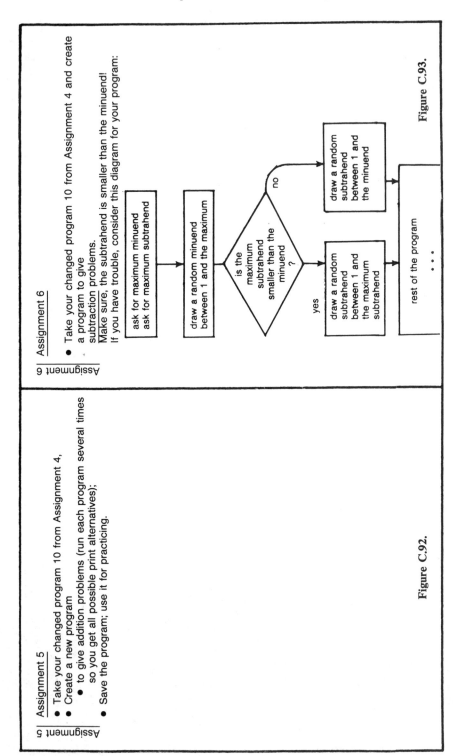

Assignment 6

- Take your changed program 10 from Assignment 4 and create a program to give subtraction problems.

Make sure, the subtrahend is smaller than the minuend!
If you have trouble, consider this diagram for your program:

ask for maximum minuend
ask for maximum subtrahend

draw a random minuend between 1 and the maximum

is the maximum subtrahend smaller than the minuend?

no → draw a random subtrahend between 1 and the minuend

yes → draw a random subtrahend between 1 and the maximum subtrahend

rest of the program
...

Figure C.93.

Assignment 5

- Take your changed program 10 from Assignment 4,
- Create a new program
  - to give addition problems (run each program several times so you get all possible print alternatives);
- Save the program; use it for practicing.

Figure C.92.

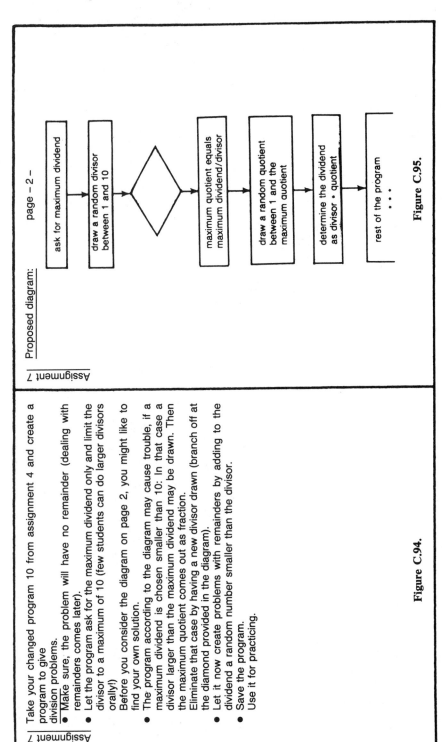

Proposed diagram: page – 2 –

ask for maximum dividend

draw a random divisor
between 1 and 10

maximum quotient equals
maximum dividend/divisor

draw a random quotient
between 1 and the
maximum quotient

determine the dividend
as divisor • quotient

rest of the program
· · ·

Figure C.95.

Take your changed program 10 from assignment 4 and create a
program to give
division problems.

● Make sure, the problem will have no remainder (dealing with
remainders comes later).

● Let the program ask for the maximum dividend only and limit the
divisor to a maximum of 10 (few students can do larger divisors
orally!)
Before you consider the diagram on page 2, you might like to
find your own solution.

● The program according to the diagram may cause trouble, if a
maximum dividend is chosen smaller than 10: In that case a
divisor larger than the maximum dividend may be drawn. Then
the maximum quotient comes out as fraction.
Eliminate that case by having a new divisor drawn (branch off at
the diamond provided in the diagram).

● Let it now create problems with remainders by adding to the
dividend a random number smaller than the divisor.

● Save the program.
Use it for practicing.

Figure C.94.

Assignment 9

- Type in Program 7 with your changes from Assignment 3,
- Run it,
- Change it
  - to ask "do you want another series of problems?"
  - make sure, that after an answer other than "yes" or "no", there comes a print "please answer with yes or no only", and then the same question again.
- Save the program.

Figure C.97.

ASSIGNMENT 8

- Type in Pr. 14
- Run it several times and answer in such a way that you get each of the different print answers;
- Change it (and run each several times as before!)
  - to ask another question, like "is 72432 divisible by 9?" (and to respond to the operator's answer in a mindful way!)
  - to make up a random number. Use RND (3): at 1 make up a divisible number, at 2 make up one that is not. Draw a diagram first.
  - to ask the operator which of the divisors 2, 3, 4, 5, 6, 8, 9, 10, 11, 12 he is able to check and to give mixed questions accordingly. Draw a diagram first. (Did you know that you can ask for more than one number with an INPUT statement?) It would look like this:
    50 PRINT "Which divisibility do you want to check? Type in all wanted numbers between 2 and 10, separated by commas, o.k.";
    60 INPUT A, B, C, D, E, F, G, H, I. If the operator types less than 9 numbers, the remaining variables would get assigned the value 0.
- Save the program, use it for practicing.

Figure C.96.

ASSIGNMENT 11

- Type in program 26, run it;
- Change it
  - to move the dot over the whole screen (the screen of PACS is smaller than others, its x runs from 0 to 31, its y only from 0 to 23. Find out the size of your screen: If you SET or RESET a dot outside of the screen, you receive an ERROR message);
  - to move a triangle instead of one dot (4 dots:);
  - not to SET and RESET the whole figure with each step, but only the dots, which change in that step;
  - to move slower;
  - to move the figure off the screen without an ERROR message; (there is no simple way; you have to design special loops for the last steps).

Figure C.99.

ASSIGNMENT 10

- Take your variations to program 10 from assignments 4, 5, 6, 7 and create an introduction (as a diagram first):
  Let the computer ask:
  "Do you want to do addition (+), subtraction (−), multiplication (*) or division (/)? Type in the sign you want." Let the program then present the respective problems.
- Before stopping after the chosen runs, ask: "Want more of this?" "Want another kind of problem?"
- Save the program. Have it available for practicing.

Figure C.98.

ASSIGNMENT 13

- Type in program 27, run it,
- Change it according to the steps in assignment 11.
- Let the figure move in diagonals of different inclinations.

Figure C.101.

ASSIGNMENT 12

- Take your program from assignment 11 and design a similar program:
  - Have a *simple* shape like the Space shuttle stand on the bottom of the screen next to its launch tower.
  - Let the Shuttle take off and move vertical up, off the screen;
  - Put in a count down time between the appearance of the Shuttle and its take off;
  - Let a counter show the countdown time in approximately seconds;
  - Let the Shuttle start slow and become faster as it goes;
  - Put decorations to it: Some dots as smoke at the launch place, some flickering dots at the bottom of the Shuttle as fire.

Figure C.100.

ASSIGNMENT 14

- Type in program 25, but in a way that allows you to move the figure.
- Change it,
  - to draw the figure in different places chosen by the operator;
  - to move the figure in different direction;
  - so the figure becomes longer, wider, shorter, skinnier in rythmic patterns.

Figure C.102.

Program II, 2

```
 10 REM Rounding numbers to full 1000s
 15 CLS
 20 PRINT "What number shall be rounded";
 30 INPUT N
 40 LET M = N/1000 + 0.5
 50 REM + 0.5 takes care of rounding up
 60 LET P = INT (M)
 70 LET R = P*1000
 80 PRINT "The rounded number is "; R
 90 GOTO 20
100 END
```

Operator: Stop the program with BREAK

Figure C.104.

Program II, 1

```
 10 REM Division with remainders
 20 CLS
 30 PRINT "What is the dividend";
 40 INPUT D
 50 PRINT "What is the divisor";
 60 INPUT S
 70 LET A=D/S
 80 LET J=INT (A)
 90 PRINT D;"/"; S; "="; J
100 LET R=D−J*S
110 PRINT "Remainder"; R
120 GOTO 30
130 END
```

Operator: Stop the program with BREAK

Figure C.103.

Program II, 3

```
10  REM time loops as subroutine
20  CLS
30  PRINT "Wait!"
40  GOSUB 200
50  PRINT "I am back"
60  PRINT "Wait again!"
70  GOSUB 200
80  PRINT "Are you still there?"
90  GOSUB 200
100 PRINT "I'm still looking for you"
110 GOSUB 200
120 PRINT "Bye, bye, now!"
130 END

200 FOR T = 1 TO 3
210 REM time loop, does nothing
220 NEXT T
230 RETURN
240 END
```

If you run this on a real computer you may change: 200 FOR T = 1 TO 300

Figure C.105.

Program II, 4

```
10  REM Drawing figures with DATA
20  CLS
30  READ X, Y
40  IF Y= 999 THEN 140
50  SET (X, Y)
60  GOTO 30
70  DATA 29, 7, 30, 7, 31, 7, 32, 7
80  DATA 33, 7, 28, 8, 34, 8, 26, 9
90  DATA 27, 9, 29, 9, 33, 9, 35, 9
100 DATA 36, 9, 27, 10, 31, 10, 35, 10
110 DATA 27, 11, 35, 11, 28, 12, 30, 12
120 DATA 31, 12, 32, 12, 34, 12, 29, 13, 33, 13
130 DATA 30, 14, 31, 14, 32, 14, 999, 999
140 END
```

Figure C.106.

Program II, 5

```
10 REM Chattanooga Choo Choo
20 CLS
30 FOR X = 1 TO 20
40 IF X > 12 THEN 60
50 ON X GOTO 130, 120, 110, 100, 90, 90, 80, 70, 70,
70
60 RESET (X-13, 15)
70 SET (X-10, 15)
80 RESET (X-9, 15)
90 SET (X-6, 15)
100 RESET (X-5, 15)
110 RESET (X-3, 14)
120 SET (X-2, 14)
130 SET (X-1, 15)
140 NEXT X
150 PRINT "End of the line!" "Chattanooga main station!" "all out!"
160 END
```

If you run this on a real computer, you might like to change it:

```
30 FOR X = 1 TO 100
131 IF X < 81 THEN 140
132 FOR T = 1 TO 3* (X-80)
133 NEXT T
155 GOTO 155
```

Figure C.107.

Program II, 6

```
10 REM Sorting numbers using subscripted variables
20 DATA 3, 2, 4, 1
30 DIM N(4)
40 FOR A = 1 TO 4
50 READ N(A)
60 NEXT A
70 PRINT "original order"
72 FOR P = 1 TO 4
73 PRINT N(P),
74 NEXT P
80 FOR R = 1 TO 3
90 FOR S = 1 TO 3
100 IF N(S) < N(S+1) THEN 150
110 LET X = N(S)
120 LET N(S) = N(S+1)
130 LET N (S+1) = X
140 PRINT "I exchanged ";N(S);" and ";N(S+1)
150 NEXT S
160 FOR P = 1 TO 4
170 PRINT N(P),
180 NEXT P
190 NEXT R
200 PRINT "all sorted"
210 END
```

Figure C.108.

Assignment II, 1

Assignment II, 1

- Take your program from assignment 4 and change it to give division problems, where the operator chooses the dividend and divisor and where the answer is expected and checked as a whole number and a remainder.

(This program will be very useful since no other calculator will give such an answer in division.)

Figure C.109.

Assignment II, 2

Assignment II, 2

- Type in program II,2
- Change it
  to ask "to what category do you
  want your number rounded?"
  and to perform accordingly.

Figure C.110.

Assignment II, 3

Assignment II, 3

- Take one of your math practicing programs of earlier assignments and put timeloops between screen displays to allow time for reading; organize these time loops as a subroutine.
- Make the time delays of different lengths, still using one subroutine (use a variable in the FOR command and assign different values to it in the main program).
- Let the time delays become shorter every time the same line is on the screen (the reader knows it by then and does not need so much time for reading).

Figure C.111.

Assignment II, 4

Assignment II, 4

Design a program to practice spelling:

- Let the program READ a pair of words from DATA lines at the end of the program; the first word in those pairs may be misspelled, the second shows the right spelling; have the first word printed.
- Let the operator answer "R" (or "W"), if he thinks the spelling is right (wrong).
  PRINT "No, check again", if it was the wrong answer.
- Print the correct spelling now, let it stay a while, clear the screen and ask the operator to type in that word. Provide repetition, if he typed a mistake.
- Go this way through all DATAs. (Provide a pair of end words.)
- Provide different sets of DATAs for this program which can be loaded from a cassette or disk.

Figure C.112.

Assignment II, 5

Assignment II, 5

Take your program from assignment 10, which presented a choice of either + , − , ×, or ÷ problems by combining four programs.

Make that program shorter:
Have four different parts for the making up of the problems only, then let all the rest be done by one same part: The printing and checking of the answer, the other prints, etc. That part will have ON-GOTO statements, where it goes back to one of the 4 first parts.

Figure C.113.

Assignment II, 6

Assignment II, 6

Look at program II, 6.
Make a similar program, which sorts names according to the alphabet:*

- Type as DATA the names of all the students in your class,
- DIMension your computer for that number of subscripted string variables,
- have both loops run the number of times as the number of students less one,
- have only the final order printed.

---

* Since letters are represented as numbers inside the computer, you can treat them like numbers. So you may apply the IF commands with <, > or = ·
< means then: Earlier in the alphabet.

Figure C.114.

d. Directions for Assembling the PACS

1. *Copy the Cards from Section C on Cardstock;*

This is what you need

a) To be assembled in the PACS

1 card to be cut into label PACS, ticket ENTER, ticket BREAK, sign CPU.	Figure C.18,19
4 RAM dividers (will be different after cutting)	Figure C.20
20 RAM statement cards (all the same)	Figure C.21
10 RAM variable cards (all the same)	Figure C.24
4 RAM string variable cards (all the same)	Figure C.22
4 RAM subscripted variable cards (all the same)	Figure C.23
1 ROM card frontispiece	Figure C.25
27 ROM command cards (all different)	Figures C.26-52
1 Calculator card frontispiece	Figure C.53
5 Calculator cards (all different)	Figures C.54-58

b) To be stored in the operator's box:

1 list of programs	Figure C.59
27 program cards	Figures C.60-86
1 list of assignments	Figure C.87
15 assignment cards (no. 1-14 incl. one page 2)	Figures C.88-102
12 program and assignment cards Level II	Figures C.103-114

c) screen   Figure C.17a&b

The screen could not be printed on one page. Glue the 2 parts (at beginning of section c) together at the —.—.— line, that line not showing. You may want to copy then again.

2. *How to Prepare the Cards*

- Cut all cards along the black margin line.

- Cut top part of RAM dividers, ROM command cards and calculator cards along the line to let the tab with the key word stand out for easier access (the RAM dividers will then each have a different key word left).

- Color in red the commands on ROM cards (only the word in capitals) with transparent marker. Do the same with the labels on the frontispiece cards (ROM, RAM, CALCULATOR).

- Cut out the tickets and the sign CPU, and paste them on red poster board. Make a string for the sign CPU to hang it around the student's neck. Draw the "prompt", the sign ⟩, on the back of the ticket ENTER (see teacher's manual).

- Make a second copy of the frontispieces and cut out the labels (ROM, RAM, calculator).

- Laminate all materials.

3. *How to Put Them Together*

The point of this material is to give an impression of the distinct parts of a computer: the calculator, the ROM (Read Only Memory) with the commands, the RAM (Random Access Memory) with the program and the variables, the CPU (Central Processing Unit), and the screen.

To provide this impression, make the three card sets into three booklets, one with the RAM cards, one with the ROM cards, and one with the CALCULATOR cards: In the bottom of the cards, punch two holes. Combine cards with metal binder rings (or chicken rings), so the hinge of each booklet is at the bottom. The booklets then can be opened 180 degrees without bending cards.

- Cut heavy cardboard in two pieces:
  17" × 7" and 17" × 4.5";
  Cover with neutral color contact paper (wood grain, green, grey);
  Punch 6 holes in each piece at the 17" side, so that the holes match the

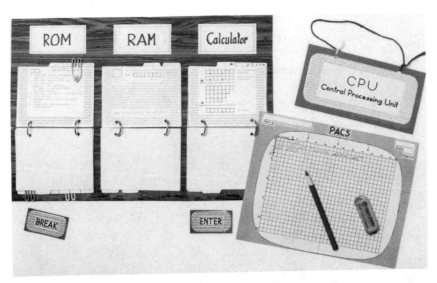

Figure C.115 PACS shown in opened position.

holes of the card booklets and the binder rings or chicken rings combine the booklets and the two cardboard covers into a book like unit;

- Glue the labels on the free space of the larger cardboard, as shown in the drawing.

- Glue the label PACS on the outside of the book.

4. *The Tool Box*

- Provide *grease pencils* (special pencils that write on plastic) and *matching erasers,* (Try different products. "Blaisdell China Marker" gave fair results.) to write on the laminated material.

- Provide three *paperclips.* They will be clipped onto command cards (where it says [working on 1/2]) to mark those cards to which you will need to return after completing other commands. These paperclips should be numbered 1, 2, 3, or color coded (green, yellow, red as in the traffic light) in order to mark the sequence in which you work your way back (large plastic clips come in colors).

- Provide a box for all the tools (grease pencil, eraser, paperclip markers) and for the tickets (ENTER and BREAK).

5. *The Screen*

- The children may write on the screen with the grease pencil the same way as they write on the cards and should do so through the first programs. Later, you may want some of their work to go in the finished work box. For that reason, provide consumable copies of the screen.

- Provide a pouch for the screen and the consumable copies of it.

6. *The Operator's Box*

- Provide a card file box for all the other cards, which stay on the shelf, while only one of them is chosen to work with;

- Provide dividers for these cards:
  "Programs 1–14"
  "Programs 15–27"
  "Assignments 1–14"
  "Programs & Assignments II."

If your students all start at the beginning of this work, you may want to hold back the material needed only later: The assignment cards and all the cards for level II (see teacher's manual), including the ROM cards of the commands DIM, GOSUB, INT, NEXT, ON-GOTO, READ, RETURN, DATA, FOR and the RAM cards for subscripted variables.

V. A SIMULATION MODEL FOR ECONOMICS—AN IDEA FOR A NEW MATERIAL

a. The Purpose

The following simulation model for studying economic laws is not yet developed into ready-to-apply material. An idea is presented, with the starting steps outlined in more detail. This is primarily meant as a help for better understanding Chapter A, section VII, where examples were given to illustrate the technique of simulation as an educational tool. This example starts on a level where it is still simple enough to be handled with mechanic models. On that level, the material could be made up of sticks or cardboard strips, functioning as levers, pinned to a corkboard and connected with wire hooks. Simple representations of isolated economic facts can be explored on these levers. But as the model grows in sophistication, the computer then may take over, simulating the growth or decline of economic data according to the underlying numerical and mathematical relations.

Today's economy is part of our everyday life and preparing children to function in this society means preparing them to face questions such as, "Why does Reaganomics work or not work?," "Why does Volcker (head of The Federal Reserve Board) keep the money supply low to curb inflation and why does that slow down economic growth?" Preparation to understand the basic facts behind these terms may be as important, interesting, and easy as square roots, which also is easy for Montessori children when built up with didactically fine-tuned steps and materials.

Economic processes cannot, however, be observed easily in reality. Even the very simple interdependencies of production and consumption in society are studied through appropriate models, provided by card materials, which simulate the real aspect of society to this point. Going beyond this and exploring the relationship of economic factors would necessitate simulation material that allows manipulation and builds up the understanding in small steps.

b. The Money Equation

This sequence could start with the basic money equation:

$$money = goods\ bought \times prices$$

A little introduction, starting from the study of production and consumption could show that the sum of all goods bought in a country times the prices,

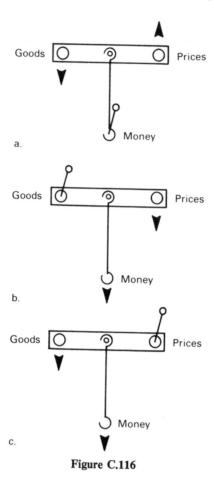

Figure C.116

would add up to the amount of money in circulation. This fact allows for certain exploration, which could be done by a simple simulating model, created from sticks pinned to a corkboard:

The model, as it is set in part a of Figure C.116, shows that if for any reason the availability of goods goes down in a country, then the people are willing to pay more and prices will rise, as long as the money supply remains stable. This holds true the other way around as well: If prices go up for any reason, for example, because the oil producers increase their prices, then with a limited supply of money, the goods that can be bought will go down, which means a slowing down of the economy. The condition of a fixed money supply is created in our model by pinning down the part labeled "money" with a pin on the board, while all the other parts are freely movable.

Part b of Figure C.116 shows that by tightening the money supply, which can be done by the Federal Reserve Board, it may be possible to bring down prices.

Part c, however, shows that if prices for any reason are fixed, as they are here with a pin to the board and as they might be in reality because producers cannot produce any cheaper, then a decrease in the money supply is followed by a decrease in the amount of goods bought on the market, which again means a slowing down of the economy.

c. Circulation of Money

This simplified model of the economy may be extended by adding a further step considering the circulation of money:

The money equation now looks like this:

$$\text{money} \times \text{circulating speed} = \text{goods} \times \text{prices}$$

Here the expanded model is shown in Figure C.117; part a shows a configuration where people, fearful of unemployment, save and hold back their money: the money circulation speed slows down which, in reverse, with the assumption of fixed prices and money volume, decreases the amount of goods bought and causes a further slowing of the economy. Part b shows the opposite situation where people are scared of increasing inflation and, therefore, try to spend their money as soon as they get it, thus speeding up the money circulation, which causes even more inflation. We call this galloping inflation.

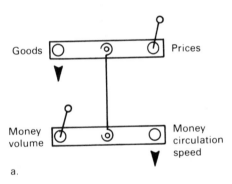

a.

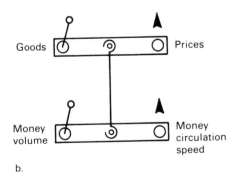

b.

Figure C.117

d. The Law of the Market Place

We may add another step by considering the law of the market place: With higher prices, the supply of goods increases. It goes without saying that each step needs a careful isolated introduction, for example, a story of the producer who buys new machines as the rising prices promise better profits.

Follow-up activities may also include role plays of producers, workers, consumers, bankers, and so forth.

Each step should also be introduced with its part of the model by itself in isolation. After this has been done, the whole model, put together, could look like this:

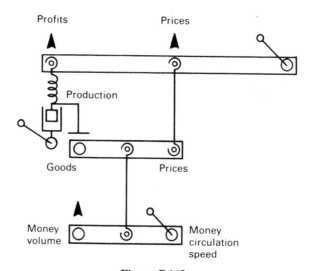

Figure C.118

If with increasing volume of money, prices are allowed to rise, profits also rise. That would trigger an increase in production with certain flexibility and delay, as symbolized by the little spring and shock absorber.

As the model shows, an increase in production would not automatically increase the volume of goods bought, but decreasing production would limit the goods available.

e. Rising Prices Trigger Increased Wages

If a next step considers that rising prices trigger increased wages and reduced profits, with a certain flexibility and time delay, then the model would look like Figure C.119.

If one manipulates this model by moving the money volume up, prices would increase and would, in the long run, trigger an increase of wages; that in turn would bring down profits, slowing down production and reducing the number of goods available, which in turn would increase prices even more. This is the cycle of inflation, still in a simplified way.

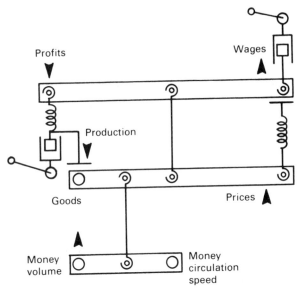

Figure C.119

f. For More Parameters, We Need a Computer

We have not yet introduced interest levels, taxes, the impact of the national debt, imports, exports, and the difference between goods for consumption and goods for investment. However, it is obvious that our mechanical model is already unable to represent the reality considered this far. A computer would be helpful at this point to put the picture on the screen and perform the changes according to the formulas and with the respective delays. That simulation would be closer to reality and would allow a better sensorial impression of any changes and a wider variety of exploration.

This model does point out certain problems involved in simulation programs: the program is only as good as the programmer's knowledge of the reality. In this case, however, the formulas of econometrics are pretty well developed to a level that is reasonable in teaching children.

The next problem is to select the facts to be considered and those to be left out. The isolation of difficulties is the most important procedure because a simulation model giving everything would end up being a replica of the reality. But isolation of difficulties also includes leaving out part of the reality and, therefore, making a choice. That choice can influence the view of reality that the children are going to acquire through their work with the simulation model.

Simulation models should be checked carefully before being put in the classroom. This is, of course, true for all educational software.

BIBLIOGRAPHY

Abelson, Harold. "A Beginner's Guide to Logo, Logo is not just for Kids." *BYTE, The Small Systems Journal,* August 1982, pp. 88-115.

Abelson, Harold. *Apple Logo.* New York: McGraw-Hill Byte Books, 1982.

Abelson, Harold, and diSessa, Andrea. *Turtle Geometry: The Computer as a Medium for Exploring Mathematics,* Cambridge, Mass. MIT Press, 1981.

Ahl, David H. "The State of the Art in Educational Software." Paper read at National Educational Computing Conference, June 1983, at Baltimore, Md.

Atari Inc., Sun Valley, CA. Unpublished Instructions for a Computer Camp, 1982.

Bearden, Donna, and Muller, Jim. *The Turtle Source Book.* Reston, Va.: Reston Publishing Co. Inc., 1983.

Bell, Mina. "Joystick/Keyboard Applications in Preschool Computer Program." Paper read at: Church, Marilyn and Wright, June, "Using the Microcomputer Creatively with Young Children," in *Proceedings of National Educational Computing Conference 1983, Baltimore Md.* Silver Spring, Md.: IEEE Computer Society Press, 1983, p. 272.

Bennin, John. "The Talking Wheelchair." *Computers Closing the Gap for Handicapped* 2. Dolores Hagen, Henderson, Minn. June 1983, p. 7.

Brown, Warren R. "Project CAISH Second Year Update." In Horan, Rita; Brown, Warren R.; Russo, Mary; Jones, Dr. Nancy; Smaldino, Sharon; and Schloss, Patrick: "Computing for the Learning Disabled or Handicapped." In *Proceedings of National Educational Computing Conference 1983, Baltimore, Md.* Silver Spring Md.: IEEE Computer Society Press, 1983.

Bunnell, David. "From The Publishing Jungle." *PC Magazine* 1. Software Educations Inc., San Francisco, CA, August 1982, p. 17.

Clurman, Carol. "Pack Your Own Computer for College." *USA Today,* 17 August 1983, p. 1.

"Creative Programming" Inc., Charleston, Ill., 1982.

Dagless, Erik L., and Aspinall, David. *Introduction to Microcomputers.* Rockville, Md.: Computer Science Press, 1982.

Digital Equipment Corporation. *Introduction to Computer Based Education.* Marlborough, Mass., 1983.

Dillon, E. T. "Do Your Questions Promote Thinking?" *Learning, The Magazine for Creative Teaching.* McMillan Publishing Co., New York, October 1982, pp. 51-57.

Fiske, Edward P. "Computers Alter Life of Pupils and Teachers." *New York Times,* 4 April 1982, p. 42.

Goble, Frank. *The Third Force, A. H. Maslow's Contribution for a Psychology of Psychic Health.* New York: Grossman Publishers, 1970.

Goldenberg, E. Paul. "Logo–A Cultural Glossary." *BYTE, The Small Systems Journal,* Petersborough, N.H., August 1982, pp. 210-229.

Grady, David. "What Every Teacher Should Know about Computer Simulations." *Learning, The Magazine for Creative Teaching,* McMillan Publishing Co., New York, March 1983, pp. 34-46.

Grammer, Virginia Carter; Goldenberg, E. Paul; and Klotz, Leigh, Jr. *The Commodore 64 Logo Tutorial.* Cambridge, Mass.: Terrapin Inc., 1983.

Grazzini, Camillo. *Unpublished Lectures on New Math.* Bergamo, Italy: Centro Internazionale Studi Montessoriani, 1983.

Harwey, Brian. "Why Logo? Logo is designed to Encourage Development of Problem-Solving Skills." *BYTE, The Small Systems Journal,* Petersborough, N.H., August 1982, pp. 163-193.

Hellbruegge, Theodor, and Montessori, Mario, eds. *Die Montessori-Paedagogik und das behinderte Kind.* Munich: Kindler Verlag, 1978.

Heller, Rachelle S., and Martin, C. Dianne. *Bits 'n Bytes about Computing, A Computer Literacy Primer.* Rockville, Md.: Computer Science Press Inc., 1982.

Hirschfelder, John J. "Karel The Robot." *Creative Computing,* Ahl Computing Inc., Morristown, N.J., April 1983, pp. 154-156.

Holladay, David. "Programs for the Visually Impaired." *Computers Closing the Gap for Handicapped* 2. Dolores Hagen, Henderson, Minn., 1983, p. 6.

Hughes, Charles E., and Moshell, J. Michael. "A Programming Environment for Preliterate Children." In *Proceedings of National Educational Computing Conference, 1983, Baltimore, Md.* Silver Spring, Md.: IEEE Computer Society Press, 1983.

Humanizing the VDT Workplace, Washington D.C.: The Newspaper Guild and International Typographical Union, 1983.

Kieffer, Kathleen, and Smith, Charles. "Writer's Workbench: Teaching Aid and Learning Aid." In Fosberg, Mary Dee Harris, and Ross, Donald: "Word Processor in the Composition Classroom." In *Proceedings of National Educational Computing Conference 1983, Baltimore Md.* Silver Spring, Md.: IEEE Computer Society Press, 1983.

Lafrance, Jacques. "Crisis in Programming, or History Does Repeat Itself." In *Proceedings of National Educational Computing Conference 1983, Baltimore, Md.* Silver Spring, Md.: IEEE Computer Society Press, 1983.

Lawler, R. W. "Designing Computer Based Microworlds." *BYTE, The Small Systems Journal,* Petersborough, N.H., August 1982, pp. 138-162.

Lewis, Lawrence P. "Individualized Instruction, is it Montessori?" *Montessori Elementary Newsletter* III/3, Cleveland Heights, Oh., 15 January 1984, pp. 1-4.

Luehrmann, Arthur, and Peckham, Herbert. *Computer Literacy, A Hands-On Approach.* New York: McGraw-Hill, 1980.

McCormack, Patricia. "Political Action." *National Education Association Press Report,* NEA, Washington, D.C., January 1983, p. 3.

Malone, Tom. "On Intrinsically Motivating Games." *Classroom Computer News,* Intentional Educations, Watertown, Mass., April 1983, pp. 17-23.

Miller, Jean K. "Piaget and Montessori—Theory and Practice and the Development of Classification Skills." *Montessori Elementary Newsletter* III / 3, Cleveland Heights, Oh., 1974, p. a.

Montessori, Maria. *From Childhood to Adolescence.* 1948; New Engl. Ed. New York: Schocken Books, 1973.

Montessori, Maria. *The Absorbent Mind.* 1949; New Engl. Ed. New York: Holt Rinehart & Winston, 1967.

Montessori, Maria. *The Advanced Montessori Method.* 2 vols. 1913. Reprint. Madras, India: Kalakshetra Publications, Inc., 1965.

Montessori, Maria. *The Discovery of the Child.* 1909; Rev. Engl. Ed. Madras, India: Kalakshetra Publications, Inc., 1966.

Montessori, Maria. "The Four Planes of Education." (Lecture given at the Seventh International Montessori Congress, Edinburgh, 1938, combined with another lecture, London 1939), Mario Montessori ed., published in AMI Communications 4, 1971, p. 5.

Montessori, Maria. *The Secret of Childhood.* 1936; Rev. Ed. New York: Fides/ Ballantine Books, Inc., 1966.

Montessori, Maria. *To Educate the Human Potential.* 1948. 5th ed. Madras, India: Kalakshetra Publications, Inc., 1973.

Montessori, Mario. *The Human Tendencies and Montessori Education.* 2nd rev. ed. Amsterdam, The Netherlands: Association Montessori Internationale, 1956.

Montessori Elementary Training Course. *Unpublished Lectures.* Washington Montessori Institute, Washington D.C., 1982.

Montessori Special Education Course. *Unpublished Lectures on Montessori Primary Materials.* Munich: Aktion Sonnenschein e.V., 1976-77.

Naisbitt, John. *Megatrends.* New York: Warner Books, 1982.

Nienhaus-Montessori: Catalogue of Montessori Apparatus. B.V. Zelhem, Holland.

Papert, Seymour. *Mindstorms, Children, Computers and Powerful Ideas.* New York: Basic Books Inc., 1980.

Peckham, Herbert D. *BASIC, A Hands-On Method.* New York: McGraw-Hill, 1981.

Piaget, Jean. *Science of Education and the Psychology of the Child.* 1969 Engl. Ed. New York: Orion Press, 1970.

Prueitt, Melin L. "Cray on Art." *Discover,* Time Life Publishing Corp., Chicago, November 1983, pp. 69-76.

Pulaski, Marianne Spencer. *Understanding Piaget.* New York: Harper & Row, 1971.

Rasmussen, Carol. "Computers in the Kitchen?" *The Washington Post,* 19 September 1982, p. H4.

Schwartz, Helen. "Aids to Organization." In Fosberg, Mary Dee Harris, and Ross, Donald: "Word Processor in the Composition Classroom." In *Proceedings of National Educational Computing Conference 1983, Baltimore, Md.* Silver Spring, Md.: IEEE Computer Society Press, 1983.

Snyder, T. S. *The Search Series, Five Simulations in Social Studies and Science.* New York: McGraw-Hill, 1982.

Solzbacher, Hildegard. "Screiben und Lesen." In Theodor Hellbruegge and Mario

Montessori, eds. *Die Montessori-Paedagogik und das behinderte Kind.* Munich: Kindler Verlag, 1978. Quotation translated by Peter Gebhardt-Seele.

Spinnaker Software. *Delta Drawing.* Cambridge, Mass., 1982.

Standing, E. Mortimer. *Maria Montessori, Her Life and Work.* 1957; New ed. New York: New American Library, 1962.

Stephenson, Margaret Elizabeth, *Unpublished Lectures.* Washington Montessori Institute, Washington D.C. 1982-83.

Stoy, Diane. "Trends: The Job Market By The Year 2000." *The Washington Post,* 2 January 1984, p. C5.

Terrapin Inc. *Instant Logo.* Cambridge MA: 1982.

Tinker, Robert. "Logo's Limits Or Which Language Should We Teach?" *Hands On! Microcomputers in Education–Innovations and Issues* 6, Technical Education Research Centers (A Non-Profit, Public Service Corporation), Cambridge, Mass., 1983, pp. 1-5.

Tinker, Robert. "Special Interfaces for Special Students." *Hands On! Microcomputers in Education–Innovations and Issues* 6, Technical Education Research Centers (A Non-Profit, Public Service Corporation), Cambridge, Mass., 1983, pp. 5-8.

Vester, Frederic. *Denken, Lernen, Vergessen.* Stuttgart: Deutsche Verlagsanstalt, 1975.

Wallace, Alan S. "Ten Questions and Answers on Computers in the Montessori Elementary Class." *American Elementary Alumni Association Newsletter,* Summer 1983, pp. 2-4.

Watt, Daniel. *Learning with Logo.* New York: McGraw-Hill, 1983.

Watt, Daniel. "Logo in the Schools." *BYTE, The Small Systems Journal,* Petersborough, N.H., August 1982, pp. 116-137.

Waynant, Priscilla, "Creative Ways of Introducing Language Arts Instruction." Paper read at: Church, Marilyn and Wright, June, "Using the Microcomputer Creatively with Young Children," in *Proceedings of National Educational Computing Conference 1983, Baltimore, Md.* Silver Spring, Md.: IEEE Computer Society Press, 1983.

Weizenbaum, Professor Joseph. M.I.T. Quoted after *New York Times,* 4 April 1982, p. 42.

Wilson, I. R., and Addyman, A. M. *A Practical Introduction to PASCAL.* New York/ Heidelberg: Springer Verlag, 1978.

Zeidman, Ed. *The Function Game.* Baltimore, Md.: Muse Software Inc., 1982.

INDEX